PRAISE FOR CH

MW01491505

"Chasing the Grid is a *Walden* for the Garmin age, a beautiful and powerful reminder of what running is—or should be—all about."

— Matt Fitzgerald, author of *Life Is a Marathon*

"Through a slow-motion and sometimes painful personal transformation, Long Path record-setter Ken Posner brings us the magic and majesty of the Catskills. His journey will have you too shedding your shoes and leaving behind your GPS, cell phone, and even maps. Among the living mountains, Ken reshuffles his priorities to find fresh insight and new appreciation for going light."

— Joan Burroughs, President, John Burroughs Association and great-granddaughter of John Burroughs

"This is not just a story about running and hiking in the mountains. It's the story of a pilgrimage, which means an exercise in discipline and a journey into the gap where creativity begins and where connection is found. A very interesting, entertaining, and educating read!"

— "Barefoot Sue" Kenney, author of *My Camino*, the story of her pilgrimage on the Camino de Santiago

"Moving through a natural environment doesn't require technology—it takes curiosity and enthusiasm. Ken's account is a roller-coaster ride through the mountains of New York amid a series of increasingly minimalist adventures. Along the way, he falls back in love with nature, learns to study the signs and clues, discovers the art of natural navigation. And ends up showing the reader how to reconnect with the world around us."

— Tristan Gooley, internationally acclaimed navigation expert, award-winning and bestselling author of *The Natural Navigator* and *The Lost Art of Reading Nature's Signs*

"In this fascinating account, Ken undertakes a daunting physical endeavor. A Big Fitness Goal. A journey in which he leaves behind digital distraction. Ventures deep into the solitude of the mountains. Wrestles with the primitive challenges of life on the trail. Discovers the important values which we need so badly to instill today. Relevant, timely, and inspiring!"

— Mike Erwin is CEO of the Character and Leadership Center, founder of veteran organization Team Red White & Blue, and a West Point grad and former U.S. Army Intelligence Officer

"This is the story of a pilgrimage, but an especially wild and intense one, as Posner fights to escape the depressingly comfortable prison of modern life. The result is what can only be described as an aesthetic experience, and a one-way trip into the unknown."

— John Kaag, professor of philosophy at University of Massachusetts Lowell and author of *Hiking with Nietzsche: On Becoming Who You Are*

"Once again, Ken takes us into the laboratory of human performance, which this time consists of the rugged mountains in upstate New York. This time the experiment is to find out whether an aging ultrarunner can keep moving despite thick vegetation, deep snow, rocky trails, and injury. What will he discover and learn? The result is a case study in important American values, like determination and acceptance—and a wild read."

— Vinnie Totorich is a celebrity fitness trainer, author, radio and podcast host, film producer, and international motivational speaker

"Running can be more than just exercise; it can be a powerful meditative practice that brings the gifts of stillness and presence to all other aspects of our lives. Posner's account of his transformation from conventional to natural runner is a wild mix of energy, adventure, and determination. It draws on themes of the American Transcendentalist tradition and is enriched by the beauty of the Catskill Mountains, not just backdrop but another character in Posner's story. This book will inspire runners of all levels of experience to pursue their own journeys of empowerment and transformation."

— Vanessa Zuisei Goddard, Zen teacher and author of *Still Running: The Art of Meditation in Motion*

CHASING THE GRID

Also by Kenneth Posner

Stalking the Black Swan: Research and Decision-Making in a World of Extreme Volatility

Running the Long Path: A 350-Mile Journey of Discovery in New York's Hudson Valley

KENNETH
POSNER

CHASING THE GRID

An Ultrarunner's Physical and
Spiritual Journey in Pursuit of the
Ultimate Mountain Challenge

VELO.
press

Text copyright © 2025 Kenneth Posner.
All rights reserved. No part of this publication may be reproduced, stored in
a retrieval system, or transmitted in any form or by any means, electronic,
mechanical, photocopying, recording, or otherwise, except for brief quotations
in reviews, educational works, or other uses permitted by copyright law.

Published by

 velopress®

an imprint of The Stable Book Group
32 Court Street, Suite #2109
Brooklyn, NY 11201
www.velopress.com

Library of Congress Control Number: 2025933939
ISBN: 978-1-64604-852-6

Aquisitions editor: Kierra Sondereker
Managing editor: Claire Chun
Editor: Renee Rutledge
Proofreader: Cathy Cambron
Design and production: Abbey Gregory
Artwork: front cover © Steve Aaron Photography

Printed in the United States
10 9 8 7 6 5 4 3 2 1

Please note: This book is independently authored and published. No
endorsement or sponsorship by or affiliation with movies, celebrities, products,
or other copyright and trademark holders is claimed or suggested. All references
in this book to copyrighted or trademarked characters and other elements of
movies and products are for the purpose of commentary, criticism, analysis, and
literary discussion only.

To Mom and Dad

Peak bagging, the pursuit of climbing with the aim only of securing bragging rights, strikes me as vulgar. But climbing with the intention of learning, admiring, and sharing can be a good and decent pursuit, even noble.

—Marshall Ulrich, ultrarunner, adventure racer, and mountaineer, in *Both Feet on the Ground: Reflections from the Outside*

CONTENTS

INTRODUCTION...1

PART I: DISCOVERING THE GRID 5

CHAPTER 1: A SIGNAL FROM THE NORTH.................................. 6
❋ The Mountains Call 9

CHAPTER 2: HOOKED BY A NEW CHALLENGE 11
❋ The Badwater Double 12
❋ The Cave Dog Take-Down...13

CHAPTER 3: RACING AFTER CAVE DOG 16
❋ A Final Test Run.. 17

CHAPTER 4: BATTLING WITH NATURE OFF-TRAIL 21
❋ A Summer to Train..23
❋ The Many Challenges of Bushwhacking 24

CHAPTER 5: SLIPPING FROM MY GRASP..................................26
❋ The Barefoot Experiment...28
❋ Foiled by Injury..29

CHAPTER 6: A NEW OBSESSION 31
❋ Burroughs on Barefoot 33
❋ Channeling Thoreau 35

CHAPTER 7: GOING LIGHT 40
❋ Lessons from the Light Infantry 44

CHAPTER 8: TAKING MINIMALISM TO THE NEXT LEVEL 46
* The Quad 46
* Back in Boston 47
* Askesis in the Catskills...48

CHAPTER 9: SHIFTING GEARS AGAIN 53
* A Tendon in the Ankle 54
* Completion of the Barefoot 35................................. 55
* Devil's Path Double 57

CHAPTER 10: THE 35-PEAK CHALLENGE 58

CHAPTER 11: CHRISTMAS IN THE MOUNTAINS.................67
* Learning to Observe 68
* Novel Bushwhack Routes..69
* The Life of Quiet Desperation...................................70
* The Christmas Run That Changed My Life................72
* A Spreadsheet Is Born 74

PART II: EMBRACING THE GRID..77

CHAPTER 12: WINTER TINTS 78
* Impressions in the Dark 79
* Sharing the Winter Sights with Friends....................80
* With Odie in the Moonlight 82
* A Dicey Nighttime Climb up Kaaterskill.................. 83
* Running into the Storm..84
* Nighttime Bushwhack up Panther and Slide........... 85

CHAPTER 13: FIFTY MILES THAT NEVER END 88

CHAPTER 14: FLOWING DOWN AND UP........................... 93
* Sauntering Through May 94
* The Nature of Flow State 97

CHAPTER 15: INTO AN ALIEN PLANETSCAPE 99
* Seeking Diversity, Not Sameness 99
* Springtime in the Mountains.....................................100
* A Glimpse into the Foundry 101

CHAPTER 16: RACING THE SUN 105
 ❋ Physical Training, Spiritual Development 105
 ❋ Insignificance Is Liberating 107
 ❋ Seeing Ego in Its Absence 108
 ❋ My First Time on Moon Haw Road 110

CHAPTER 17: A SPEAR OF SUMMER GRASS 115
 ❋ A First Attempt at Natural Navigation 115
 ❋ On the Indestructibility of Mind by Time 117

CHAPTER 18: BRINGING FRIENDS AND FAMILY TO THE
MOUNTAINS 121
 ❋ A Natural Navigation Fail 121
 ❋ Mystery Bus 122
 ❋ Insect Symphony 124
 ❋ A Family Hike 125

CHAPTER 19: LEARNING TO TOE THE LINE 127
 ❋ Mindfulness and the Spirit of Exactitude 128
 ❋ The Mind Is as Turbulent as the Wind 130
 ❋ A Hike Poised on the Boundary of the Seasons 131

CHAPTER 20: FACING THE WINTER PROBLEM 134
 ❋ Congratulations to "Tigger" 136
 ❋ The Winter Problem 137
 ❋ A Free Man, But Injured 138
 ❋ Learning from the Iceman 140

PART III: COMPLETING THE GRID 145

CHAPTER 21: BLACK TOES 146
 ❋ Southwest Hunter in the Snow 147
 ❋ Natural Navigation in the Frost 149
 ❋ Wishing It Were Summer 150

CHAPTER 22: A DAMNED CLOSE-RUN THING 152
 ❋ Some Breakfast Might Help 153
 ❋ Zombie Death March Up West Kill Mountain 154
 ❋ Back to the Pathless Ridge 156

CHAPTER 23: A GRUESOME SLOG 158
❊ Snowshoeing in Slow Motion 160
❊ Why Runners and Birches Both Get Bent 162
❊ Another Trekking Pole Bites the Dust.....................164

CHAPTER 24: THAT SPECIAL SONG.....................166
❊ Hello, Inner Daemon 166
❊ Back to Going Light 168
❊ A Long Loop Teaches an Important Lesson 169
❊ Return of the Migrant Birds...............................172

CHAPTER 25: A NEW RECORD FOR THE CATSKILLS.....................175
❊ Another Lesson in Patience 176
❊ A Lesson in Catskills History from Night Dog 178
❊ Cave Dog's Record Is Finally Taken Down 179

CHAPTER 26: A NEW RECORD FOR THE LONG PATH.................181
❊ Meeting Will and Dustin 182
❊ Will and Dustin Reach New York City 183
❊ Caught in the Nettles' Kill Zone 184
❊ We Cannot Separate Ourselves from Nature.............185
❊ Rediscovering the Magic of Childhood 187

**CHAPTER 27: AN UNCONVENTIONAL UNIFORM FOR SUMMER
BUSHWHACKING** 189
❊ Stubbing Toes on Rusk 191
❊ Minimalism Requires Mindfulness 192
❊ Nearly Naked Among the Nettles..........................193

CHAPTER 28: BACK TO WORK...............................197
❊ Climbing Friday with Ralph and Kelly 200
❊ Autumn Fog in the Mountains.............................200
❊ Why Barefoot? 201
❊ Do We Run Too Fast? 202
❊ Closing Out the September Grid, One Peak at a Time...............202

CHAPTER 29: A LOST GOOSE 205
❊ Climbing Southwest Hunter with My Inner Daemon...............205
❊ Blown Off Course 208

CHAPTER 30: THE NINE, THE SIX, AND THE ONE 212
* The World Demands Productivity 212
* The Last of Autumn 214
* A Celebratory Climb 216
* Goodbye, Inner Daemon 217
* An Ill-Conceived Operation 218
* Back to Friday, No Room for Error 220

CHAPTER 31: THE FINAL ASCENT 222
* Inside the Scene and Part of It 222
* Running as Attitude 224
* The Philosophy of Trying Harder 225
* Goodbye, Pathless Ridge 226
* Goodbye, Doubletop 227
* The Grid as Personal Transcendence 228
* Tallying Up the Costs, Regrets, and Benefits 230
* The Final Countdown 231

APPENDIX A: THE GRID 235

APPENDIX B: LIST OF SPECIES OBSERVED IN THE CATSKILLS 238

APPENDIX C: RUNNING-RELATED INJURIES 251

APPENDIX D: SAMPLE OPERATIONAL PLAN 252

REFERENCES AND SUPPLEMENTAL INFORMATION 258

ACKNOWLEDGMENTS 269

ABOUT THE AUTHOR 271

INTRODUCTION

THIS IS A STORY ABOUT TRANSFORMATION, ALTHOUGH THAT WAS never my intention. I'm a good example of the modern knowledge worker—completely comfortable behind a laptop or on my phone. Critical and pragmatic. Inclined to take incremental steps then reassess. Hardly a free spirit or a flower child (actually, I'm a CPA, financial analyst, and former Army Ranger). But as I spent more time in the mountains, my practice began to change, until I was running through the forest nearly naked.

This story takes place in New York's Catskill Mountains, located about 100 miles north of New York City, but it could have happened almost anywhere. Over the years, I've visited mountains up and down the East and West Coasts and some overseas. Regardless of the location, I've always felt the same emotions. The wonder. The energy. The sense that somewhere there was a path for me.

It doesn't matter if you're a runner (like me) or a hiker (once I overdid the running and got injured) or a walker (I love walking) or have some other practice for getting out there. What I really hope to share with you is the passion.

Technology shields us from pain and helps us be more productive, but these benefits must be weighed against the costs. If you'd like to transcend the limitations of modernity, you may find, as I did, that mountains make excellent instructors.

Kenneth Posner
Ulster County, New York, 2025

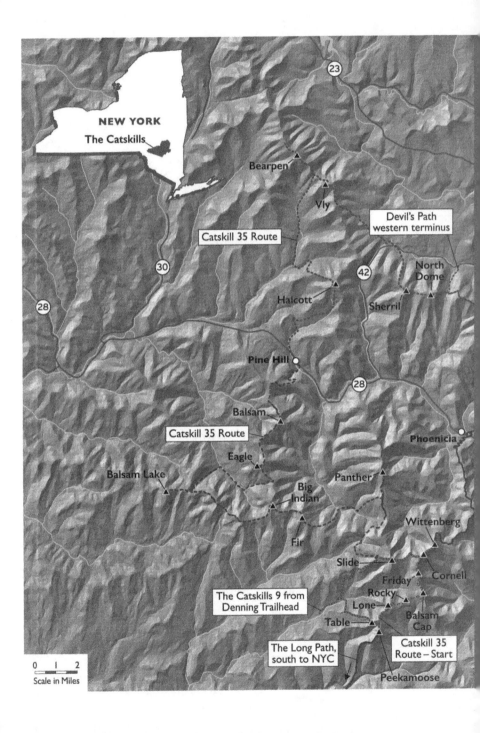

NEW YORK
The Catskills

Bearpen

Vly

Catskill 35 Route

Devil's Path
western terminus

North
Dome

42

Halcott

Sherril

Pine Hill

28

Balsam

Catskill 35 Route

Phoenicia

Eagle

Balsam Lake

Big
Indian

Panther

Wittenberg

Fir

Slide

Cornell

Friday

The Catskills 9 from
Denning Trailhead

Rocky

Lone

Balsam
Cap

Table

Catskill 35
Route – Start

The Long Path,
south to NYC

Peekamoose

0 1 2
Scale in Miles

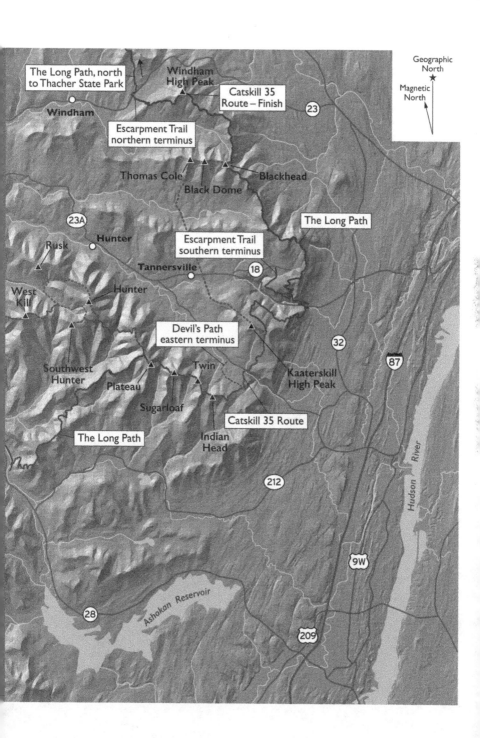

PART I
DISCOVERING THE GRID

I sometimes think I climbed enough peaks this summer to render me a candidate for a padded cell—at least some people look at the matter in that way. However, I get a lot of enjoyment from this rather strenuous form of diversion.

—*Norman Clyde, legendary Sierra mountaineer*

CHAPTER 1

A SIGNAL FROM
THE NORTH

WALT WHITMAN WROTE THAT EACH OF US MUST FOLLOW OUR OWN path. It is not far. It is within reach. "Perhaps you have been on it since you were born and did not know." Indeed, I did not know that Windham and Blackhead would count as the first two mountains on my path when I showed up on July 31, 2005, for the Escarpment Trail Run. I did not know I was embarking on a journey that would so radically change me.

The Escarpment Trail Run is a 19-mile trail race in the northern Catskills, which draws about 250 runners every year. It has a notorious reputation. The trail for which the race is named follows the spine of a long, rugged ridge with multiple peaks, and the route includes nearly 10,000 feet of cumulative elevation change, equivalent to climbing and descending a vertical mile. The path is a jumble of roots and rocks snaking through damp, tangled forest. The race website shows a runner with blood oozing from her knee.

I had come here in search of adventure, but now that I was riding to the start, peering out a dirty school bus window, the steep wooded slopes looked dark and menacing. I was 42 years old, an undistinguished athlete with little to my credit besides a couple of marathons with mediocre times. As a child, I was uncoordinated and hated gym. As a teenager, I was plagued by chronic shin splints. Part of what impelled me now was a sense of duty to preserve my fitness, as I'd seen colleagues struggle with health problems. However, I had never participated in a trail race. I don't recall having ever run on a trail.

Once the race started, I discovered that trail running is totally different from pounding the pavement. Scrambling up ledges, hopping across roots, jumping from rock to rock was great fun—I just had to pick my feet up a little higher. That is, it was fun until the halfway mark, when my calves began to twinge. I fought off cramps until a mile from the finish, at which point a rock caught my foot, both legs locked up, and I went flying. As I was lying on the ground, muscles spasming, another runner neared and gave me a doubtful look. I waved him on then dragged myself to the finish, where I lay in the grass until the twitches calmed.

At this point in my life, I was living in New York City with my wife, Sue, our two teenaged kids, Emeline and Philip, and Odie, the family Labradoodle. After a bumpy start in investment banking, I'd gained some traction as a research analyst. My job was to recommend stocks for institutional investors, which was a mission I pursued with great enthusiasm. Indeed, I was relentless in tracking down any scrap of information that might shed light on a company's fate. And I worked diligently, toiling late into the night on my models, forecasts, and reports. Sometimes I felt like a hunter tracking prey. Sometimes I got surprised and became the prey myself. Wall Street research took a toll, but it was exciting; the stakes were high and the markets always volatile. Over time, I became more established in my career, but work remained incredibly intense, like riding on one of those old-fashioned roller coasters where the wooden beams shiver and creak as the cars rattle by.

To keep my mental balance, I kept up with running, heading out in the mornings for a jog and signing up for races on the weekends. Inspired by the Escarpment Trail Run, I screwed up my courage and registered for a 50-kilometer (30.5-mile) ultramarathon. I completed it successfully, crossing the finish line in second-to-last place. It didn't take long for me to raise my sights. A few months later, I finished a 50-mile race, this time in third-to-last.

Ultrarunning was a good fit for me, since it rewarded grit, rather than athletic skill, of which I had little. By simply trying harder, I could cover longer distances. By trying harder, I could go faster, too. I was no elite, and I was no longer young, but with additional training, my times became respectable. I was thrilled to become decent at something that was physically demanding. After so many hours in meetings, on calls, and sitting behind the computer, it was such a blast to disengage from the complexity, get outside into the sun and open air, and run!

A few more years passed. I was promoted, and my workload expanded. As I took on more responsibility, I managed the incremental stress by seeking out bigger ultrarunning challenges. In 2010, I survived California's Death Valley to complete the 135-mile Badwater Ultramarathon. The next year I ran the 100-mile Leadville Trail Run in the Colorado Rockies, just barely making it over Hope Pass (12,600 feet elevation) before the cut-off. I wasn't the only person participating in the sport—at this point the sport of ultrarunning was beginning to take off.

As my fiftieth birthday drew near, the idea occurred for a special adventure: a solo thru-run of New York's 350-mile Long Path, which stretches from New York City to the John Boyd Thacher State Park a few miles west of Albany. I set off on August 25, 2013, and, with help from Sue, who brought me food when I ran out, completed the trail 9 days 3 hours and 6 minutes later, beating the prior record of 12 days.[1]

For someone like me, setting a record was an empowering experience. I'd never before distinguished myself at sports. I'd never won a race. As a kid, I was so bad in gym, I was the last one picked for teams or games. Now, I basked in the recognition, taking pride in having shown people what was possible with a little effort and feeling like I'd made the world a slightly better place.

The Long Path led me from New York City, through the Hudson Valley, then into the Catskill Mountains, where, over the course of 100 miles, the trail took me up and over 11 mountains: Peekamoose, Table, Slide, Cornell, Wittenberg, Plateau, Sugarloaf, Twin, Indian Head, and (for the second time) Blackhead and Windham. This part of the thru-run took three days. It left me blistered, injured, and out of food. While at the time it seemed like a great deal of work, it was only a tiny fraction of what was to come.

---

1 I wrote a book about this adventure entitled *Running the Long Path: A 350-Mile Journey of Discovery in New York's Hudson Valley*.

By this point, it'd been almost 20 years since I'd first set foot in the Catskills. Perhaps I'd fallen under the mountains' spell and simply did not know.

THE MOUNTAINS CALL

One cold and windy December day, three months after my Long Path run, Sue, a friend of hers, Odie, and I went for a hike in the Shawangunk Mountains, situated halfway between New York City and the Catskills. After arriving in Berme Road Park in the town of Ellenville, we split up. Sue and her friend headed off for a scenic overlook, while Odie and I set out for the summit.

Odie and I were partners; we'd been running together for years. In the city, Odie spent most of his time asleep, as there wasn't much for him to do indoors. But in the mountains, he came alive. How he loved to run!

We now picked our way up the side of the ridge on a rocky, washed-out trail, stepped through the shadows of stately hemlocks, then emerged into the vast pitch pine barrens that rolled in green waves across the plateau. A final scramble brought us to a vantage point from which we could see the Catskill Mountains, 30 miles away. With wind thundering out of the north, I took shelter behind a boulder with Odie. When I finally raised my eyes and squinted into the blast, I saw a distant mountain wall flashing in crystal bands of blue and white.

Even today I remember the scene distinctly—how it felt like a signal was emanating from those peaks, with a code that unlocked something deep inside me. How I felt anticipation and a surge of energy, as if I could sense the whine of engines powering up. Suddenly I understood that the mountains were calling to me—and had been all my life—only before this moment, the sound had been drowned out by the roar of work, family, and the day-to-day distractions of life in the modern world.

During his first summer in the Sierra, the author, environmentalist, and mountaineer John Muir heard "many still, small voices, as well as the noon thunder" inviting him to come higher. "Every rock, mountain, stream, plant, lake, lawn, forest, garden, bird, beast, insect seems to call and invite us." But to me, the call sounded like a warning. *Behind these mountain walls temperatures are colder, winds stronger, conditions rougher than where you stand now. People get hurt out here and sometimes die. Don't expect help or sympathy or acknowledgment of any kind because to us you are nothing. Nothing but a spark—flickering in the breeze for an instant—gone in a blink.*

I thought about this message, while the wind whistled through pine needles and the mountains glittered blue-white in the frigid light. I'd never set foot in the Catskills during winter. But now I pictured myself running the 30 miles from here to there, even pushing on to the boreal forests of the distant north, and felt a rush of exhilaration because I knew in theory that I could.

Odie is an intelligent dog. He looked up at me with an expression that seemed to say he knew his duty and would follow me to the end of the world. But there was a look in his eyes that hinted even dogs have their limits—let's not forget the fireplace and warm sofa waiting for us back home.

Odie was right. Today was not the day to take on the winter mountains. Yet I couldn't help casting one last glance back at the mysterious mountain wall. Then I shook off the sense of enchantment, and we headed back down the trail.

Over the winter of 2013 to 2014, I heeded the Catskills' warning and stayed away. But after the record-setting Long Path run, I was hungry for another challenge. I was prepared to undertake any trial, endure any test of strength and will, no matter how extreme. I would have done *anything* for another shot at distinction.

View of the Catskills' southern escarpment from a snowy
perch in the Shawangunk Mountains.

CHAPTER 2

HOOKED BY A NEW CHALLENGE

NOW 52 YEARS OLD, MY PASSION FOR RUNNING WAS OUT OF CONTROL. I was constantly racing, on roads and on trails, at distances from one mile to one hundred, and when I wasn't racing, I was training *intensely*. As I ran farther, I hungered to run even longer distances. As I ran faster, I became determined to improve my times, if only by another second. This was the mindset of a conventional runner, preoccupied with speed and distance, except that I was perhaps a little more driven than some, or in the heat of my enthusiasm took things a little further to the extreme.

Life was quiet at home. Emeline was away at school, and Philip was getting ready to join her, while Sue was busy with her own priorities. My corporate life was changing. I'd left my job as an analyst and joined a management team to help raise capital for acquisitions. For someone with my background, this was a dream assignment. But it was a different kind of role. I brought to the team a deep understanding of how investors value companies, but I had no experience in operations, while my partners were executives with long track records who had led some of the largest financial organizations in the country. At first we had some disagreements and sometimes clashed, as the stakes were high. Our success would hinge on finding acquisitions and integrating them, a strategy for which there was no established playbook. Over time, my colleagues came to appreciate the clarity of my logic and my creative approach to communications. On my part, while I would have liked to play a bigger leadership role, in practice I deferred to them and spent the greater portion of my time listening and trying to learn.

I eventually settled into the new role. I found myself on frequent conference calls, dug into complicated analyses, and drafted memos and presentations, eager to tell our story in a clear, concise manner (but with a touch of flair where possible). I was good at these tasks, but it was largely left-side-of-the-brain type work. Sometimes I tired of the endless calculations. Sometimes I craved the feeling of intensity that comes from marshaling an all-out effort.

THE BADWATER DOUBLE

In early 2014, I turned my attention to California's Death Valley. At the base of the Funeral Mountains lies a small depression with a seep of brackish water called Badwater Basin. At 282 feet below sea level, this spot is the lowest point in the continental US. One hundred forty-six miles away by road and trail lies the summit of Mt. Whitney. At 14,505 feet in elevation, this spot is the highest point in the continental US. On July 1, 2014, I set out to attempt the so-called Badwater Double, a 292-mile round trip from Badwater to the summit of Mt. Whitney and back again. The goal was to run, survive, and, if possible, break the record of 96 hours 7 minutes, set in 2001 by the legendary ultrarunner, mountaineer, and adventure racer Marshall Ulrich.

The Badwater Double was a challenging endeavor, with three mountain ranges to climb each way, temperatures that peaked at 127°F, and gale-force headwinds that hit me toward the end of the run, when I was struggling from the accumulated fatigue. But I was in excellent condition, with an exceptional support team by my side. On the third day, as my tired mind began to struggle with hallucinations, the mountains took on the appearance of sinister faces, and the white line along the shoulder swirled and faded. By this point, I could no longer talk. Each step seemed like the hardest thing I'd ever done, but as my pacers trotted into the wind, I made a supreme effort and followed them. After going four days with a total of four hours of sleep, I sprinted across the finish line in an elapsed time of 94 hours and 39 minutes, breaking the record by a small margin. I fell asleep instantly and woke up the next day feeling on top of the world. I didn't even have a blister.

Sue was relieved that I hadn't died—she'd seen from Facebook posts that my crew had pushed me hard. My boss at work, who'd completed 33 marathons in his time, located a photograph of me during the run wearing a desert hat with flaps that draped around my neck, which he had framed and placed in the company's small reception area. I was embarrassed yet delighted by the attention. I was brimming with confidence. I was eager to do more.

"Life is an ecstasy," wrote Ralph Waldo Emerson, the nineteenth-century founder of American transcendentalism. "Each man is a jet of flame." That is exactly how I felt.

THE CAVE DOG TAKE-DOWN

That fall, hardly had I settled back into my routine when out of the blue there arrived an email from a group I'd never heard of, called the Hardcore Hikers of New York. The "Cave Dog Take-Down" was about to take place. This would be an opportunity "to be part of history."

Some inquiries among Catskill-savvy friends revealed that "Cave Dog" was the nickname of Ted Keizer, a hiker and ultrarunner who owned an intriguing speed-climbing record for the Catskill Mountains. During September 2002, he'd climbed all 35 high peaks in a single trip, finishing the 137-mile route in 2 days 15 hours and 24 minutes. It was this record the Hardcore Hikers were trying to overturn.

Further research revealed that Keizer's Catskill record was one of many. He'd completed similar speed-climbing exploits in the Adirondacks, White Mountains, Colorado Rockies, southern Appalachians, and on Vermont's Long Trail. Keizer had been christened Cave Dog while working in Colorado and living in a cave 45 minutes by snowshoe from the nearest road. According to his website, Keizer hiked and climbed extensively. He wrote that he loved all forms of wilderness, "from the peaks to the canyons, from the swamps to the desert, from the woods to the tundra," and most of all the wildlife and wildflowers.

The record intrigued me, but Keizer was intimidating. He seemed like an authentic Mountain Man, whereas I felt like a pretender. Sure, I loved to run, but deep down I was quite comfortable sitting behind a computer. (It had never occurred to me to try living in a cave.)

Yet a spark had landed in my imagination and kindled a small flame of interest, and I couldn't help pondering the "how." As a New York resident, the Catskills were right in my backyard, which meant I could train on the course extensively. I also had some experience navigating with map and compass, dating back to a four-year career in the US Army as an infantry officer and briefly as a Ranger. These skills would help me find my way on the Catskill peaks that had no paths. As a runner, maybe I could pick up some time where the trails were flat.

I heard nothing more from the Hardcore Hikers.

That fall I began to organize a few training runs to familiarize myself with Keizer's route, including visits to some of the Catskill peaks I hadn't climbed before. Today, these memories have a distant dreamy quality, but I still remember some interesting discoveries. For example, on the way up Peekamoose, I recall startling an adolescent black bear, which slid down a tree like a fireman on a pole. Later that evening, I spotted the bear back up in the branches. I tiptoed by, careful not to disturb the animal as it was getting ready for bed, then paused and snapped a surreptitious photo, which came out blurry.

Another bear encounter happened on Halcott. On this trip, I was accompanied by Odie and my son Philip, then 16 years old. As we approached the summit from the southwest, following a compass heading through a tangle of berry brambles, I looked up and found myself face-to-face with another black bear, this one big and old. It looked mortified to have been caught by surprise—*by humans!* Odie pricked his ears but was too low in the brush to see. Philip told me later he heard a growl. When I looked again, the bear had magically vanished.

We descended from the summit. Heading back to the car along a quiet country lane, we sauntered beneath a row of maples blazing like colored candles against a swirling chrome-blue sky. Philip and Odie trotted along together, and I felt so happy watching them. They seemed so full of innocence and joy.

I hadn't made a firm commitment to take down Cave Dog's record, but feeling cocky, I started dropping hints among my running friends about how there might be something special going down in the Catskill Mountains.

Odie on the way to Peekamoose. January 18, 2015.

CHAPTER 3

RACING AFTER CAVE DOG

T<small>HERE WAS LEGITIMATE REASON TO FEEL COCKY</small>—I <small>WAS IN THE BEST</small> shape of my life. Over the last 18 months, I'd set one new personal record after another. Of course, I knew that age would one day slow me down, but I wasn't going to give in without a fight.

I hadn't forgotten the Catskills' warning to beware the winter mountains. Over the winter of 2014 and 2015, I stayed away but for a single trip (I have a photograph of Odie peering down from atop a snowy ledge on the way to Peekamoose). Otherwise, I ran on roads and at the local track, in preparation for a busy schedule of spring races, including the Boston Marathon, where I woke up on race morning to chilly, wet conditions and a head cold, but persevered and set yet another personal best.

On the train ride back from Boston, as sunlight filtered through the leafless trackside trees, my thoughts swung back to the Catskills. The best window to take on Keizer's record would be late May, when days would be lengthening and temperatures rising, but before the foliage had leafed out fully and made it hard to navigate.

There were still a handful of mountains left to scout, including Kaaterskill High Peak. Saturday morning, five days after Boston, I woke up with a headache and cough (the head cold still lingering) but somehow pulled myself together. Sensing something was up, Odie was jumping in circles and barking even before I opened the car door. He hopped in, and we raced up to the Platte Clove parking area on the Catskills' eastern rampart, a little more than an hour's drive away.

From the trailhead we followed a footpath up the mountain's shoulder, then cut through the woods to a muddy snowmobile trail circling the summit. From here, a short scramble took us up a steep, unmarked trail and onto a sunlit ledge. We came upon Kaaterskill's summit a few steps later, where I was surprised, so late in April, to find a dusting of snow. Continuing north down the mountain's backside led to another scramble, but now the surfaces were slick with ice. I was stepping with extreme caution when one of my feet slipped out from under me—and suddenly I was flying. The acceleration frightened me, but the slide lasted just a couple of yards. I stood up tentatively and dusted off, furious with myself, for that misstep might have led to injury.

But there was no harm done. Down a little farther, the sun was beaming through the leafless trees, and the ground was bare again. As we jogged back to the car, I noticed that my cough and headache had vanished, while Odie, who'd had no trouble with the ice, bounded along enthusiastically, ears flapping and tongue lolling.

The next weekend, I ran a 50-mile race in the Shawangunk Mountains called Rock The Ridge. I'd come up with the idea for the event a few years back, convinced the Mohonk Preserve to host it, and recruited my friend Todd Jennings to design and direct the race. This year I ran shirtless, carrying nothing, slipping through the trees like the breeze, the sunbaked ridgeline and vernal woodlands sliding by in a dreamy mist of amber-mottled light. I was thrilled with my time, a little over seven hours and less than 90 minutes behind the winner, a runner named Ben Nephew, who was the undisputed champion of New England trail racing (among many other victories, he'd won the Escarpment Trail Run almost every year). Ben was also 12 years younger. In hindsight, I was, like Icarus, flying dangerously close to the sun. In my case, borne aloft mainly by exuberance.

A FINAL TEST RUN

A week after Rock The Ridge, it was time for a final test run to determine whether I was ready to challenge Keizer's record and seize the title for the Catskills. The plan was ambitious: to bag 17 peaks over 50 miles.

It was the second Saturday in May and a bright spring morning when I arrived at the base of Peekamoose Mountain. I took a deep breath, clicked the start button on my GPS watch, and just like that, 3.8 miles to the summit passed in a flash. From here it was less than a mile to the next peak, Table Mountain.

However, from Table to the next five peaks, there was no trail. I would have to travel straight through the forest, which is not the kind of challenge runners face in a typical ultramarathon. So now I backtracked a short distance, searching for the point of departure where I'd leave the trail and plunge into the pathless thickets that cloak this rugged ridge. Pausing for a moment, I stared into a chaos of fir and spruce. A wall of trees. Spindly. Mute. Bristling with broken branches. It looked about as welcoming as barbed wire. Feeling hesitant, I stepped into the forest and began threading my way between the trunks, aiming for the saddle (the low point on the ridge) between Table and my next objective, Lone Mountain. Somehow I missed the saddle and ended up too far downhill, an error that forced me to claw my way back up, spending extra time and effort. I finally reached Lone's summit, but with the navigation error and the thick vegetation, unstable footing, and steep terrain, I wasn't moving at the pace I'd hoped to.

Navigation on this ridge was vexing. The forest was too thick to see the lay of the land, so I followed a compass heading. But this method invariably led me straight into the worst obstacles—boulders, impenetrable clusters of saplings, deadfall heaped in tangled piles. The GPS-enabled map on my phone showed my location, but it was hard to tell the direction I was moving. Sometimes the display seemed to orient the wrong way, as if I were holding the device upside down. When I'd first scouted this ridge the summer before, I'd marched along, staring at the phone instead of looking where I was stepping, and ended up going in a circle!

I staggered a few steps forward from Lone's summit, then paused to peer uneasily into treetops, as the slope fell away precipitously in front of me. The scene was unsettling. Not only was there risk of injury in a remote location with no way to summon help, but even the smallest navigational errors were enormously costly—and how I hate wasting time! Especially when trying to challenge a record.

I tried to run, only to stumble when my foot punched through a rotten log. I squeezed between two saplings, only to have my hat knocked to the ground. I clambered over a mess of fallen trees, tiptoed through a tumble of slick, mossy rocks, and hoisted myself up a sandstone ledge, my fingers clawing for a secure hold. This wasn't running; it was more like climbing on a jungle gym. For someone used to hustling along on roads and trails, the mental focus needed to navigate these obstacles was draining. All I got for trying to move quickly was scratched and bruised, and the sluggish pace was discouraging.

Once again a branch knocked my hat to the forest floor. Stooping to pick it up, I saw a shoelace had come untied. With a sinking heart, I realized I was falling apart. I didn't need to glance at my watch to know my grandiose plans were crumbling. I was moving too slowly to threaten Keizer's record.

I plopped down on the ground and tried to collect my thoughts. Next to me, a trillium flower with three maroon petals was sprouting from the earth. It stared at me with a questioning expression on its one-eyed face, as if it had never encountered someone like me before and couldn't fathom what I was doing in its neighborhood.

After some thought, I decided to cut the run short, go back home, and spend the rest of the weekend with the family. My relentless battle with the thickets resumed until I finally regained the trail. A few hours later, I pulled up on Panther Mountain's summit ledge, where I stopped to eat a snack and marvel at the secluded valley spread out below, echoing with chirps and hoots as it slowly awakened from the deep sleep of winter.

It was dusk, and I was almost down in a narrow valley when, looking up, I spied a yellow glow. My first thought was of headlights in the parking lot. Then I realized this was the last of the sun, spilling out from between low cloudbanks and a distant mountain wall. A story from *The Iliad* came to mind, of how the god Hephaestus forged a magic shield for the warrior Achilles. For a moment it seemed I might be staring straight into the forge on Mount Olympus where Hephaestus worked the precious metals with tongs and a massive hammer, while 20 magic bellows blew upon the flames.

I blinked. The vision vanished. A few minutes later I was trotting along a road in the valley, heading to where my car was parked many miles away. Night fell. Up above on darkened slopes, deer eyes flashed in my headlamp's glow.

I'd climbed 10 peaks and covered close to 40 miles, but I'd failed to achieve my goal. I wasn't ready to take on Keizer's record—not even close. Disappointed but nowhere near ready to give up, I knew I'd just have to try harder.

Trillium.

CHAPTER 4

BATTLING WITH NATURE OFF-TRAIL

RETIRED MARINE CORPS GENERAL JIM MATTIS COUNSELS YOUNG leaders: "If you haven't read hundreds of books, you are functionally illiterate, and you will be incompetent, because your personal experiences alone aren't enough to sustain you." I'd spent four years in the Army, during which time I'd read a lot of military history for just this reason, and afterward I turned my attention to other subjects, hungry for insights that might help me achieve my various goals.

It was around the time when the Catskill thickets had foiled my plans to take down the Cave Dog record that I discovered the work of another well-regarded general, the second-century Roman emperor Marcus Aurelius. "Nothing is evil which is according to nature," he'd written in his *Meditations*, explaining that if you feel pain from an external object, it's not the object that disturbs you, but your attitude. It should be in your power, he argued, to set your own mind straight.

In my case, I caught myself blaming the fir-spruce thickets for my slow pace and the frustration I'd felt as I fought my way through them. But rough terrain is part of nature. It doesn't do any good to blame it.

After some reflection, I came up with a new plan. I would take another shot at Cave Dog's record in the fall. In the meantime, what I needed was more practice on this surprisingly rugged terrain, which meant devoting the summer to training. As soon as I made this decision, my frustration was forgotten, and the enthusiasm came rushing back. I was still on track to realize my dreams—it was merely the timetable that had changed. And how thrilling it would be to spend the summer in the mountains!

If I could have, I would have spent not only every weekend there, but every weekday, too. At least that's how I felt at the time. Over the years, my hunger for nature had been gradually intensifying until by this point it seemed insatiable. No doubt, my job was partly to blame. I'd chosen to rent an office in New York City without windows because it was less expensive, but as I spent long days working on presentations and analyses, the smooth white surfaces, humming lights, and occasional whiff of toner began to wear on me. Sometimes, feeling short of air, I'd take a break and walk around the block. I would push my way through the hustle of tourists and smartly dressed professionals and peer up at the office buildings, studying their stark geometry and trying to appreciate the long lines and hard angles. But the architecture didn't move me. It was too sterile. In the distance, at the end of long avenues flanked by towers, I caught glimpses of sunlit clouds hurrying across the harbor.

Even when I flew out of the city for a board meeting, I listened with one ear to a succession of reports while doodling on a note pad, but what kept attracting my attention was a pair of French doors that opened onto a putting green, beyond which stood a grove of oak trees shimmering under the hot spring sun. I couldn't help but stare. How I wished I could be outside!

I read a survey stating that contemporary Americans spend on average 93 percent of their time indoors, which struck me as outrageous. The American transcendentalist Henry David Thoreau wrote that he could not preserve his health and spirits without passing at least four hours a day outside. He professed surprise that the shopkeepers and mechanics of his time could tolerate working endless hours indoors: "I think they deserve some credit for not having all committed suicide long ago."

Compared to Thoreau, I was flexible. I worked diligently in my windowless office during the weekdays and hung out with my family in the evenings. But the weekends were sacred; they were my time to train.

A SUMMER TO TRAIN

It occurred to me that to break the Catskills record, I might need to navigate off-trail during periods of darkness. To prepare for this scenario, I headed back to the mountains in late May to run a circuit called "The Nine," which summits nine peaks, including those on the pathless ridge cloaked with those nearly impenetrable fir-spruce thickets.[2] Starting after sunset, I clawed my way through the tangled vegetation all night long, my awareness limited to the obstacles within my headlamp's cone of light and the blue dot representing my position on my phone. It was steady, methodical work, and grueling. At one point, I reached up to clamber atop a sandstone boulder, when my fingers slipped and I lost my grip and fell—but luck was with me as I landed on my back in a bed of moss. After eight or nine hours of this, I emerged onto Wittenberg's summit ledge in the orange haze of dawn.

That summer I ventured to the Catskills for training runs as frequently as possible, driven by my desire for Keizer's record and an insatiable hunger to be outdoors. While my purpose was to practice moving faster, I was also fascinated by what I saw. On one run, it was a quiet grotto where the headwaters of the Esopus Creek pool beneath a grove of hemlocks, which stood around the water like sentinels. Or a sandstone boulder draped with a complex tapestry of moss and ferns and lichen. On another run, it was graceful pink flowers with long curling stamens growing by a sandstone ledge, which later I learned are called *pinxterbloom azalea*, and how those hot pink flashes contrasted with the misty blue of distant ridgelines.

On one visit I was creeping through first-growth forest when a movement caught my eye. I froze behind a tree. A black bear materialized out of thin air—a stout, shaggy creature—and shambled off into the woods. I stood in place, hardly breathing, while a quiet voice inside my head said *don't move yet*. A moment later a second bear lumbered into sight. I held my breath and waited an extra moment before venturing on.

---

2   The Nine consist of Peekamoose, Table, Lone, Rocky, Balsam Cap, Friday, Wittenberg, Cornell, and Slide.

THE MANY CHALLENGES OF BUSHWHACKING

The sport of running takes place on roads or trails where the obstacles have been cleared away. Moving through the mountains is altogether different. Navigating off trail is called "bushwhacking," and for me, a constant theme was the aggravation of encountering endless obstacles when trying to move quickly.

For example, take hobblebush, so-called because its arching branches sprout roots where they touch the ground, creating cage-like tangles that snag the legs of unwary hikers. Covered with heart-shaped, prominently veined leaves and, in late spring, clusters of small white flowers, these bushes often reach overhead.

Beech saplings are also extremely annoying, and the Catskills have a lot of them. When mature beech trees become diseased (evident from the pockmarks on the bark) they thrust up legions of young suckers, whose whiplike branches lash at face and chest.

Arguably, deadfall presents the most complicated barrier. Picture piles of fallen trees with sharp broken limbs radiating in all directions, which makes climbing over the trunks a delicate operation. To avoid these traps, I tried to scan ahead, but this made it hard to see where I was stepping. So I'd find myself groping forward, one hand stretched out to deflect beech branches, the other clutching compass, while my feet had to feel their way across an unpredictable mix of spongy moss, twisted roots, and slippery, tilting rocks.

Of course, steep grades make everything worse. Trying to climb or descend through tumbles of slanted rocks, often slicked with moss or shrouded with fallen leaves, while at the same time pushing through vegetation, is an exercise in instability that often left me out of breath, off-balance, and out of sorts.

For someone like me, used to the rapid pace and steady rhythm of pounding pavement, bushwhacking was mentally demanding. Sometimes I'd glance at my GPS watch and see the pace reading out at one mile per hour. This was disheartening. But I persevered, reckoning that practice would make me faster.

I remember on one trip bagging five peaks along a 30-mile circuit, half of which was off-trail. The sun was setting, the last rays slanting through the foliage, the hobblebush flowers floating like tiny white boats in a sea of green shadows. Somewhere nearby a barred owl called once ("hoo-hoo hoo-hooooo") and then again ("who cooks your food?"). For a moment, I was floating along the trail, mind empty. Then the feeling passed. I missed my family and was anxious to be home.

CHAPTER 5

SLIPPING FROM
MY GRASP

The bushwhacks were painful, but I was slowly becoming more adept at navigating the thickets, even if it still felt like I was plowing straight into almost every obstacle. The practice was paying off.

In June I ran a 53-mile trail race in the Catskills called Manitou's Revenge. This was an excellent training exercise because the course closely follows the second half of Keizer's route, including a section of the Devil's Path, a trail notorious for the brutal scrambles. It was a dark, misty day, and the rocks were slick and treacherous, forcing me to scoot down certain slabs on my butt. Going uphill, though, I was able to power-hike aggressively, and I beamed with pride when someone called me a "hill-climbing ninja." Throughout the 17 hours it took me to reach the finish, I felt strong and steady, and what a thrill it was to pass some runners near the end!

Later that summer I showed up at my favorite track at the SUNY New Paltz campus, a 400-meter oval with a bright blue surface and a spongy feel underfoot, overlooked by the Shawangunk Mountains to the west and the Catskills to the north. I made a point to relax my mind and ran the fastest ¼-mile splits of my life. Two weeks later, I came back and ran the splits even quicker. This was pure exhilaration.

There was one last race on the calendar, the 100-mile Beast of Burden, which takes place alongside the Erie Canal a few miles east of Buffalo, New York. The event, held twice a year, gives runners a chance to experience both winter and summer conditions. I'd run the race back in February and not only set a personal record for the 100-mile distance, but won third place overall, a rare podium finish. The August edition would be an opportunity to practice skills for the upcoming Catskills run, such as managing nutrition, hydration, and pacing. Perhaps I'd beat my prior time and set yet another personal best.

As race day dawned, conditions looked ideal. But warming up before the start, something didn't feel quite right. The first few miles went well, but suddenly I tripped. And while I executed a combat roll and was back on my feet immediately, I felt somewhat troubled to have fallen where the path was smooth and flat

By mile 35, I was struggling. A strain had developed somewhere in my hips or groin, and my legs ached all over. By mile 40, my pace was barely faster than a walk. I'm cautious about taking pain relievers while running, not wanting to mask information about my body, but there are exceptions to every rule, especially in difficult circumstances. So I popped a couple of pills, which loosened up the sore muscles and helped me swing my legs more easily. I trotted along the canal path, taking in the sight of boats docked alongside the banks, and later, when dawn broke, of the morning mists drifting through an orchard of apple trees, only to fall apart again with a handful of miles to go, when another runner overtook me and I couldn't marshal the strength to catch up.

For all the drama, my finishing time was only a couple of hours slower than in February. And there wasn't anything necessarily *ominous* about this injury—I'd had plenty of strains over the years and always bounced back quickly. But recovery took longer than normal. It was two weeks before I could run again, and the hip strain or groin pull—whatever it was—continued to bother me intermittently.

After a busy summer, maybe it was time for a break. Sue had organized a special treat for the family: a vacation in the European Alps filled with great food and wine, beautiful sights, and friendly people. Although there was some conflict—when it came to museums, Sue and the kids liked to take their time, whereas I would fly through them, typically in 30 minutes or less, my goal being to focus on a few items that made a strong impression rather than trying to take in everything. Then the tables were turned on me. It was my turn to lag behind when Philip and I went out for an easy jog, and I could not keep up (understandably, as Philip was now co-captain of his high school cross-country team, but also my recent injury had not yet fully healed).

THE BAREFOOT EXPERIMENT

On the last day of vacation, I had an idea for an experiment. I'd read Christopher McDougall's bestseller, *Born to Run*, in which he argues that shoes increase the risk of injury because they alter a runner's gait compared to running barefoot, the natural way to move. Not far from our hotel, an inviting dirt path led up a ski slope. The experiment would be to work on natural form while taking a break from the stress of running—by hiking barefoot.

Honestly, the results of the experiment were inconclusive, although I did surprise some cows who looked at me wide-eyed, as if they'd never seen a person walking without shoes before. Whether I'd improved my gait, I couldn't tell. Nor was it much of a revelation to find gravel was irritating, mud slippery, and grass soft. But one thing surprised me—walking without shoes was fun. I felt like a kid again, admittedly a strange reaction for someone who'd *never* gone barefoot as a child.

Upon returning to New York, I decided to repeat my barefoot hiking experiment on a Catskill trail. One morning in early September, Odie and I headed out to Peekamoose Mountain. I stepped out of the car wearing sandals (which I'd bought for the minimalist feel and recently started running in), and removed them with some trepidation. Gingerly, I began picking my way along the rocky trail, feeling off-balance and awkward as I tried to tiptoe between the stones. Odie was ecstatic to be outdoors. He scampered ahead, spotted a chipmunk, and sprinted after it. Within half a second, a dozen nearby chipmunks had dashed to the safety of their holes and were chattering at us furiously.

I advanced along the trail with exquisite care, placing one soft foot upon the ground and then the other. Small black berries littered the path, which gave way to white pebbles and gray sand higher up. On the final ascent to the summit, fir needles and twigs prickled underfoot. A puddle of black boreal mud cooled my scratched and tired feet; the moss-covered rocks felt luxurious. At the top Odie and I kicked back on a nearby vantage point and enjoyed the sunny views. Slipping the sandals back on made the return a little quicker. The trail up Peekamoose was a familiar route, but this time the climb felt different. The sensory perception from the soles of my feet added an extra layer of information and a whole new dimension to the experience. I felt more exposed to the environment, more deeply immersed, as if I'd leapt naked into a swimming hole. As if I'd become a part of the forest, instead of merely passing through.

It was now early September and time to set a date for my attempt to take down Keizer's record, but one last race was tempting me. The Fifth Avenue Mile in New York City was an old favorite. The year before, I'd set a personal best, running the mile even faster than I did in college. With the groin feeling a little better, I decided to give the race a try, hungry for a new record if only by a fraction of a second. When the gun went off, I sprung from the start, jostled my way through a wave of slower runners, flew down the smooth pavement, and soon was gasping desperately for air. I reached the ¾-mile mark and looked up for the finish line, but with my heart beating at 100 percent of maximum and leg muscles starting to quiver, it seemed impossibly far away. I put out a terrific effort and finished strong, but my time was 10 or 15 seconds slower than the year before, which came as a horrible shock.

FOILED BY INJURY

Afterward the groin strain came back. Then the top of my right foot started hurting. Over the next few days, the two injuries alternated, as if they were tag-teaming me. If the foot felt better on one run, the groin was sure to ache, and the next day would be the reverse.

I had blown my chance at Cave Dog's record. With two nagging injuries, trying to cover 137 miles and summit 35 peaks was out of the question. Now winter was on the way. The next window to launch an attempt would be the following spring, which was eight months away. It might as well have been a lifetime.

But when one plan doesn't work, I've often found that another will occur. Maybe the mountains were still whispering, because soon enough, from somewhere deep inside my mind there bubbled up a strange idea.

First barefoot hike in the Catskills. Peekamoose, September 6, 2015.

CHAPTER 6

A NEW OBSESSION

THE STRANGE IDEA WAS TO DO MORE HIKING IN THE CATSKILLS barefoot and see if I could get all 35 high peaks done this way.

Admittedly, this would be an unconventional approach, but I had a rationale. Moving slowly, as was necessary without shoes, might help me become more familiar with the mountains. Instead of trying to barrel through the thickets, I'd see more, learn more, and perhaps come to feel more at home in an environment that for now seemed alien, if not downright hostile. Greater familiarity might help me move with more confidence when the time came once again to travel swiftly.

Deeper down, I had another reason for going barefoot. For an aging athlete, an occasional break from speed was starting to sound like a sensible idea. And no matter how slowly I went at first, it would be fun to pursue a new discipline and have something to improve at, since my times in shoes no longer seemed to be getting faster.

The very next weekend after climbing Peekamoose, I raced back to the Catskills for a barefoot attempt on Hunter and Southwest Hunter. It was another slow-paced, cautious operation, but the intense concentration required for each step, the contrast between edgy rocks and smooth cool dirt, and the feeling that I was prowling through the forest like an animal made the experience wildly exhilarating. When I woke up the next morning, the soles of my feet were tingling—hungry, it seemed, for more sensations. Next up was Rusk Mountain, which would be my first barefoot bushwhack.

Odie and I were on the road before dawn. This morning, we were witness to a vision phantasmagorical: golden-orange clouds flaming so brightly it seemed the horizon had caught fire. The Catskills loomed in the north, gleaming purple under lilac sky, as if they'd dropped their shaggy robes and stood there naked.

Arriving at the Spruceton Road parking area, we started out along a gravelly trail. Odie dashed ahead, exuberant and full of energy as always, then looked back quizzically as I crept along in slow motion, wincing as the crunchy gravel jabbed into my feet. At a bend in the trail, I pulled out my compass, dialed in a northwestern azimuth (or compass heading), and led us into the woods. We crossed a creek and splashed through cold water swirling over mud and mossy stones. Then it was onto layers of beech leaves—papery, crinkly, slippery. The surprise was that without shoes, the forest floor was softer and easier to walk on than the trail.

We stumbled upon a faint path, perhaps a thruway for bear and deer, which soon petered out among a patch of berry canes. Extricating myself from the thorns, I blundered next into a growth of stinging nettles, so-called because the leaves and stems bristle with toxin-filled needles that impart a burning sensation when they brush against the skin. Fortunately, these had lost their vigor. I pushed through thickets of whip-like beech that lashed against my face and chest, while Odie slunk underneath, before ducking under dead fir branches which showered dried-out needles down my back. The slope steepened. Above us loomed a blue-gray wall of rock splashed with white lichen, the only channel between the slabs choked with brush. Odie was undaunted, but I had to take a few deep breaths to keep from feeling overwhelmed. We edged around to the right. Groped through more tangles. Stepped across matted thorny stems, which pricked the bottoms of my feet. It required such constant focus to navigate this chaos, it seemed to take forever to reach the summit, although later when I checked the data from my watch, the elapsed time was just two hours.

This experience left me with the impression that the worst bushwhacks get progressively steeper and more tangled the farther you go. It's like getting caught in a snare, where the more you struggle, the more tightly you get stuck. Sometimes I get that feeling at work, when a project turns out to be more involved than it first appeared, and it starts to dawn on me just how much effort it will take to get it done. We talk about following a "path" through life, but bushwhacking might be the better metaphor because we often grope our way through confusing circumstances, never quite sure which direction to go.

BURROUGHS ON BAREFOOT

One of my favorite authors is John Burroughs, the Catskills nature writer whose essays were immensely popular at the turn of the twentieth century. Burroughs was on friendly terms with John Muir, although he found Muir's personality overwhelming ("You must not be in a hurry, or have any pressing duty, when you start his stream of talk and adventure. Ask him for his famous dog story... and you get the whole theory of glaciation thrown in").

In one of his essays, Burroughs extols the naked foot:

> *Occasionally on the sidewalk, amid the dapper, swiftly moving, high-heeled boots and gaiters, I catch a glimpse of the naked human foot. Nimbly it scuffs along, the toes spread, the sides flatten, the heel protrudes; it grasps the curbing, or bends to the form of the uneven surfaces,—a thing sensuous and alive, that seems to take cognizance of whatever it touches or passes. How primitive and uncivil it looks in such company,—a real barbarian in the parlor!*

"Barbarian in the parlor" is the same phrase Burroughs used to describe his friend, the poet Walt Whitman, whose poetry was too sensuous for conventional tastes of the time. Both men believed that exposure to the rough stimuli of the outdoors world was necessary for people to develop a direct connection with nature. Without this connection, the shelter of civilization becomes a prison.

Burroughs continues:

> *Though it be a black foot and an unwashed foot, it shall be exalted. It is a thing of life amid leather, a free spirit amid cramped, a wild bird amid caged, an athlete amid consumptives.... That unhampered, vitally playing piece of anatomy is the type of the pedestrian, man returned to first principles, in direct contact and intercourse with*

> *the earth and the elements, his faculties unsheathed, his*
> *mind plastic, his body toughened, his heart light, his soul*
> *dilated; while those cramped and distorted members in*
> *the calf and kid are the unfortunate wretches doomed to*
> *carriages and cushions.*

Here Burroughs is echoing Emerson, who warned (in one of his famous lines) that "the civilized man has built a coach, but has lost the use of his feet."

As far as I knew, Burroughs wore shoes habitually. But in another of his essays, I found him reminiscing about his youth as a farm boy, how in the spring he'd search out a smooth flat section along a local road, remove his boots, feel the packed dirt beneath his naked soles, and exult in a sense of light-footedness as he ran barefoot: "What a feeling of freedom, of emancipation, and of joy in the returning spring I used to experience in those warm April twilights!"

Inspired by Burroughs, I returned to my new quest with enthusiasm. But time was of the essence—it was already October, and winter was on its way.

It was 45°F and raining lightly when Odie and I reached the McKenley Hollow trailhead deep in the heart of the central Catskills. To make up for my cold feet, I piled on a long-sleeve shirt, sweater, jacket, hat, and gloves, although it didn't occur to me to swap my shorts for trousers.

The trail started out along a stream bed full of edgy sandstone fragments, as is typical in the Catskills. But I felt faster this morning. Maybe it was the spongy matted leaves covering the rocks. Or could it be I was starting to get the hang of this? Without the protection of Vibram soles, the entire body becomes a spring: The leg swings forward and pauses as you search for a landing spot, then the impact is taken up by arch, calves, quads, core. Such a different experience from clumping in heavy boots!

After crossing a stream, the path rocketed upward toward a ridge-top saddle 1,000 feet above. Odie romped ahead while I lunged from one cold, damp stone step to the next, soon chilling the bottoms of my feet. At the same time, thanks to all that insulation, the rest of me was getting warm. Too cold, too hot—multiple warning bells were going off. I paused, unzipped a couple of layers, and took a deep breath, trying to regain a tenuous sense of control.

Near the saddle, the forest brightened. A wind gust stirred the trees. Reaching an intersection, I gestured to the right, and Odie moved out, taking point. As we wound up through a series of sandstone ledges, I noticed little things: moss and lichen nestling among the rocks, ferns crowding the path, maple leaves carpeting the ground.

A moment later Odie nosed into a small clearing with a rock cairn. This was Balsam's summit. I peered around in the mist. Despite the layers I was feeling chilled again, so we didn't linger but pushed on toward our next objective, Eagle Mountain. On the way there we passed hobblebush dying back from the cold, the big floppy leaves turning flamboyant colors—orange-brown or purple flecked with green—before blackening, withering, and curling up around the edges. I stepped cautiously as the trail crossed slabs of conglomerate studded with pebbles that poked into the soft, wet, cold skin of my soles.

In due course, Odie found another side trail, which led to yet another clearing and another cairn. We'd arrived at Eagle. As we started back, a flash of luminescent green caught my eye. It was a large, fluffy patch of moss, composed of serrated triangular fronds, looking like a miniature forest of fir trees or feathers jutting from the top of a knight's helmet. Once home I looked it up in a guidebook and found that it's called knight's plume moss.

CHANNELING THOREAU

In *Walden*, Thoreau wrote, "Simplify, simplify. Instead of three meals a day, if it be necessary eat but one." Inspired by this advice, I planned a minimalist-style operation for the coming weekend. I would go barefoot, sleep in a lean-to, and eat and drink only once per day. Odie would be my companion. (Sue insisted that I bring an extra sleeping bag for him, since he'd never camped out before.)

The next day Odie and I arrived at the trailhead below Giant's Ledge and were soon clambering up a short scramble. The path leveled off and proceeded across a series of large flat stones laid down to keep hikers out of mud. I skipped along merrily, enjoying the smooth cool surfaces underfoot. From cliff-top ledges along the trail, Woodland Valley spread out below us, the fall forest speckled with hot orange and cherry red, while farther off, spiky mountain walls shone in iridescent blue.

Later that evening, we drove into the tiny Catskills hamlet of Phoenicia (population 268), where according to the plan, it was time for my first food and water since dinner the night before. Maybe it was my training as an ultrarunner, or the cool temperatures, or the beautiful day, but for whatever reason I hadn't felt hungry or thirsty all day. But now I happily wolfed down a cheeseburger and fries. Odie got a piece of my burger to supplement his dry food, which I'd brought along in a Ziploc bag.

After dinner, we drove to our next destination, the trailhead for Blackhead Mountain, which is located at the far end of a narrow valley in the northern Catskills. It was pitch-dark when we arrived. I pulled out a large pack with the two sleeping bags, and we headed out along a muddy trail. A mile and a half later we found a spot to camp. I gathered some wood and lit a small fire, which flared brightly and quickly died. I burrowed into my bag and zipped it tight while Odie settled on top of his.

Toward dawn, I woke up to the sound of wind rushing high in the trees. In the dim light, I saw a massive hemlock towering above us, branches swaying. Without any breakfast to prepare, we were quickly on the move. We followed the trail higher up the mountain, while far below, the rising sun cast a steely sheen on river fog. A large rock slab jutting from the ground was familiar to me from the Escarpment Trail Run. After this point, the path turned steep and rocky. I was soon huffing from the strain, struggling to keep my balance while barefoot on the rocks, and suddenly plagued by sharp hunger pangs. But there was no food in my pack.

There wasn't much to see on Blackhead's summit besides a large boulder surrounded by fir and spruce and a three-way intersection. We took the southern branch. For the next quarter mile, the path tunneled through dense forest, and I enjoyed the sensation of smooth damp dirt underfoot. Then the trail plunged down Blackhead's backside, skittered over a series of slick slabs dripping with moisture and strewn with stone chips. Slipping and stumbling in bare feet did not seem like a good idea, so I studied the path and thought long and hard about the alternatives, before selecting each new spot to place a foot. I lowered myself from a large smooth rock into a patch of slippery mud, mindful of the pack's bulk tilting unpredictably on my back, and then looked around with growing desperation for the next shaky awkward step. I began feeling anxious, fearing I would never make it down.

Then I remembered something the legendary ultrarunner Dave Horton used to say: "It never *always* gets worse."

He was right, at least this time, for the trail soon leveled out. Walking became a little easier. The anxiety dissipated. I relaxed.

After that weekend, the count stood at six barefoot peaks complete. The next weekend it increased to eight, and soon it was 10, then 12. The progress gave me such a rush—it felt like ticking off the miles in an ultramarathon, just spread out over days instead of hours.

I didn't mention my strange new interest to any of my running friends, as they wore shoes happily and many loved the new models with super-thick cushioning. I didn't breathe a word of this at work, lest colleagues think I'd lost my mind. Sue is a physical therapist, whose specialty includes fashioning custom orthotics. She expressed concern about my going barefoot, as it might place strain on tendons that were used to having some support. But trumping all points of view, the soles of my feet hungered for new textures and impressions. As soon as the nicks from one trip healed, they demanded more sensations.

Odie accompanied me on my second trip to Kaaterskill High Peak, where 18 months earlier, I'd been surprised by that icy chute. This time we arrived at night. The late October weather was cold, the path a disconcerting mix of rocks and mud, every step an unpleasant surprise. A long flat rock covered in thick moss felt more luxurious than a Persian carpet. But then the path deteriorated, becoming a "path" in name only. It was nothing but tangled roots, cold puddles, and stream crossings until it became a stream itself. Each step required unwavering concentration. The pace was abysmally slow. I began to feel deeply weary. Then I stepped off a slimy rock and plunged into ankle-deep mud, and the trek became nightmarish.

At the top of the peak, we faced about, got caught in a shower of freezing rain, and then it was straight into the mud again. Somehow, we made it back to the car. Once home I washed my feet and went straight to bed, while Odie made a beeline for the sofa.

The next weekend, with commitments during the day, I was on the road at night again. Arriving at the trailhead for Bearpen Mountain, I saw the crescent moon reflected in the rear-view mirror looking as if it had floated down from outer space and perched upon a ridge. The car thermometer read 27°F, which was unnerving, since I had no idea what my feet could tolerate before I put myself at risk. But I was here on my special mission and determined to make progress toward my goal. I wasn't about to turn back without trying.

Heading out, I soon realized the temperature of the ground wasn't my biggest problem. The trail was covered in sharp-edged gravel (or "shot rock," as I've learned it's called) trucked in from some quarry where it had no doubt been freshly crushed. The needling underfoot was so painful I almost quit, but I persevered, and once past a junction, the gravel faded. The path became much smoother, with stretches covered in fallen leaves and frosty grass. In the distance a handful of lights sparkled in the Catskills' sparsely settled northern reaches. A few snowflakes fluttered about. Skins of ice had spread across puddles—I crashed through these in a burst of childlike glee, then thought better of it, as my feet began feeling chilled.

I entered a tunnel in the woodline, looking for a shortcut to the top. But I must have wandered off course, for soon my feet were sinking into a damp, snowy mix of leaves and moss and starting to turn numb. I'd heard experienced barefooters counsel that "numb is dumb." Mindful of their advice, I retreated to the trail and settled in for the long trek to Bearpen's summit.

When I finally made it back home the next morning, I was alarmed to discover the soles of my feet had turned black, a possible sign of frostbite. It turns out, however, that black skin is also a sign of Catskill mud, and happily the color washed off in the shower.

Eager to get one last peak bagged before winter put my strange new quest on pause, I headed to Fir in early November, only to find the lower slopes already dusted. Odie scampered about with delight, stopping from time to time to rub his nose in snow, while I stepped warily through the powder, gritting teeth, hopping up and down on rocks to warm my feet. Walking on a chilly trail was manageable, as I'd found on Bearpen, but now as I climbed higher and encountered deeper accumulation, the cold became unbearable. Soon I was howling in pain. I dropped my pack, whipped out my sandals, and ran all the way back down.

Odie on the shoulder of Black Dome. October 11, 2015.

CHAPTER 7

GOING LIGHT

"OF COURSE YOU'RE SLOWING DOWN," THE SMARMY LITTLE VOICE whispered inside my head, "you're getting old."

With winter having reclaimed the mountains, I'd put barefoot hiking on hold and returned to the track to work on speed in my favorite style of lightweight minimalist shoes, only to find my split times were off from what I'd hoped.

As a financial analyst, I'd learned to listen to those little voices that piped up with strange ideas, because sometimes they were good ones. I'd also learned to weigh their counsel against the data, because sometimes they were not. Thanks to my GPS watch, I'd been collecting pace and heart rate data at the track for nearly a decade. Initially I'd monitored heart rate as a proxy for effort, to keep myself from slacking off. With practice, I was able to push my heart rate to the max. Then I looked at the relationship between heart rate and pace. How thrilling to see faster times at the same level of beats per minute, the very measurement of progress!

But that wasn't the case today. As I studied the data from my recent workout, it seemed my heart rate was a little low. Evidently, I wasn't putting out the effort. No doubt the groin and foot injuries of the previous fall had left me feeling tentative. My strategy, therefore, would be simple: Try harder.

Indeed, the strategy of trying harder had been drilled into me throughout my life: as a child, watching my father work incessantly; as a young karate student, being taught to turn "devil's eyes" on myself (meaning to demand relentless self-improvement); as an Army officer, being expected to lead my soldiers to the objective and accomplish the mission; as an analyst, always trying to help my clients with insightful research; and as an executive, having a sense of urgency and a commitment to accountability and outcomes. The strategy of trying harder was what had made me successful as an ultrarunner. On my record-setting Long Path and Badwater Double runs, I'd gone without food and sleep; braved wind, heat, and rain; climbed mountains; and pushed on even when injured. Now I resolved to fight back against age by trying harder at the track.

At the same time, I hadn't forgotten about Keizer's Catskill record. It occurred to me that some winter mountain running—up to this point studiously avoided—would help me stay in trim for a late spring attempt.

In typical fashion I set an audacious goal. I would take on the Nine, that notorious 19-mile circuit with the painful fir-spruce thickets, which I'd completed during the day and at night, although never in the cold.

The Nine was a daunting prospect for someone who'd climbed only one single Catskill peak in the winter (Peekamoose with Odie the year before), so I prepared carefully. The night before, I laid out my gear for inspection, the way I'd been taught in my Army days. There were microspikes for traction, plenty of layers for warmth, lights in case of a late return, extra batteries, water, and a compass. This was a trail-runner's loadout: no shelter, sleeping bag, stove, food, or other safety gear that a hiker might have carried. To mitigate the risk of getting lost or injured, I carried a personal locator beacon, which could broadcast an SOS message at the push of a button.

Better than high-tech gear, however, is having companions.

Iain Ridgway, Aaron Anaya, and I met at the Denning trailhead at 8:00 am on Saturday, January 17, 2016. There was a record for the Nine, I explained to them, but no one had claimed a separate record for the Nine in winter. That record could be ours. All we'd have to do was finish the course. And not get lost.

With long legs and purposeful stride, Iain set a brisk pace along the crusty trail toward Table Mountain, and at first I felt encouraged. However, by the time we'd climbed 1,000 feet, my feet were starting to slip. Snow blanketed the forest floor and covered every branch, and underneath the snow lay sheets of ice. I noticed that Iain and

Aaron's spikes had large metal fangs, while mine had lugs instead of teeth, making them "spikes" in name only. I placed each foot as carefully as I could and struggled to keep up.

Passing Table's summit, we jogged downhill a short distance and made the quick climb to Peekamoose. Soon it was time to leave the trail. We pulled out maps and stared into a maze of snowy conifers. Having already measured the azimuth on my phone map, I pointed the way. The three of us plunged into the shadows and were suddenly careening down an icy slope, zigging and zagging between the spindly trees. After a few minutes, I pulled out my phone for a map check, only to find we'd drifted too far downhill. We reoriented and moved out, but a few minutes later, the next check showed we were still off course. With every step, we seemed to be sliding a few feet down the slope, as if the forest was trying to suck us into the valley of the Neversink River, far below.

I recalled a scene from *The Lord of the Rings*, when after leaving their homes in the Shire, Frodo and his hobbit friends enter the Old Forest, only to find the trees "somehow would not yield to the left, but only gave way when they turned to the right." They couldn't keep to their intended direction but were instead deflected onto a route chosen by unfriendly spirits, a route which led "into the heart of the Forest and not out." The same thing seemed to be happening to us now.

After a couple more corrections, we eventually reached the saddle below Lone Mountain. Now the navigation became easier. A distinctive feature of topology is that if you keep moving up, you must eventually arrive at a summit. The three of us jokingly called this the "Rule of Up." Pocketing our compasses, we worked our way up the mountain, squeezing between trees and edging around rocks, until we surfaced on top of Lone.

Out came compasses and maps once again to plot our course to the next mountain. An adventure racer and former Marine, Aaron is well-versed in the art of land navigation. Listening to my directions, he made an observation—when converting azimuths from grid (on a paper or phone map) to magnetic (for the compass), I was subtracting the 13-degree westerly declination, when I should've been adding it. For a former Army officer, this was an embarrassing mistake (and painful to be corrected by a Marine). It seemed, however, a better explanation for our navigational challenges than unfriendly spirits.

Leaving the summit of Lone, we discovered fresh tracks in the snow. Evidently someone had come this way recently. Surely these people knew where they were going, I reasoned. With some luck, these tracks would lead straight to each of the next four mountains. But after a short distance, instead of taking us north, the tracks turned east. My patience frayed. We abandoned the tracks, only to find ourselves staring down icy cliffs. I rushed off in a different direction without consulting my compass, only to encounter yet another set of cliffs and then another set of tracks. I was perplexed, until Aaron pointed out these tracks were ours. I'd led us in a circle.

We paused, reoriented, and found a route down through the cliffs. Soon we were treading through the snow toward the next mountain, Rocky. I brought up the rear, traction still a challenge in my toothless spikes.

The next objective, Balsam Cap, is considered one of the Catskills' most challenging bushwhacks, but I'd been through here before. So now I strode forward with confidence, deflecting branches, scanning ahead for obstacles, twisting and shifting to free snagged clothing. I was thinking to myself how the worst tangles don't last forever ("It never *always* gets worse"), when a branch slipped from my outstretched hand and slapped me in the face with a load of snow.

In due course we were standing on Friday Mountain. As runners accustomed to speeding along roads or trails, we were by this point getting pretty tired of fighting with fir trees. I could tell that Iain's patience was wearing thin, and as for myself, I was breathing through pursed lips to stay calm.

After a final push through the thickets, we popped out on the summit of Cornell. What a relief to be back on a trail! But our trek had taken longer than expected, and we decided to skip Wittenberg. Instead of the Nine, we'd settle for the Eight. With Iain in the lead, we jogged off toward Slide, at one point Aaron reaching out a trekking pole to haul me up an icy scramble.

It was dark by the time we reached Slide's summit. The half-moon peered down at us through cirrostratus haze as we read the plaque dedicated to John Burroughs. Then we ran downhill for the next five miles, snowflakes flashing in our lights, not pausing until we reached the refuge of our cars.

My next purchase was a pair of microspikes with real teeth. The following weekend saw me out for a 10-mile spin in the Blackhead range on a cold, clear day. The new spikes worked perfectly—their teeth bit into the mounds of swirling gray ice and dug into the hard-packed snow.

When the temperature dropped one day to -5°F, I was not deterred, although I chose the popular trail to Panther Mountain and trotted along with care.

Honestly, I've never enjoyed winter. I've never lost my sense of caution about conditions. A few weeks later, I learned of the fate of a hiker who'd recently earned membership in the Catskill 3500 Club. She'd gotten wet during a solo trip in the Adirondacks, stopped to rest against a tree, and never rose again.

LESSONS FROM THE LIGHT INFANTRY

This sad news made it hard to resist when I heard about a 50-mile trail race taking place in sunny California. Not only would this be a well-timed break from New York winter, but it would take me back to some old stomping grounds. The race would take place at Fort Ord, a former Army post nestled between the Northern California towns of Monterey and Salinas. Some 30 years ago I'd served there as a light infantry platoon leader, in what had been a formative experience.

For the US Army of the 1980s, light infantry was a radical concept. The idea was to deploy foot soldiers with stamina, training, and strong leadership in terrain too rough for heavy forces. Our bible was the field manual on Ranger-style dismounted patrolling, the Army's version of small unit guerrilla tactics. One of our standard exercises was a 12-mile road march. Not a particularly long distance by running standards, but bear in mind, even a "light fighter," as we called ourselves, bore a substantial load of equipment, weaponry, and supplies. Our battalion commander had served in Vietnam, where he saw that overburdened soldiers were ineffective. When out on training missions, he'd order us to drop our rucks, and we marched more easily through the coastal chaparral and live oak groves.

As a runner, my philosophy had gradually become somewhat minimalist, and maybe the light infantry experience was part of the inspiration. For this race, my uniform would consist of shorts, shirt, lightweight trail shoes, hat, and GPS watch. There was a chocolate bar in one pocket and rental car keys in the other. No phone. No pack. No lights. I didn't even bring a water bottle.

The race started up in the hills. After a couple miles of easy running, I stripped off my shirt and tied it around my waist, only to encounter dank air down in the canyons. A bundled-up volunteer with steaming breath was surprised to see a shirtless runner so early in the morning. He wanted to know whether I'd undergone some kind of special training. Sure, I replied, laughing, right here at Fort Ord. Getting miserably wet and cold, and then baking in the sun was all part of life in the infantry.

Since I wasn't carrying water, I made a point to drink up at each aid station. A runner stared in astonishment as I headed out without a bottle, but the risk of mild dehydration was not a major concern. A bigger issue would be reaching the finish line before dark, since I wasn't carrying a light. With some extra effort, I made it there by dusk.

Going light means relying more on human strengths, like endurance and judgment, and less on gear. Running through the emerald hills of my old post, I felt the confidence that comes from intensive training, a sense of freedom from unnecessary burden, and the thrill of self-reliance. What a joyful experience it was, slipping through the coastal landscape without encumbrance, on a mission no more demanding than getting myself from start to finish. I truly felt as light as a feather.

On returning to New York, however, I felt uneasy. In three short months it would be time to take my long-awaited shot at Keizer's record. Despite all the training, all the racing, all the practice at bushwhacking and navigating, deep down I knew this wasn't going to be easy.

CHAPTER 8

TAKING MINIMALISM
TO THE NEXT LEVEL

I'D BECOME MORE CONFIDENT MOVING THROUGH THE THICKETS, but I didn't seem to be getting a whole lot faster. As far as bushwhacking, Ted Keizer might as well have been a forest spirit. I did not possess his magic.

This was probably why I was so quick to react when, out of the blue, a friend reached out to propose another Death Valley adventure.

THE QUAD

It's a maxim of the ultrarunning mindset that once you master one distance, you start imagining the next, this being the relentless logic of always trying harder—not to mention the thrill of doing something that other people can hardly comprehend. The proposed adventure was the Badwater Quad, which is two times the Double, meaning you have to run from the Badwater Basin to the summit of Mt. Whitney and back, and then the whole trip once again, for a total of 584 miles. The Quad is the ultimate Death Valley challenge, a Herculean labor that's been completed by only a handful of people. The Quad had long intrigued me, and it wasn't just the record that caught my eye. I loved the endless sweep of desert vistas, the stretches of empty space, the blackened mountains and heaps of blasted rocks and gravel washes, and the spicy smell of sage and desert holly when you crush a leaf in your fingers and take a whiff.

I floated the Quad with the members of the crew who'd supported me before, and they were all enthusiastic. So my answer was yes. And I put the Catskills on hold.

This was a calculated risk. It's a core principle of racing that training must be *specific*. Struggling along the Catskills' steep and rocky trails and muscling through its tangled thickets wouldn't help me when it came to cruising along the endless asphalt roads that cross Death Valley. With the desert now calling, it was time to hit the pavement and ramp up miles.

I didn't totally forget the Catskills. To join the Catskill 3500 Club, you need to climb all 35 high peaks and then four of them again in winter. There was only a single winter peak left for me to do. In late March, I hurried out to Balsam Lake Mountain, only to realize once I'd made it home that this was the wrong peak. There are four mountains in the Catskills with similar names: Balsam Lake, Balsam Cap, and two different Balsams. It was one of the Balsams that I still needed to bag. So, on the last official day of the winter season, I hustled back out and climbed the correct Balsam. At the club's annual dinner in early April 2016, I proudly strode across the stage to accept my certificate and patch.

BACK IN BOSTON

A week later it was time for the Boston Marathon, which is held each year on Patriots Day, the third Monday in April. This would be my fourth time at Boston. In light of the Quad coming up and the need for road mileage, the race took on special significance. I took the train up to Boston a few days early to attend a conference on Native American running held in conjunction with the race. One of the panelists, Chief Oren Lyons of the Onondaga Nation, made an interesting comment. When asked what advice he gives young athletes, he uttered a guttural-sounding phrase in his native tongue, which he translated as, "Try hard—try harder!" It was meaningful to hear someone from a different culture voicing the same philosophy I'd been taught all my life, as it indicated that physical and mental effort is a universal value among all different kinds of people.

After the conference, Sue met me in Boston, and we enjoyed the weekend in town. But Sunday evening, the night before the race, I felt apprehensive. Not only had those injuries of the previous fall disrupted my training, but my back had started aching on the train ride into town.

Race morning, the cannon fired and off I went. For the first few miles, everything went according to plan. But then my pace began to slip. I tried hard and then I tried harder, but with each mile my time fell further behind target, while each glance at my watch provoked a feeling of despair. I finally crossed the finish line a full 17 minutes slower than the year before.

That smarmy voice—the one that warned I was getting old—was right.

I packed my bags and flew off for business meetings. My boss congratulated me on completing Boston, which he had run several times. When I mentioned my disappointing performance, he counseled me with one of his favorite sayings: "There are only two kinds of people who care about time: those who are trying to win the race and those who are serving in prison."

I tried to focus on work, but my heart was not in it. Instead, my thoughts kept returning to the Quad, which was looming four short months away, and the question—what next? I couldn't afford to slack off on training, although recovery from Boston dictated something moderate. But even so, my hunger for intensity was insatiable. I could not slake it with another easy jog. In between meetings, calls, and business dinners, that quirky goal came back to mind, to complete the Catskill high peaks barefoot. A plan began to come together in my mind. I would return to the Nine and attempt them without shoes. Plus, for extra challenge, I wouldn't carry food or water.

ASKESIS IN THE CATSKILLS

This time the inspiration for this minimalist expedition wasn't Thoreau's call for simplicity or my experience with light infantry, but rather the ancient Greek concept of *askesis*, which refers to a program of rigorous training undertaken for athletic and spiritual development.

Especially favored were practices that entailed endurance, resistance to the elements, and going without sustenance.

The Cynic philosopher Diogenes of Sinope (413–323 BCE) practiced askesis as part of a lifestyle of simplicity and self-reliance. Inspired by the legend of Hercules's labors, Diogenes exercised on hot sands during summer, walked barefoot in snow during winter, and lived outdoors year-round with no possessions other than staff, satchel, cloak, and drinking vase. One day Diogenes saw a child drinking from a creek with cupped hands, so he threw his vase away. This was a commitment to simplicity before which Thoreau would have paled. Diogenes is believed to have said, "Nothing in life has any chance of success without self-discipline. With it, anything is possible."

I'd long thought of running as a form of training, with the goal of making myself stronger. More in control. Better able to confront fear and manage stress. More reliable and dependable and thus more useful to other people. My practice already incorporated certain aspects of askesis—for example, running without food and water, which I no longer saw as necessary for races up to marathon length (at least in mild temperatures). Now it occurred to me that going without could be considered a form of training in and of itself, and a perfect way to add intensity when speed and distance weren't the focus. Practicing askesis in the Catskills suddenly seemed like a thrilling proposition— as if the mountains were daring me to show them what I could do!

The idea seemed less thrilling on Saturday evening, five days after Boston, when I pulled into the Denning trailhead. It was dark already, and the temperature was falling like a rock. I started out on a trail full of mud and standing puddles, gritting my teeth at the sensation of frigid water on naked soles and even worse, the sensitive skin around my ankles. An owl hooted. My flashlight flickered out. I groped around in my pack for the extra batteries and inserted them by feel. Light restored, I resumed the march, only to find after a short eternity that I hadn't even reached a mile.

The trail began to climb. The full moon hung over a distant ridge, a baleful white reflector, all-seeing and indifferent. The wind thundered overhead and then came rushing down the mountain, whirling through the trees around me. It took endless hours to reach the lean-to on Table Mountain. But it was occupied, so I staggered another mile along the trail and sheltered next to a boulder.

Sometime later, I awoke. It was only at the last minute that I'd decided to bring a sleeping bag, and I hadn't bothered with an insulated pad. I'd been thinking back to my Army days, when I'd wrap myself in a nylon quilt for an hour's rest, brush off the frost, and get on the move again. But now, the cold was seeping into my bag from the ground. I shivered, curled up tighter, closed my eyes. And woke again. If I concentrated on warming myself, this seemed to keep the cold at bay, so I marshaled all my mental focus, tried not to shiver, and dozed off. Then woke up shivering. This pattern repeated itself for the duration of the night.

My eyes opened to a blood-red sun suspended above the horizon. The night had been a little grim, but the only thing that mattered now was making progress toward the next objective. I steeled myself against the prospect of discomfort from cold, hunger, fatigue, and scratched-up feet and started out with a determined mindset. I stepped cautiously over frozen puddles and slipped past rocky ledges dripping with white fangs. After a mile on the trail, I reached the familiar point of departure. Here I turned into the woods, treading on dry fir needles and broken branches, threading my way between the spindly trees, and skidding downhill on frozen moss and leaves that were slippery in bare feet.

I made better progress as the slope leveled out. My mood lightened as I recognized the familiar floppy leaves and cheerful white flower buds of the ubiquitous hobblebush. It had become a cloudless day, with bracing crisp air and bright skies. Breaks in the forest revealed distant peaks. I stepped into a small clearing where the sun-baked soil felt deliciously soft and warm underfoot. Then it was back into shadows.

Despite a creeping pace, I reached the first three pathless summits without issue. Five of the Nine were now complete. It was on the way to Friday Mountain that I started to fall apart. I was stuck in an impenetrable thicket, the young trees growing so close together I couldn't squeeze between without breaking off the knife-like branches or catching them on my clothes. I got stuck in a pile of deadfall where I had to crawl across an enormous fallen trunk without impaling myself on sharp broken branch-spikes while at the same time pushing through a screen of prickly boughs. Frustration at the slow pace had been gradually building all morning. Now it boiled over into a feeling of helpless rage. I started swearing out loud, and with each obstacle, my shouts got louder. Anxiety was spreading across my mind like smoke from a burning forest. It was partly because I'd promised Sue I'd be home by 6 p.m. (that wasn't going to happen) and partly because I couldn't fathom how people like Ted Keizer moved so quickly through this stuff. *Why couldn't I be as good?*

I marched along beneath a small, dark cloud of angst, bellowing at each new barrier. One part of me wallowed in this bad attitude, while another part recognized this behavior as childish. By the time I reached Friday, I'd had enough. I pulled out my sandals and stomped off toward the nearest trail, when looking down, I spotted a mound of peat moss. Instead of green, it was bright red. I'd never seen red moss before; I would never have imagined such a thing was possible. I stared in astonishment for a moment longer. The dark cloud of angst began to break up and drift away.

Back on the trail, I paused at a spring near the top of Slide to sip a handful of water. Then limped the last few miles down to the car, having completed only seven of the nine, and only six of them barefoot.

The next day at work, a big project dropped onto my lap without warning, a meeting left me feeling frustrated with colleagues who didn't share my point of view, and then it was off to the airport for a one-day trip with my boss deciding at the last moment to tag along and supervise. All of this was irritating, but upon reflection, it wasn't as painful as going barefoot through those fir-spruce thickets.

One of the Roman Stoics, Epictetus, wrote that while wool takes up certain colors immediately, there are others which it will not absorb unless soaked and steeped repeatedly. He was referring metaphorically to the long period it took to learn to live in accordance with Stoic principles. Even a wise man may tremble, feel pain, and turn pale, he commented, "therefore let us press on and persevere."

After this adventure, I did press on. I resumed training for the Quad and pushed the mileage, running twice on many days, knocking out 40-mile training runs and logging 100-mile weeks.

By late July, I'd run 2,400 miles year-to-date, which was 30 percent more than the year before.

I persevered. But I wasn't hitting speed and distance milestones the way I had two years earlier, when I was training for the Double. The Quad would be the biggest running challenge of my life, and I was starting to feel uneasy.

CHAPTER 9

SHIFTING GEARS AGAIN

MY PROBLEMS WEREN'T JUST PHYSICAL. ON SOME LONG RUNS, I'D feel apprehensive. Sometimes bored. And often I felt this way on short runs, too. It seemed as if my conscious mind was growing anxious about the effort, then becoming anxious about its own anxiety.

The ancient Hindu text Bhagavad Gita was a favorite of Emerson and Thoreau. There's a passage where the warrior Arjun complains that "the mind is restless, turbulent, powerful, violent . . . trying to control it is like trying to tame the wind!" In response, Lord Krishna counsels him to "strive to still the mind."

That's ironic, isn't it? Today we're taught to manage stress through relaxation techniques. Deep breathing. Visualization. Yoga. But Krishna's saying you might have to "strive." In other words, you might have to *make an effort* to relax.

I decided to experiment. I started with everyday situations that tested my patience: waiting for an elevator, filling up the car with gas, standing on a subway platform. Now I made a point to take a deep breath. Suppress the irritation. Put away my phone. Instead of fretting, I shifted my attention to my surroundings, which seemed to calm my thoughts.

When doing speedwork at the track, I made an effort to focus only on the current lap. When my mind leapt ahead, I gently reined it in. Sometimes I visualized a gear selector and imagined shifting my thoughts into neutral. This helped the laps pass more fluidly.

With my thoughts under slightly better control, I went back and pushed myself hard. I reasoned there are times in life to focus on work and family, and times to run. For me, the time to run was now.

A TENDON IN THE ANKLE

And so I did, with a mix of long runs for endurance and speedwork to build strength. To work on climbing, I set the treadmill to steep inclines and did jogging intervals on the StairMaster. Hiking on the weekend brought some variety, while I programmed in walking breaks just to stay in motion, whenever I had the chance. Until one evening, when out for an easy barefoot jog, I stumbled on a hidden rock. The pain brought me to a halt. I put on sandals and stumbled along a short distance. My calf felt strained.

Two scenarios started flickering in my mind. In one, the strain was a minor ache of no consequence. In the other, it was a serious injury that would derail my training and defeat the Quad. I limped along, frustrated and grim, thoughts rushing about chaotically.

A few days later saw me running on the roads in shoes, ankle wrapped with tape to support the calf, trying to log some miles without making things worse. At first the sky was overcast, but then the sun broke through and the clouds rolled back in—and so it was with me. My calf started feeling better on the flats, ached on the hills, and then I was running smoothly for a mile or two, my mood darkening and lightening as my mind recalculated the probabilities of those two scenarios.

The next day I remembered Marcus Aurelius and the lesson from the fir-spruce thickets—don't blame the obstacle; recast your plan and get back on track. This insight helped me come up with a solution to my turbulent thoughts. I would attempt a short, slow, cautious jog and see what happened. This plan helped me feel purposeful again. And for the first time I reflected that as I got older, a point would come when I'd be grateful to still be moving at any pace.

The short slow jog went fine, but when I got home and took off the tape, there was a faint bruise beneath my ankle, which indicated internal bleeding. The solution changed once again. It was time to take a break.

COMPLETION OF THE BAREFOOT 35

Giving the ankle some time to heal, I invited a friend of mine named Steve Aaron on an easy-paced Catskill hike. Like me, Steve's a corporate worker, but he has a calming, laid-back manner. And a shrewd eye. Outside of work he's a photographer who specializes in landscape images of the Hudson Valley.[3] Hiking with Steve would be a chance to slow the pace, moderate the intensity, appreciate the views, and share the experience with a friend.

We climbed to the top of Twin Mountain, me in bare feet, still working on my quest, and Steve with his 35-mm slung over one shoulder. From the summit, we looked south, searching for the Shawangunk Mountains, and soon spotted a distant ridgeline, curling like a breaking wave. Steve pointed to a stone tower called Sky Top, some 25 miles due south according to the map. Then he gestured to the right. Squinting, I could barely make out another tower, so far off it looked no bigger than a pin. This was the Monument Tower in New Jersey's High Point State Park, 62 miles away to the south-southwest. Between the two towers stretched a long plateau. This was the point where I'd stood some three years back on a windy winter day with Odie by my side. I looked this way and thought I heard a special call. It felt like a thousand years ago.

To give the ankle even more time to heal, I attempted another easy climb, this time a barefoot ascent of Sherrill Mountain, where the forest floor was sprinkled with spring flowers: trilliums with three maroon petals, which I'd seen before, as well as a version in electric white; yellow-flowered trout lilies with mottled green-brown leaves (John Burroughs gave them this name because the color of the leaves reminded him of the fish's skin); boreal lilies with shyly drooping yellow petals; spring beauties with delicate white petals with purple stripes; and an odd little creature with deeply cut fern-like leaves and tiny white flowers shaped like pantaloons, which I later learned is called Dutchman's breeches.

---

3 Steve's landscape images can be seen at www.steveaaronphoto.com.

I'd finally achieved my goal of climbing all 35 high peaks barefoot. Had there been a certificate for this accomplishment, I would've happily added it to my collection.

In total I gave my ankle two and a half weeks off from running and then threw myself back at the roads, determined to rack up miles. But my training log was filling with complaints. One entry read "ankle hurting from last night." The next day, my ankle "felt sore at first then fine." A day later, "tendon ached a little but ran through it." I ran hard when that was possible and backed off when not, but the volume took a toll. "Very tired and slow" read one entry. "Felt slow and lethargic, groin ached." "Top of right foot starting to feel sore again."

I signed up for a trail race but skipped it due to the sore ankle. I signed up for Manitou's Revenge, and skipped it, too.

Then a key member of my support crew changed jobs and dropped out. Another friend had a conflict. Soon the whole team unraveled. You don't take on an extreme environment like Death Valley unless you're ready, both physically and logistically. I was neither, so I canceled the Quad attempt.

It was a huge relief to stand down. In my condition the outcome would probably have been a disappointment. Maybe a disaster.

But at the same time, I felt adrift. It was August, the best time of the year to do great things, and I had no goal or plan. Then it occurred to me—this might finally be the chance to attempt the Catskill record.

It no longer seemed realistic to challenge Keizer's time, given my frustrating bushwhack splits, the injuries, and the decision to forsake the mountains and spend so much time training on roads. Keizer also had been supported by an enthusiastic team when he set his record, but my crew had just dissolved, and there was little time to recruit a new one. Accordingly, I decided to undertake the 35 peaks on an "unsupported" basis, that is, without relying on anyone for help, which would be a different format from Keizer's run.

There was an unsupported record for the Catskills of 4 days and 13 hours, set in 2011 by Jan Wellford and Cory DeLavalle. For the 137-mile course, this was equivalent to 30 miles per day. It seemed feasible. Possibly. But Jan was an intimidiating athlete. He held the course record for Manitou's Revenge and had broken Keizer's speed-climbing record in the Adirondacks. He was another Mountain Man.

DEVIL'S PATH DOUBLE

If I was to have any hope of challenging this record, I'd need to whip myself back into mountain-running shape. To do so, I decided to take on the Devil's Path, that notorious steep and rugged trail, which climbs five high peaks (Indian Head, Twin, Sugarloaf, Plateau, and West Kill) and crosses within a mile of Southwest Hunter, for a total elevation gain of 14,000 feet over 24 miles.

Ben Nephew, the runner who won the Escarpment Trail Run almost every year, owned the FKT (fastest known time) for the Devil's Path. He first set the record in 2010, only to lose it in 2014. He returned in 2015 but failed to regain the title. Then he failed again. It took him three tries before he finally set a new record of 4 hours and 53 minutes. According to Ben's report, the Devil's Path is "incessantly steep and rough, has several spots that are outright dangerous, and there are no easy miles."

I was not the runner to challenge Ben. But I'd noticed there was no record for a Devil's Path Double, which would be a 48-mile out-and-back run. I could win another record. I could gain more of that distinction I so craved. All I had to do was survive.

There were some high points during this run: the views across the Hudson Valley, the colorful plants and mushrooms along the trail, the steep descent from Plateau Mountain where someone seeing me trotting down the trail commented to a friend, "that's one fit man." And there were some low points: a passing rainstorm, muddy trails, and the climb back up Plateau Mountain on the return, which nearly killed me.

I finished the Devil's Path Double in just under 24 hours, returning to the start as a chorus of hermit thrushes greeted the dawn. For the next few days, my leg muscles ached so badly that I could hardly walk. But that didn't stop me. Once my legs recovered, I set a date two weeks out, arranged to take time off from work, and briefed Sue on my plan to take on the 35 peaks unsupported (she shook her head).

The odds of success did not seem high, but the time had finally come to throw myself into the heart of the mountains. The idea was strangely seductive and a little frightening. Like casting off into a lake whose glittering sun-swept surface is enticing, but whose waters run cold and unknowably deep.

CHAPTER 10

THE 35-PEAK CHALLENGE

I PRESSED THE START BUTTON ON MY WATCH. IT WAS 8:14 A.M. ON THE morning of August 23, 2016.

I'd woken early. Made the 90-minute drive to the base of Windham High Peak, the Catskills' northern sentinel, where I hoped to finish in four days' time. From Wyndham I was ferried by Smiley's Taxi Service to the base of Peekamoose Mountain in the south. As the taxi rolled off, I stood there for a moment, staring at the steep trail, frantically stuffing supplies into my trouser pockets and a tiny runner's pack, double-tying the laces on my favorite trail-running shoes. My thoughts raced with excitement. And a touch of dread.

After starting the watch, I charged up the familiar trail, but not too fast—there were 137 miles to go, and none of them would be easy. Arriving at the summit shortly before 10:00 a.m., I sent a signal from my personal locator beacon to document completion of peak number one. A few minutes later I bounded up to the small cairn on Table's summit. Two down, thirty-three to go.

It was time to turn into the woods and aim for the saddle below Lone. Recalling the embarrassing mistake I'd made here once before, I'd double-checked all the compass headings. But unfriendly spirits must have been at work, because I still dropped too far downhill and had to claw my way back up to reach the saddle.

I then fought my way to the top of Lone, where I sent another signal from my personal locator beacon, marking completion of peak number three.

On the way to Rocky, I was moving through a clearing full of blowdown when I caught a glimpse of the far side of the valley.

Looming there was Slide Mountain's asymmetric dome. If all went well, I'd be inching my way up the steep eastern face later that afternoon. Reaching Rocky's summit, I saw a trekking pole hanging from a tree. Someone must have lost it, and someone else must have found it and hung it there.

Onward to Balsam Cap, which involved navigating through the notorious balsam fir thickets that "cap" the summit. To stay cool and avoid sweating, I was going shirtless. As I pushed past fir branches, the cool green needles brushed against the skin of my chest and shoulders, as if the trees were reaching out to stroke me, curious about the visitor slipping between their boughs. The dead branches, however, poked and scratched me, as if they resented the presence of the living.

From Balsam Cap on to Friday I slunk through more thickets. Spiderwebs hung from branches everywhere; I was constantly brushing filaments from my hat and shoulders. I took a sip from one of my water bottles, my first drink since starting six hours earlier. At the summit of Friday, a rabbit hopped off into the brush. In the distance, there was a persistent nasal squawk: *yank yank yank*.

Descending from Friday, I stepped over a Yankees cap moldering in a bed of peat moss. Then it was back into the thickets. It was just before 4:00 p.m. when I reached the trail and a moment later the summit of Cornell Mountain. A short distance past Cornell, the trail took me through a vertical fissure in a sandstone ledge called the "Cornell Crack," a three-inch groove where two slabs come together and a vertical drop of about 20 feet. I jammed my feet into the crack and worked my way down to a narrow ledge, then hopped back on the trail.

A few minutes later I arrived at Wittenberg's summit ledge, where I pulled off shoes and socks, shook out needles, and paused to eat some food. A small bird with white and black stripes across its face and a russet-colored chest hopped out on the rocks, gave me a curious look, flitted off. Later I would identify it as a red-breasted nuthatch, the same kind I'd heard going *yank yank yank*.

From Wittenberg, I backtracked past Cornell (climbing back up its Crack) and made my way over to the base of the steep climb up Slide Mountain, only to find that one of the trekking poles strapped to my pack had gone missing. I hesitated for a moment, then sprinted back a mile along the trail searching for the pole, until I'd crossed the Crack again. At this point I concluded that the pole must have gotten knocked off in the thickets. Also missing, I soon discovered, were my car keys, which I'd left in a pocket, having forgotten to secure them inside the pack. Turning back, I crossed the Crack (for the fourth time) and made my way back to Slide, wondering if someone would find the missing pole and hang it from a tree.

I worked my way up Slide with my remaining pole in one hand, navigating a series of scrambles, a set of stone steps, and a pair of stout wooden ladders bolted to the side of the mountain. Just below the summit, I stopped to filter water from the spring, having so far gotten by all day on a single liter.

It was dusk when I arrived at Slide's summit—peak number nine. Orange light pooled along the horizon. Then it was down 1,500 feet into the valley, where it was pitch-black. I marched along an asphalt road feeling purposeful, while a solitary tree cricket called on the left and the Neversink River trilled on the right.

At 11:00 p.m., I arrived on Panther's summit to the sound of a soft wind stirring with a rhythm like ocean waves. I maneuvered down the backside of the mountain, where once upon a time I'd seen two bears ambling by, but this time it was a field mouse desperate to avoid my tread, flinging itself from rock to rock. The rumble of tires wafted up from below. Soon I was marching on pavement again, marveling at silver flashes along the shoulder, which may have been dewdrops sparkling on the waxy leaves of jewelweed.

Then it was back into the forest for a lengthy bushwhack in the dark. I scrambled over the banks of the Esopus Creek and paused to filter water, drink, and refill my bottles, as this would be the last water source for quite some time. I started scrambling up toward Fir's summit, 2,000 feet above. My flashlight caught a large toad sitting motionless in the leaves, a spider hanging in its web, clumps of coral fungus glowing eerie white. I reached the top at 4:00 a.m., having been on the move now for almost 20 hours.

On the way to Fir Mountain. August 24, 2016.

At one point, I was creeping along a sandstone ledge, searching for the narrow saddle that connects Fir with the next peak on the route, when suddenly my headlamp flashed out across what seemed to be a lake. But there was no water up here. Rather, where I was standing, I realized, the mountain wall dropped off abruptly, and I was staring into space. I quickly stepped back from the brink before turning and climbing higher up onto the rocky and heavily forested ridge. In the dark it seemed to take forever. By the time I was back on track, the dawning sun was spattering the foliage with spots of blood-red neon.

I passed across Big Indian and pressed on to Doubletop. Elbowed my way through saplings. Slipped past a small peat bog. Stole through a dense boreal grove of lichen-shrouded branches and moss-covered stumps. Just past the summit, the slope fell off at a sharp angle. I paused to study the descent, then it was down one shaky step at a time, wary of rocks that could slide out from under my feet. I reached out for scrawny stems, giving them a tug to make sure they'd hold my weight. By the time I reached the saddle, my head was spinning. The climb up Graham came almost as a relief, although the summit was tangled with bristly berry canes. I wanted to take a break on the summit, but a horde of flies chased me off.

Finally, I was back on a trail, a welcome relief after bushwhacking for 12 hours straight. But my energy was beginning to fade. I sank to the ground, nibbled feebly on a chocolate bar, and sipped some of the small amount of water remaining in my bottles. While long runs always have their ups and downs, sometimes there are moments of clarity. Now I reflected on what I loved most: running fast, spending time on the trails with friends, exploring nature. Maybe this record attempt was one small bridge too far.

I got up and staggered along the trail toward Balsam Lake Mountain. My energy ebbed further. Nutrition and hydration were becoming problems. My pack held four pounds of homemade pemmican, a Native American recipe consisting of dried beef and tallow, and several bars of dark chocolate. These items had served me well in past events, but now I was having trouble eating. Dehydration was a possible factor. I was carrying two bottles that together contained a single liter of water, a deliberate strategy to conserve weight. But it had been 12 hours since I'd crossed the Esopus Creek the night before. The next water source was still five miles away.

I sat down again and tried to force down another square of chocolate, wondering whether I was in over my head (to put it mildly) when another runner appeared. He gave me a friendly nod and then a questioning glance before he bounded off toward Graham. I noticed that he had the same brand of trekking poles as me, but he still had two.

I struggled on toward Balsam Lake Mountain. Never had this trail felt so impossibly steep. Never had three-quarters of a mile seemed so incredibly long. Finally at the summit, it was time for a short break, another square of chocolate, and a sip of water. I was stumbling back downhill when here was that same runner again, this time standing on the trail with three other people and a large black dog. From the goatee and gray eyes, I finally recognized him as a local trail runner named Mike Siudy.

We exchanged greetings. I explained my quest to complete the 35 and break the unsupported record. Mike nodded. He knew about the record.

I knew a little bit about Mike. He'd set a record for the Nine that was so fast, it was positively baffling. I couldn't resist asking how he moved so quickly off trail.

"For every bushwhack," he replied, "there's one good route, and a multitude of bad ones."

Mike went on to explain that he'd spent a lot of time training in the mountains, and it was this experience that allowed him to find and follow the best routes. In fact, today he had finished a project called "the Grid." Graham Mountain, from whose summit he'd just returned, was the final peak in this quest. He pivoted so I could read the homemade banner pinned to his pack:

$$35 \times 12 = 420$$

I stood there, confused. Had he climbed 420 peaks within a single year? I tried to imagine how a person with a job or family could spend so much time in the mountains. The project made no sense, so I pushed it out of my mind. But I had a small epiphany. With his speed and experience, Mike might well be the right person to break Keizer's Catskills record. If he did, it would be a magnificent accomplishment and one that I could take great pleasure in, even if I wasn't the runner. Suddenly I understood that what matters is the achievement, not the personal identity of the achiever.

The clock was ticking. I said goodbye to Mike and his friends and moved on.

After a long and difficult descent along an ancient forest road shot through with saplings and stinging nettles, I finally reached the valley floor and found a stream, the first water source in 18 hours. What a joy it was to drink!

I passed the Seager trailhead and walked along Dry Brook. I kept stopping to filter more water and drink and drink and drink.

A little while later, I felt a huge sense of relief upon reaching the Shandaken lean-to. I hooked up my watch and phone to a power charger, forced down some pemmican, and spread out on the wooden floor, trying to avoid positions that triggered cramps. I gave myself permission to take an hour and a half of rest.

Ninety minutes later, I was on the move again.

The sun was sinking when I reached Eagle. I gave a quick nod to that special patch of knight's plume moss I'd seen before. It was a few minutes after 8:00 p.m. when I reached Balsam, sweating from the uphill climb. The temperature, however, was plummeting, and my breath was steaming.

I needed a break. The map showed a lean-to in three miles. Upon arrival, I bundled up in a long-sleeved shirt and lightweight jacket, which was all I'd brought for warmth. But now that I was no longer moving, the cold was unbearable. I curled up to conserve warmth, but this triggered cramps. I gave up on rest and got moving again.

The trail swept downhill for two long miles, taking me into the tiny hamlet of Pine Hill. The Birch Creek was rushing through a channel in the middle of town. The air was cold and dank. Parked cars lined the road, their windshields wet with dew.

A paved road followed Birch Creek out of town and took me to the base of Halcott Mountain. Once again it was into the woods. Once again it was into the dark world of toads, spiders, and coral fungus.

From the summit of Halcott, a ridge led down to the west, but in the darkness, I wandered from one side to the other. Then, trying to follow a compass heading more closely, I slipped off the top and started sliding down one side. The slanted terrain was killing my hips and ankles. I didn't want to climb back up, but if I ended up trapped in a creek bed full of boulders, I would probably just lie down and die.

After endless slanted walking, I finally stumbled off the ridge. At a nearby stream, I knelt to fill my bottles, then slunk past a house and stepped back onto pavement. On the march again, thighs aching. A wild profusion of roadside plants greeted me: blackberry canes full of ripe fruit, which I helped myself to frequently, goldenrod, chicory, orange jewelweed, and myriad ferns, including shoulder-high clusters of interrupted fern (so-called because the fertile leaflets wilt, leaving gaps in the frond) and clumps of sensitive fern (so-called because the fronds wilt quickly in the cold), which had shriveled and turned black.

On the climb up Bearpen, there were more blackberries, the canes arching across the trail, the fruits dancing before my eyes. I kept stopping to eat them. I arrived at the summit at 10:00 a.m. It was now T + 50 hours, or two hours into day three.

At the saddle beneath Vly, I was overcome with fatigue and had to lay down on a rock and close my eyes. Ten minutes later I opened them, stood up, and followed the unofficial but clearly blazed path to the summit, which was graced with the most extraordinary profusion of blackberries yet. On a wide, grassy path leading down from the summit, a black bear looked up at me and turned into the woods. The path became indistinct, so I followed GPS waypoints from a prior visit and emerged onto a grassy forest road crowded with Queen Anne's lace, its waist-high clusters of white flower heads shaped like the doilies my great-grandmother used to sew.

I was back on pavement once again, walking downhill, thighs burning, while spread out before me lay the West Kill Valley and the next set of mountains in the mist. Cloying scent of basswood trees in bloom (also known as linden). Flock of wild turkeys picking their way across a field. A solitary bald eagle drops from a limb and sails north.

Passing through the small collection of buildings that constitutes West Kill, I reached New York City water supply land, turned into the woods, and marched straight up to the summit of Sherrill, navigating perfectly for once, arriving a few minutes before 4:00 p.m.

Then it was on to North Dome, where I was greeted with a sprinkle of cool drops across my face and shirtless chest. I made my way downhill through an ocean of stinging nettles. Moss-covered rocks and rotting logs were turning slick. I stumbled and caught myself, one hand plunging into a nettle and burning for a few minutes.

I emerged from the woods and was back on a trail. Suddenly feeling energetic, I rocketed to the top of West Kill, only to discover that this wasn't the summit, but a bump along the way called St. Anne's Peak.

Now it was fully dark and raining steadily. The trail had morphed into a demonic roller coaster. I plodded along the twists and turns, single trekking pole clutched in one hand, my tired brain perceiving the forest sounds as eerie elevator music playing in the background.

I reached West Kill at 9:37 p.m. This was peak number 23. I'd been on the move for 61 hours. My pace was now quite slow, and I needed food and rest. The next objective, Rusk Mountain, was a steep bushwhack and a difficult prospect at night and in the rain. But after Rusk, there would be a lean-to along the trail. The plan: Keep moving. I saw an aged man tottering along the trail with a single trekking pole grasped in a gnarled hand, and I hoped he could keep up with me—and then with a start I realized that he was me.

I stumbled around a large rock ledge, worried that I'd gotten turned around. Consulting my GPS showed that this was indeed the case. I turned around again and kept moving, the part of myself that felt in charge taking the lead, the old fellow with the single pole keeping up as best he could, while the weird music echoed in the woods.

Feeling increasingly unsteady, I lurched down the backside of West Kill. The rain prattled in the leaves. Food and rest were becoming ever-more pressing priorities, while fighting my way up Rusk—in the dark, wet, tangled, slippery forest—was starting to seem like a really bad idea.

The legendary ultrarunner Pam Reed, two-time Badwater champion and winner of countless other titles, makes a simple point: "Even in extreme racing it is important to keep a perspective on how extreme is too extreme."

My mind was tired, but the logic of my situation was crystal clear. Without shelter from the rain, there was no way to get meaningful rest, and in my current state of total exhaustion, it wasn't realistic to mess with Rusk. So I made a command decision—I decided to abort the thru-run.

There was no sense of disappointment, at least not in the present moment, because it was unquestionably the right call. In fact, I felt pleased that my sense of judgment was still operating, even as the rest of my mind was breaking down.

However, now I faced the question of how to exit the field. There was no cell service. No one was going to pick me up. There were three routes out, and for a while I wandered back and forth wavering between the alternatives, as if my feet would make a better choice than my brain, until I finally decided to climb up and over the shoulder of Southwest Hunter, hoping to get some rest in the Devil's Acre lean-to. But it was occupied. I kept moving, only to take the wrong turn at the next trail junction, recognizing the error after nearly a mile. I staggered downhill along the devilishly steep trail, taking breaks every few minutes to close my eyes. I reached the Devil's Tombstone campground at dawn, stretched out atop a picnic table, and tried to doze, only to get harassed by a cloud of mosquitoes. I rolled off the table, wandered off in search of the caretaker's cabin, found a phone, and called for a ride to the nearest town. After 72 hours in motion, climbing 23 peaks, and covering over 90 miles, I left the mountains and made my way back home (having lost my car keys, I had to take a bus ride home).

CHAPTER 11

CHRISTMAS IN THE MOUNTAINS

MY INTENTION WAS TO GET BACK OUT THERE IMMEDIATELY AND TRY again. But first I assessed what had gone wrong.

The explanation seemed simple enough: I was trying to go *too* light. "Carry as little as possible, but choose that little with care," advised Earl Schaeffer, the first person to thru-hike the Appalachian Trail, and himself a former infantry soldier. I'd chosen poorly because without a tent or at least a tarp, I couldn't stop in the rain and rest.

Upon further reflection, though, I discovered a deeper root cause. I'd become enthralled by the idea of minimalism. On one of his trips into the wilds of Maine, Thoreau hired a guide named Polis, a Native Penobscot who traveled exceptionally light. "All the baggage he had, beside his axe and gun, was a blanket, which he brought loose in his hand." At the end of their trip, Thoreau asked Polis if he was glad to be home, but he found "there was no relenting to his wildness," for Polis said, "It makes no difference to me where I am." During the record attempt, this became my mantra. When tired or frustrated, I'd remind myself it made no difference where I was, which is to say, being out in the mountains was as good a place to be as behind a desk. The spirit of wildness, it seemed to me, required independence from comfortable places, just like the spirit of lightness required freedom from excessive gear. In hindsight, I don't think the attitude was wrong, just a little overdone.

After getting some rest, I ordered new gear. Soon a one-man tarp, lightweight sleeping bag, inflatable pad, and slightly larger pack were at my doorstep. This modest quantity of equipment, which might have made the difference between failure and success, weighed less than four pounds.

The next thing I did was go out and injure myself. With hindsight, the Thacher Trail Running Festival Marathon, held an hour north of the Catskills in the John Boyd Thacher State Park, was probably not a sensible recovery exercise. Especially on the very next weekend after I returned from my 35 peaks attempt. From the start, I was practically in tears. Afterward the old groin injury flared up. A week later I strained a muscle in my butt while working with a weedwhacker. It seemed a break from running was necessary, so I worked out on the StairMaster. But I did too many sessions, or at too aggressive of a pace. The result was an injury to the quadriceps tensor tendon in my left knee, which forced me, tragically, to spend a beautiful fall weekend indoors, barely able to walk.

By this point in my running career, I'd completed over 70 races of marathon distance or longer. Now aged 53, I'd dealt with plenty of injuries over the years. But never so many at once. Or from such a variety of causes. Or so reluctant to heal.

LEARNING TO OBSERVE

Sometimes a blocked path forces us to stumble off in a new direction. That fall, instead of 30-mile training runs, I wandered around and looked. Even in the past when I'd been running hard, my eyes had been drawn to so many interesting patterns. Now that I had time to observe, I became fascinated by the sparks of color in the autumnal forest; the textures of leaves and rocks; and the geometry of streams, slopes, and clouds, which seemed to offer hints of meaning.

When John Muir wrote that the mountains were calling, he explained that he would go and work on while he could, "studying them incessantly." He took notes, pressed flowers, and made detailed sketches, regretting once that he could not pencil in every single needle of a sugar pine. A journal entry reads: "Perched like a fly on this Yosemite dome, I gaze and sketch and bask, oftentimes settling down into dumb admiration without definite hope of ever learning much." I didn't have much talent for sketching, but I had my phone to take pictures, and there were guidebooks, websites, social media groups, and a few knowledgeable friends who could help me identify some of what I saw.

When it came to studying nature, Muir considered himself a disciple of Thoreau. One damp weekend midway through September, as I was meandering in a nearby forest, I noticed maple leaves dotting the ground, splashes of scarlet among the prevailing greens and browns. This brought to mind Thoreau's essay, "Autumnal Tints," in which he observed that as early as the twenty-fifth of September, a small red maple had turned color, becoming "one great scarlet fruit full of ripe juices," with "every leaf, from lowest limb to topmost spire, all aglow, especially if you look toward the sun!"

Turning to the calendar, I saw that next Sunday would be September 25. I invited my photographer friend Steve Aaron to join Odie and me in a hunt for the first red maple. That Sunday, we met Steve at a Catskills trailhead, turned into the woods, and toiled upward on the ridge that leads to Fir Mountain. Once atop the crest we wandered into a sun-lit clearing full of pale green wispy ferns—such a contrast to the steep, shadowed forest—and there, standing right in the middle of the clearing as if waiting for us, was a solitary red maple, bright scarlet from head to toe.

On every hike or run that fall, I was conscious of the colors. Venturing out to Harriman State Park on a rainy afternoon, a colorful flash caught my eye—mountain cherry leaves turning orange and red around the edges. In the Shawangunks, I found a grove of crimson cherry trees standing watch over bronze-hued berry heather. And then it seemed there were cherry trees blinking everywhere. Between the cherry and the maple leaves, it was like walking through a scarlet mist.

Yet for all the beauty of the autumnal tints, something was lacking. There was no mission. No sense of urgency. I missed the intensity of racing.

NOVEL BUSHWHACK ROUTES

Then another idea occurred to me. I was reading an essay by Burroughs. In 1885, he set out to climb Slide Mountain, but instead of taking the trail, he decided to bushwhack. At first, I was perplexed. Why would you struggle through the forest when you didn't have to? Then a light bulb went off. It would be a new experience.

Inspired by Burroughs's adventure, I decided to reenact his bushwhack ascent of Slide. For some company, I invited a friend named Alan Davidson, a young attorney with a thoughtful and soft-spoken manner. I'd met him at a race in the Shawangunks, where I tried hard to pass him but couldn't quite catch up.

Back in the days before GPS and topographic maps, Burroughs faced a huge challenge getting up the mountain. The Catskills' rugged slopes and thick forests block the views, rendering "the eye of little service," as he wryly noted. He'd heard of people who attempted this route only to turn back "baffled and bewildered."

For Alan and me, armed with GPS-enabled smartphones, there was no chance of getting lost. Even so, the ascent of Slide from a new direction was a memorable experience. When we finally reached the top, we paused to admire the views. Suddenly the clouds parted to reveal streamers of mist swirling past distant ridges. Burroughs had experienced something similar:

> *The fog in our front was swiftly whirled up by the breeze, like the drop-curtain at the theatre, only much more rapidly, and in a twinkling the vast gulf opened before us. It was so sudden as to be almost bewildering. The world opened like a book . . . the forests and mountains looked surprisingly near; in the heart of the northern Catskills a wild valley was seen flooded with sunlight. Then the curtain ran down again, and nothing was left but the gray strip of rock to which we clung, plunging down into the obscurity.*

THE LIFE OF QUIET DESPERATION

Following new bushwhack routes was a novel way to experience the mountains. But it didn't change the fact that my injuries were not healing. This was the first time in years that I wasn't training intensely for a race, a record attempt, or some other ambitious goal.

Time passed, the holidays drew near, and soon it was Christmas Day. Emeline and Philip were home from school. Sue was cooking the traditional family feast, which included a standing rib roast with lots of garlic. But instead of appreciating quality time with my wife and kids, I sat by myself in the living room in a deep funk. The idea of eating a large meal repulsed me. I felt I'd done nothing to deserve it.

Other frustrations were emerging. My job had required a significant adjustment. As an analyst, I'd had a major impact when I made a differentiated call on an important company. To be honest, I'd enjoyed the notoriety. In my new job, however, while my work was appreciated, I had little autonomy and worked mainly behind the scenes. I was tiring, too, of the endless meetings and conference calls. The long sedentary hours inside my windowless office were becoming difficult to endure. Staring at the screen, I felt my body going slack and my mood turning stale. There was this nagging thought, as irritating as a splinter, that something was wrong with the world. Here I was working endlessly for money, but money to spend on what? On fancy food and drink, expensive clothes, a renovated and redecorated apartment—in other words, on things that didn't matter. Whereas there was such vast wealth, namely the joy and beauty experienced outdoors, available for free.

For thirty years I'd been working steadily, with hardly a complaint, and maybe it was because the intensity of running had balanced out the endless left-brain calculations that represent the stock-in-trade of a professional analyst. But now, in my injured state, I found myself longing even more for the physical vitality and emotional vibrancy I experienced in the mountains. Thoreau wrote that the mass of men led lives of "quiet desperation." Surely these were people who sacrificed themselves to work and never made time to run. Now it dawned on me that unless my injuries healed, this group would soon be welcoming a new member—me.

Glancing out the window, my eyes were drawn to the sunbeams dancing among the leafless trees, and my thoughts began to drift. John Muir wrote that California's Sierra mountains radiated "spiritual beauty" and "divine thought." He saw the twilight alpenglow "kindle to a rapt, religious consciousness," while the peaks "stood hushed and waiting like devout worshipers." His passion gave me an idea. Instead of gorging on fancy food, maybe we could celebrate the holidays in a more spiritual fashion—with a family hike in the Catskills.

I tried to pitch the idea to Sue and the kids but stumbled over the words. Sue gave me an odd look. Understandably she was loath to change plans in the middle of her preparations. Emeline did not respond. Philip did not look up from his device. Even Odie seemed uninterested.

I went back to staring out the window and considered my options. If I got up, left, and went out to the mountains by myself, the family would be mystified at this behavior (and Sue would be upset). If I stayed, my gloomy mood would dampen the festive atmosphere and might contribute to irritation and conflict.

I have a philosophy: I can be of no use to others if I am not squared away myself. And another philosophy: The quietly desperate life is not worth living.

THE CHRISTMAS RUN THAT CHANGED MY LIFE

The drive from our house north to the Catskills follows the I-87 Thruway. At one point the road dips and rises, offering a brief glimpse of the Catskill's southern escarpment. This morning, I was treated to a special vision of a vast plateau floating in the north with rounded slopes, softly mottled tan and brown and dappled with blue cloud-shadows. It might have been a lost world or Shangri-la.

An hour later, I pulled into the Devil's Tombstone Campground and stepped out of the car onto ground glazed thick with ice. I strapped microspikes over my running shoes to begin the steep ascent, stepping cautiously on account of all those injuries, but this morning my knees and ankles felt OK.

After reaching the crest, I took off for the summit of Southwest Hunter along an unmarked trail, tunneling through snowy fir, spruce, and paper birch, running where the path was clear, dodging drooping branches, exhilarated to be in motion. At the tiny clearing on the summit, the snow-crusted trees were dazzling.

The summit logbook showed two hikers named Dmitri and Natalya had signed in earlier. A few minutes later I caught up to them. We chatted briefly, while sunbeams flashed around us. Dmitri mentioned that he was working on the Grid and looking forward to January. I remembered that chance encounter with Mike Siudy and my confusion over this strange-sounding project.

"How could anyone with a job or family find the time to climb all the 35 high peaks in every month?" I asked. "That would be 420 peaks in a single year."

"You don't have to do them all in the same year," Dmitri explained. "Each peak has to be completed in each of the 12 months. But you do them as you can and keep track."

Now I understood. The Grid wasn't a race. It was more like a pilgrimage.

I thanked Dmitri for this information and took off downhill, jogging and sliding through sun-warmed slush. Once down in the shadowed valley, I trotted along a gravelly trail still crusted over. A few minutes later I reached the trailhead below Rusk Mountain, the spot where four months earlier I'd made the decision to abort. Now I felt fresh and energetic. Reveling in bracing cool air and bright sun, I stripped off my shirt, followed the horse path toward Hunter Mountain, and where the path wasn't too steep, I ran slowly and felt triumphant. Where the grade increased, I power-hiked in a steady and determined manner, all the while turning over in my mind Dmitri's interesting explanation. To complete the Grid, you didn't have to climb all the peaks in a single year.

At 3,500 feet, a line of frost sliced through the middle of the trees, crisp white branches above the line, damp brown trunks below. At 4,050 feet, the sun blasted down on Hunter's summit, lighting up the wide snowy clearing. The snow-crusted fir forest, the rime-flecked cabin and fire tower, everything was blazing white, and I couldn't stop thinking about what I'd learned.

On the drive back home, I was feeling much more festive. Indeed my mind was positively spinning, for the Grid seemed like an opportunity to channel my energy into a distinctive goal where speed would no longer matter. It would give me an excuse to spend a lot of time outdoors, which at this point in my life felt essential for my mental and spiritual health. And there would be flexibility to schedule Catskills trips around work and family obligations, instead of walking out on them.

I felt somewhat guilty that evening when I pulled into the driveway, tiptoed into the empty kitchen, and helped myself to leftovers. I'd done what I had to do, and it was the right decision. But that doesn't mean there wasn't any cost. I would have to find some way to make it up to my family. I would have to find some way to share the passion I was finding in the mountains or at least do a better job of explaining it.

A SPREADSHEET IS BORN

The next day it occurred to me that after so many years hiking and running in the Catskills, I had surely accumulated a large number of peaks that would count toward the Grid. Curious, I opened my laptop, created a spreadsheet table with the 35 high peaks down the side and the 12 months of the year across the top, and started filling in cells with dates for all the climbs I could remember. Further research took me back through training logs, photographs, routes uploaded from my GPS watch, and a few more cells were filled. I thought of family camping trips we'd taken many years ago and went tearing through the house, rifling through drawers and shelves and files, searching for further clues.

Evidently, I'd been working on the Grid without knowing, for once it was complete, my spreadsheet showed a total of 117 qualifying peaks. That was 28 percent of the total. At the time, this seemed like a huge head start.

Of course, this meant there were 303 peaks left to do, or 72 percent remaining. It did not occur to me then how much effort this would entail, or how the experience would change me.

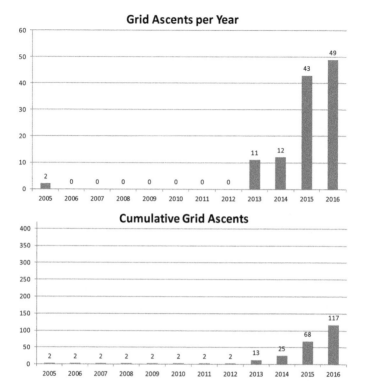

PART II
EMBRACING THE GRID

To those who have struggled with them the mountains reveal beauties they will not disclose to those who make no effort. That is the reward mountains give to effort. And it is because they have so much to give and give it so lavishly to those who will wrestle with them that men love the mountains and go back to them again and again.

—*Sir Francis Younghusband, Mount Everest,*
The Reconnaissance, 1921

CHAPTER 12

WINTER TINTS

I KICKED OFF THE GRID WITH BOUNDLESS ENTHUSIASM, MY CAUTIOUS attitude toward winter all but forgotten, as the whole point of this new quest was to experience the mountains' qualities in every single month. I felt like a scout with a high-stakes mission—to reconnoiter uncharted territory. My orders: To report back on the sights and sounds of unfamiliar places. To share what I found there. To share what I learned.

The very first weekend in January found me on the road before dawn, the mountains barely perceptible, a faint line separating blackened slopes from still-dark sky. Last fall I'd studied Thoreau's autumnal colors. Today my purpose was to observe the distinctive tints of winter.

Arriving at the Mink Hollow trailhead, I found the forest dim under gray cloud cover and a pen at the trail register whose cold ink wouldn't flow. Two miles later, Mink Hollow Notch floated into view through leafless trees, while Sugarloaf Mountain towered overhead. I was scrambling up the mountain's shoulder when a small bird fluttered onto a branch a few feet above my head. Head down, it pecked at a spot of peeling bark, revealing the familiar striped face and russet chest, then glanced my way inquisitively. John Burroughs wrote, "You must have the bird in your heart before you can find it in the bush." Six months ago, I'd never heard of a nuthatch. Now they followed me everywhere.

Up an icy scramble, spikes barely biting, I jogged across the summit of Twin Mountain. The air was dead calm. To the south, a shadowy haze signaled a storm front churning through. To the north,

I spotted Blackhead, Black Dome, and Thomas Cole Mountains, lolling against the winter sky. These three peaks constitute the Blackhead Range, which forms the Catskills' northern wall. Behind them glimmered a band of pale yolky yellow, lingering dawn effects from a sun crawling low across the sky.

I ran, jumped, skipped, and slid down into the next notch, then made the quick ascent to Indian Head. Paper birch was everywhere, the trunks varnished in ice, outer bark shiny white and where it'd peeled away, the inner layers glowed with a warm russet hue redolent of the nuthatch's red-brown breast. Long slender branches encrusted with a full inch of crystal accumulation bowed to the ground, clattering softly.

I turned around, retraced my steps over Twin and Sugarloaf, and butt-slid down an icy scramble. Brushing off, I looked up, and there was the Blackhead Range again, watching me.

I climbed and descended Plateau and passed one last time through Mink Hollow Notch, where I saw a young beech tree with pale beige shriveled leaves vibrating in the breeze.

IMPRESSIONS IN THE DARK

With days short, the search for the mountains' special winter qualities took me into the evening hours. Now the question became, What could I observe at night?

The second weekend in January I drove north again, the mountains now a sooty wall beneath an ashen sky. It was 4:00 pm when I reached Woodland Valley Campground, as a group of hikers was descending.

"How's the view on Wittenberg?" I asked.

"It was great," one replied, "but you'll miss it by the time you get there."

Undeterred, I charged upward in the fading light, only to encounter another hiker descending. He warned of ice-covered ledges, explained how he struggled to get up them, added that he saw another party give up and turn back. Soon enough, I came upon the tall ledges slick with ice, but my spikes gave adequate traction, and there were plenty of holds to grab. I was up and over in a snap, feeling energized.

At the summit, the view was as dark and boundless as the midnight sea. The wind slipped through the trees behind me, and I heard it off to one side, as if a serpent of celestial size was uncoiling from around the mountaintop and slithering into the valley.

Later that evening, after returning from Wittenberg, I drove out to Windham. An hour or so later, I was standing on the summit in a grove of stunted birch and maple with beard lichens pendent from barren branches, gazing at the familiar three-humped Blackhead Range silhouetted against the night sky, black on black. The moon passed behind a film and became a vaporous circle with concentric rainbow rings.

SHARING THE WINTER SIGHTS WITH FRIENDS

With this handful of climbs, I'd advanced the count of Grid peaks completed to 124. The sights and sounds were exhilarating, and the momentum felt unstoppable. Saturday morning, the last weekend in January, I was on the road racing north again, the early morning mists tinged with red, and then, as the road snaked higher into the mountains, a smoldering disc appeared in the rearview mirror, as if a burning eyeball were peering from behind the clouds. On reaching the trailhead, a few flakes twirled about, and all was gray again.

I'd last seen Amy Hanlon at Manitou's Revenge, the 53-mile ultramarathon I'd run two years before. She passed me early on and called out, "I'll see you again when you catch me." But I never did. Amy is an accomplished runner, and she has a quirky sense of humor; I've never seen her without a sparkle in her eyes. I'd invited her to join me on today's adventure, and soon we were sauntering out along the trail, laughing, talking, crunching on firm snow, spikes and snowshoes strapped to packs.

After two miles, it was time to leave the trail and turn into the woods. Along the way, I mentioned to Amy how John Muir sometimes referred to plants as "people." In one of his journal entries he wrote, "Here, too, are most of the lowly plant people seen yesterday on the other side of the divide now opening their beautiful eyes." In another he described the plants growing along the mountain passes in California's High Sierra as "beautiful and tender and enthusiastic plant-people." Once in Alaska, a companion observed him running from one flower cluster to another, falling to his knees, addressing his favorites as if they were long-lost friends: "Ah! My blue-eyed darlin', little did I think to see you here. How did you stray away from Shasta?"

Amy and I tramped through the forest until we discovered an enormous black cherry with three trunks fused at the base, each reaching separately into the sky. We stared at this magnificent individual, and I wondered, could such a beautiful, substantial specimen have feelings? Even if it has no brain?

After Fir, it was on to Big Indian, which requires a tricky left-hand turn (during the first night of my failed run, this is where I imagined I saw a lake). But this morning, we kept on course precisely, and soon the saddle was hanging to the front like a suspension bridge between two peaks. A feeling of elation swept through me: "I'm so happy!" I shouted, almost giddy, "We're exactly on the crest!"

We marched across the saddle in high spirits and followed the far slope all the way to the summit of Big Indian. Next, we trudged toward Doubletop through deep drifts and tangled forest, scrambling upward into an eerie snow-coated boreal grove. When here last spring, I'd admired the lush moss- and lichen-coated trees, but now everything was white. The "tree people" stood as if on watch, unfazed by the elements, while the lichen slept under snowy blankets, no doubt dreaming lichen dreams.

Back at the trailhead, Amy left for home while I drove over to McKenley Hollow, where the plan was to camp in the lean-to. But first, a quick jaunt up the trail to bag Eagle and Balsam. At the saddle between the two peaks, wind gusts dashed among the trees with a sense of urgency, while flakes sparkled across my field of vision. On Balsam, I switched off the light. The wind huffed on one side, then the other. Slowly the darkness resolved itself. The tree people were dim presences.

The next morning, the clouds broke apart and the sky popped out in a startling shade of electric turquoise blue, and then it was gray clouds and swirling flakes again. I'd invited Alan Davidson to join me for the bushwhack up Rusk Mountain, and he showed up right on time, carrying a winter pack full of extra gear. We found a crusty trail and fell into the groove, toiling our way up a very steep slope when suddenly the clouds broke, the woods flashed with light, and the sky flipped back to turquoise. I reached for my sunglasses, but a moment later the light was gone.

At the summit the sun splashed around us one last time. We stumbled back down in those crusty tracks, but it was painful going on the broken surface, especially for my left ankle, the most persistent of my nagging injuries. I stopped and looked around for a better route. To the right, the ridge flowed all the way down to the valley floor, all fresh snow and trackless, so we went that way, weaving between the trees, careening, skidding. "I'm so happy!" I shouted once again, "this is how winter bushwhacking's supposed to be!"

WITH ODIE IN THE MOONLIGHT

It was Friday night, the first weekend in February, with the Grid count now at 131. After work and the long drive north, Odie and I crunched along a snowy lane. Looking up, I took in the saddle between Bearpen and Vly looming 1,000 feet above us in the dusk. Odie trotted along light on his feet, while I trudged and panted. My watch beeped off a mile, and a few steps later we turned onto the path to Vly. I placed my snowshoe cleats into steeply angled snowbanks and grasped for branches, while Odie jogged along nonchalantly, pausing from time to time to clean snow from his paws.

It was too cold to loiter at the top, so I turned about and was soon clumping back down the path, sometimes skidding a foot or two, while Odie flew ahead, a wild expression on his face, eyes glinting in my headlamp's beam when he paused to look back at me. We marched on to Bearpen's summit, where we found the moon casting crisp branch shadows on the shimmering trail. I unclipped my snowshoes and tied them to my pack, turned out the headlamp, and stood there in the brilliant darkness. Then the two of us started running. We flew down the mountain in the moonlight, not stopping until we reached the base.

A DICEY NIGHTTIME CLIMB UP KAATERSKILL

Two weeks later, the descent from North Dome was slow, exacting work as Alan and I picked our way through soft snow sitting on sheets of ice. Then we had to cross the West Kill, whose frigid currents were running knee-deep. The sting left tears in my eyes.

But we were eager for more, and a change of socks later, it was off to the Platte Clove trailhead for an attempt at Kaaterskill High Peak. Enough bushwhacking, we agreed, let's stick to trails. I switched from snowshoes to spikes, and these gripped the trampled surface as we hustled along. A little later, as dusk fell, we were standing next to a shoulder-high cairn, looking around for the faded dark blue blazes painted on the trees that would take us up 500 feet to the summit. Even with lights on, we soon lost the blazes and wandered off the sketchy trail.

"Let's work around to the left," I suggested.

But the slope was so steep I was soon on hands and knees.

It was pitch-black now. I scanned around for a route, but our headlamps lit up only the tangled welter to the front, blinding us to what lay farther off. I crawled a few feet up, shoes slipping on ice-glazed rocks, my normally reliable spikes failing to purchase even when I pressed down hard. Up ahead stood another smooth gray wall. I scouted left, Alan scouted right, but the cliffs were unyielding.

We fell back and regrouped. The new plan was to push right and get back on the trail. But we didn't see the blazes. Alan seemed unfazed—indeed, he's as steady as they come, exactly the companion you'd want on a dicey climb like this. But I was concerned. If one of us slipped off an icy ledge, it would take a long time to summon help. Suddenly my feet flew out from under me, sending my face into a pile of snow.

"I'm OK if we don't make it to the top," I panted.

Alan concurred with my assessment, but we decided to make one last try. Moving right, we encountered another cliff, but this time a small tree was growing from a crack. Grunting with effort, I heaved myself up onto Hurricane Ledge, Alan right behind me, and a few seconds later we stepped onto the summit.

Here I discovered that my spikes had slipped off the front of my shoes and bunched up around the heels, which explained why I had so little traction. Having no appetite to return the way we came, we opted instead for the longer route home down the mountain's northern scramble, sliding much of the way on our butts. This memorable climb was Grid peak 136.

RUNNING INTO THE STORM

I'd read how John Muir had once ventured into the Sierra Mountains specifically to observe a gale: "When the storm began to sound, I lost no time in pushing out into the woods to enjoy it," he explained, "for on such occasions Nature has always something rare to show us." He scaled a 100-foot-tall Douglas spruce, whose top whipped back and forth in the wind, remaining there for hours to study the wild scene.

With a major storm expected to hit the Hudson Valley, I pulled out the map and planned a run in the Blackhead Range, timed to be in and out just as the front arrived. I briefed Sue on my destination, as I always do (but not mentioning the forecast) and then drove off to the Big Hollow parking area in the Northern Catskills, arriving around 2:00 p.m. to overcast sky, calm air, and temperatures hovering in the 50s—weird conditions for February.

I headed out first to Black Dome, where I paused and peered across the way at its neighbor, Blackhead. The mountain stared back at me, an enormous, rounded mass, like a giant head, mist curling about its shoulders, while the currents thundered in transit high above.

I was nearing the saddle between the two peaks when the wind began to rage. A gust roared across the path no more than 20 feet in front of me, clutched the trees and shook them violently. Where I stood, only a gentle ripple touched my cheek.

Heading up Blackhead, I was mindful of escape routes should the storm burst suddenly upon me, but it was still calm. Somewhere beyond the heavy clouds, the sun was setting; warm hues seeped into the mist until the tawny grass and stunted brush were glowing softly.

Almost back at the trailhead now, it was still strangely warm, with just a light drizzle when suddenly the heavens opened. The temperature crashed. Sleet was stinging my face and chilling chest and shoulders. When I reached my car, it was already covered in an inch of slush. On the drive out, the vehicle slid around on the pavement, shuddering in the wind and hurtling rain, and then a white flash lit up the night.

NIGHTTIME BUSHWHACK UP PANTHER AND SLIDE

By working steadily during the winter months, I'd pushed the count to 153, and now there was time for one last adventure before the end of March. It was after dark when Amy, Alan, and I converged on the Woodland Valley Campground, geared up, and headed out. A short distance later we turned off the trail. Even with snowshoes, it was hard work, each step sinking three or four inches into soggy snow. With Alan in the lead, the three of us groped around some ledges, found gaps between the slabs, inched upward onto the crest of a ridge, which was so narrow that even in the limited play of our headlamp beams the slope could be seen dropping off to either side, as if we were walking atop a castle wall.

The ridge broadened and turned more steeply up, and it was back to work, two steps forward, one back, but we inched along with a semblance of rhythm. The mist parted, revealing stars above the mountain's spine. Nearing the top, we found a small clearing, snowy and starlit, such a surprise after deep forest. It was as if the mountain had worked some magic, rewarding our perseverance with a small gift of open space.

On the summit ledge a little before midnight, we stared out across Woodland Valley, a pool of inky blackness, totally devoid of light.

From Panther, we followed the trail back down the mountain. The surface was soft and squishy in some places, in others frozen hard and lumpy, everywhere full of postholes punched in the snow by hikers without snowshoes. My left ankle began to ache. Three months into the year, it still hadn't fully healed.

We reached a junction, turned into the woods, and began a second bushwhack, this time up the shoulder of Slide Mountain.

We crunched steadily through fresh snow until we encountered a dense thicket of fir saplings. Now we ducked branches and squeezed between spindly trees growing inches apart. Our pace slowed almost to a halt. "It *never* always gets worse," I muttered, reminding myself that Catskills thickets don't go on forever—but this one seemed like it might.

We saw some tracks in the snow, big round holes with blurry claw marks along the edges, probably a few days old. I'd never seen a bear in winter but had heard they sometimes woke from hibernation and wandered around in search of food. A few steps later, more of these tracks appeared, but these ones unmistakably fresh (the claw marks were sharp-edged).

The nightmare thicket began to thin. We struggled uphill through deep snow, reaching Slide's summit just in time to witness a line of ruby light glowing along the horizon, filling the space between mountain walls and cloudbanks, as if we were inside a cauldron and the lid had been cracked open. The ruby line expanded into a band of churning purple. Vapors drifted ghostlike across the scene.

The plan had been to descend into the Neversink Valley and then climb more peaks, but no one was game. We decided instead to return to Woodland Valley along the trail. We descended awkwardly, snowshoes twisting as we scooted over boulders and clambered down icy ladders. Sheets of mist curled around Cornell and Wittenberg. The trees along the trail were varnished with a thin glaze of ice, and so, I noticed, was Alan's hefty pack. By the time we reached Wittenberg's summit, rain was splattering against the rocks.

On the final descent to Woodland Valley, Alan took the lead, I struggled after, while Amy lagged to fix a snowshoe strap. The trail was badly chewed and full of frozen holes. Our snowshoes stuck on ice, sank in snow, tilted unpredictably, and when we took them off, the footing was slippery and uneven. For my sore ankle, this was becoming an ordeal. I hung on grimly, determined not to get left behind.

Sugarloaf Mountain, January 7, 2017.

CHAPTER 13

FIFTY MILES THAT NEVER END

I POURED SO MUCH ENERGY INTO THE GRID. IN THE FIRST THREE months of 2017 alone, I bagged 40 peaks, which was almost as many as the entire year before.

Otherwise, my running wasn't going well. The sore left ankle wasn't healing. Back in late November, while doing calf raises in the gym, I'd felt a burning sensation in the posterior tibialis tendon, which lies underneath the ankle on the inside of the foot and connects the calf muscle to the navicular bone. Sue rummaged in her physical therapy supplies, produced a roll of special tape, and showed me how to wrap the ankle for support. But even so the tendon felt tight and irritable. I worried that it would become a chronic problem.

I dialed back on training. There was no more speedwork at the track. I limited total mileage. I canceled all the springtime races I used to run, except for one. Rock The Ridge, the 50-miler in the Shawangunks, held special significance: Not only had my friend Todd and I developed the event, but it raised funds to support conservation, and I wanted to be part of this important cause. But if there was to be any hope of completing the run—or even starting it—I'd need to modify my approach.

At work, the lull in acquisitions continued, and without this avenue for growth, there was talk about putting the company up for sale. Still, there was plenty of work to be done, for the regulators demanded that we build out our risk management infrastructure, which is a preoccupation for banks, or at least it's supposed to be.

We got to work, and soon every aspect of operations was tracked and reported in color-coded dashboards so that the key risks stood out. I appreciated the systematic approach to measuring and managing risk, for tactical discipline had been drilled into me in my Army days, and later on as an analyst I watched a procession of companies crash and burn that were once considered Wall Street darlings.

It occurred to me that I could borrow from this corporate playbook for my own purposes. As a first step, I started color-coding entries in my training log: green for normal days, yellow when aches and pains signaled a need for caution, and red to indicate injury. This simple system forced me to listen more carefully to what my body had to say. To keep in the green as much as possible, more of my training consisted of walking, whether around the block during lunch, on the treadmill, or in the park with Odie.

With this more measured approach in place, and a couple of longer training runs complete, I was starting to feel confident about the race. Then, with a couple weeks to go, the ankle flared up again: condition red.

After deliberating on the risks, I decided to attempt the race, but at a very cautious pace. Two years earlier, I'd been close behind the leader, but this year the only goal would be to finish. Then I had an idea—I could make the experience more interesting with some askesis.

The ideas I brought to my practice, whether called askesis or minimalism or going light, reflected a growing sense of skepticism toward conventional wisdom. For example, it's commonly thought that runners should eat and drink continuously. Typical advice is to consume 300 calories and 10 ounces of water per hour, and somehow suggestions like this are tossed out as if they were right for everyone, irrespective of important variables like body weight, fitness, pace, exposure to the sun, or ambient humidity and temperature.

My skepticism intensified after reading historical accounts in which people got by with much less. For example, in 1849, a scout named William Lewis Manley was leading a caravan toward California. He wrote of going one or two days without water. "No one who has ever felt the extreme of thirst can imagine the distress, the dispair [*sic*], which it brings. I can find no words, no way to express it so others can understand." Yet thirst did not stop him from walking a day or two ahead of the wagons, searching for the safest route through difficult, unknown terrain.[4]

In another example from the mid-nineteenth century, I read the story of a pair of White explorers who joined up with a band of Shoshone Indians on a hunting trip. Several days passed without sign of game. "These Indians did not seem to suffer for want of food," one of the explorers reported. "Even when we were starving, they appeared happy and contented. . . . It appeared that these people were accustomed to go for long periods without food, and with little apparent inconvenience."

Not only is it possible to get by with less than contemporary people think, but it's become apparent that there are risks to excessive consumption: Too much water can lead to hyponatremia, which may be fatal, while overreliance on sugary snacks is blamed for obesity, diabetes, and other chronic problems that have become alarmingly prevalent (and runners are not immune).

As an experiment, I decided to attempt the 50 miles of Rock The Ridge without food or water. If successful, this would be a first for me, and a way to add some distinction to a run that would otherwise be slow and cautious.

The race started at 6:00 a.m. on the first Saturday in May. Mindful of the ankle, I maintained a measured pace on the steep hill at the start. Up ahead I caught a glimpse of Sue, digging in with trekking poles (she was running on a relay team with Emeline and Philip). Once past the crest, I trotted along cautiously. Instead of pushing myself, I focused on the spring forests, the oak flowers and maple samaras dotting the trail, the ovenbirds and woodpeckers calling from the canopy, the floppy brown rock tripe and toadskin lichen dotting the white cliffs along the course.

Fifteen miles in, I passed Awosting Falls in Minnewaska State Park, which was thundering like I'd never seen before. A torrent was pouring over the cliff and hurtling into the basin; the wind caught

---

4 For a discussion of William Lewis Manley's adventures crossing Death Valley, see my blog post "Before Badwater," accessible at https://thelongbrownpath.com /2015/10/23/before-badwater-william-lewis-manlys-1849-crossing-of-death-valley.

droplets and whipped them across the trail. One stung me on the cheek.

At the halfway point, I caught a glimpse of the Catskills, some 30 miles to the north, crouching under a murky layer of evil-looking clouds. A rough cold wind was blowing from that direction. I passed a friend who was struggling with mild gastrointestinal distress, a common affliction for long-distance runners, especially when following conventional advice to keep eating as you run. With nothing in it, my stomach had no cause to get upset.

I jogged along at a slow but steady pace, trying to match the flowers and catkins on the trail to the trees along the side. A flash of brilliant crimson caught my eye: the buds, flowers, and seeds of a red maple. For the first time I realized these trees are as colorful in spring as in the fall.

At mile 40, my stomach began to growl, this being the farthest distance I'd ever run without taking in any calories. I was starting to feel thirsty, too. The next aid station came into view, and I felt sorely tempted to help myself to food and drink, but it would be such a shame to give up on my special goal with the end so close. So I persevered. A mile later the trail crossed a rushing creek. How I wanted to scoop up the cool water in my hands and take a long drink! But then it started to rain, and as I fumbled for the jacket in my pack, the shocking cold drops made me gasp.

Thirst forgotten, I ambled along on the last few miles to the finish, and my mind began to wander. I'd recently read John Muir's account of his first summer in the Sierra, and one of his journal entries came to mind:

> *Toward sunset, enjoyed a fine run to camp, down the long south slopes, across ridges and ravines, gardens and avalanche gaps, through the firs and chaparral, enjoying wild excitement and excess of strength, and so ends a day that will never end.*

How could a day never end?

It always felt to me like time was rushing by. At work, when I was scrambling to meet a deadline. Or when racing, the experience felt so fleeting: the ticking clock, the marshaling of an unsustainable effort, the desperate push to finish.

But suppose these experiences, and the effort we put into them, change us. Then wouldn't the impact on our lives be permanent? And wouldn't our changed lives have lasting impact on other people, too? For Muir, that first summer in the Sierras intensified his love of nature and determination to preserve Yosemite. And Muir has had a lasting impact on the world, for he went on to influence so many people, from contemporaries like Burroughs to people like me who are still reading his account more than 100 years later. Evidently, the impact of that "fine run to camp" is still rippling outward.

When I finally crossed the finish line of Rock The Ridge, it dawned on me that the 50-miler I'd just completed would never end. What I'd experienced had subtly changed me, and the new me would go on in myriad ways to impact other people too.

For what it's worth, I completed the 50 miles without food or water. I don't remember how many helpings I had, but the chili, cornbread, and watermelon at the finish line were wonderfully refreshing, although they tasted no different than how they did on other occasions. Remarkably the ankle felt OK.

Over the next few days, I limited my recovery to short walks. A week after the race, an optimistic assessment in my training log: "Ankle not too bad."

I headed to the track and tried a cautious jog—and the ankle cried out immediately.

CHAPTER 14

FLOWING DOWN AND UP

BELIEVING THAT THE BODY HEALS FASTER IN MOTION, I WALKED THE three miles to my doctor's office and told him my ankle was on the mend. But to him it looked swollen, and this assessment pricked my bubble. A week later the MRI came back. The good news was that the tendon wasn't torn, although there was a stress fracture in the bone where it attached. The bad news: "No running for six weeks." My doctor delivered this directive with an embarrassed expression, as if he sensed I would take this as poorly as defendant would a lengthy prison sentence. But at least the dreaded "boot" was not deemed necessary, and hiking was still allowed. Was barefoot OK? So long as it didn't hurt too much.

At about this time, there was news at work as well. At the board's direction, the management team had engaged in a series of confidential discussions with other banks that might be interested in acquiring us. A great deal of activity produced a single offer, which was accepted with alacrity, although we tried not to act too eager during the negotiations. A flurry of investor calls and employee meetings followed the announcement, after which it became very quiet.

For the management team, including me, the sale would mark the end of an eight-year run. Notwithstanding my frustration with indoor office work, it had been an adventure: We had raised capital during the global financial crisis, completed eight acquisitions, taken the company public, and significantly improved results. Now our mission was to keep things together until the sale closed, which would hopefully happen before year-end.

In these circumstances, there wasn't much to do in terms of investor relations, strategic planning, or mergers and acquisitions, which were my primary areas of focus. It was time for me to start looking for my next job.

Someone asked if I was interested in an M&A position at a regional bank. I hesitated. Banks are pretty stodgy. My current employer was the exception to this rule, since we had been launched as an entrepreneurial gambit, with investors betting that a small team entrusted with capital could exploit disruptions in the market. My boss used to laugh and call us a "band of pirates." Not in the sense that we raised mayhem, took hostages, or walked people off the plank, but merely that we'd eschewed steady work and instead set sail on the high seas in search of opportunity.

Meanwhile, if the world of banking wasn't calling with an invitation to come higher, the mountains continued to whisper in my ears. The table in the spreadsheet now had 165 cells filled in, meaning that roughly 40 percent of the Grid was done. The count for May was 20 peaks complete, leaving 15 to go. To finish off the Grid for May seemed within reach, which was an exciting possibility, although the stress fracture was a concern, of course. But if I took a few vacation days, that would give me time to bag the peaks while moving at an easy pace and hopefully not antagonize the injury.

I never followed up on the M&A position. I couldn't picture myself working in a suit and tie.

SAUNTERING THROUGH MAY

Thoreau wrote that "the saunterer, in the good sense, is no more vagrant than the meandering river, which is all the while sedulously seeking the shortest course to the sea." To complete the Grid for May, instead of running I'd need to learn to saunter. Instead of racing, I'd need to flow through the mountains like a river, except I'd be going uphill as well as down.

I kicked off the month with a visit to Twin Mountain with Dave Togut, a friend from New York City. Keeping things easy on the ankle was paramount, and therefore I decided to go barefoot, which guarantees a slow pace. If Dave was surprised to see me without shoes, he kept his opinions to himself (like any Wall Street analyst, he has a good poker face). On the mountain's eastern summit, we were treated to sweeping views under a glorious spring sky. And now Dave's face broke into a wide grin.

Later that evening, after Dave had left for home, I headed north and climbed Vly Mountain, pitched camp near the saddle, and passed the night listening to rain spattering against tent fabric. The next morning, I bagged Bearpen.

A day later, I was standing barefoot at the base of North Dome. I took a step onto leaves and moss and from there began moving upward through a succession of environments—first a grove of white pine, next a plantation of Norway spruce. Then it was into the Catskills' native northern hardwoods: maple, yellow birch, black cherry, ash, beech. A moment later I was floating through a grove of hemlocks, and then it was back into northern hardwoods, but now they were shrinking in stature and becoming gnarled and stunted. Somewhere past 3,000 feet, clusters of blooming hobblebush appeared, waving big floppy leaves and small white flower clusters, and soon I was winding through groves of lichen-crusted fir and spruce. The climb felt effortless, as if I were a balloon lofted by the breeze.

The descent was a different story. I threaded my way between sandstone cliffs, tottered over piles of tilting mossy rocks, blundered into that large dense field of nettle, which I recalled from last summer's failed run, only now a fresh generation was rising from the earth, hungering for a taste of flesh.

Past a small pond the trail appeared. It brought back memories of weird music and a demonic roller-coaster in the rain. Yet now it was a beautiful path of soft dirt and smooth slabs. I rolled along without much effort, the miles chirping off on my watch.

Time no longer mattered. There was a lean-to a few miles distant where I might spend the night. If it were occupied, I could pitch my small tarp practically anywhere.

Later that evening, I was filtering water from the West Kill where it flows through Diamond Notch as the light was growing dim. Some illumination returned as I climbed toward Southwest Hunter, but then it faded for good. I was moving carefully, without a headlamp, scanning the path ahead for smooth spots to place my feet; in the ambient starlight these were nothing but faint ghostly glimmers, but that was all I needed.

I reached the lean-to only to find it occupied by a porcupine. The animal hid its head in a corner, then reconsidered its options and departed.

The next morning, I felt chilled and listless. I perked up a little on the walk to Hunter, enjoying the feel of cool black mud underfoot. At the summit I was surprised by a profusion of purple pollen cones bursting from fir branches, a spring phenomenon I'd never noticed before.

The gravel trail heading down was too painful for my feet, so shoes went back on. After two miles, I turned off the trail and into the forest for the bushwhack over to Rusk, all the while dreading the steep descent. It turned out to be hellish—torture on the ankle, plus the shoes started rubbing sores on the tops of my toes. I kept drifting off course, groaning with vexation at the endless grade.

Eventually the ordeal was over. I was sitting at the trailhead retying laces while a butterfly as big as a saucer darted among the flowers, an eastern tiger swallowtail, with huge yellow and black wings, so busy gathering breakfast it didn't notice my peering face a foot or two away.

Four miles back to the car along Spruceton Road, my ankle now throbbing in earnest, but how could I complain when woolly white clouds frolicked in a crisp blue sky? When the breeze tussled the trees along the road, and they seemed to love having their limbs and leaves stroked so? Here rippled endless lilac in royal purple bloom, redolent of expensive lotions, and the Norway spruce stood so stately, the kind of trees Walt Whitman surely had in mind when he wrote, "Why are there trees I never walk under but large and melodious thoughts descend upon me?"

The ankle got a day off after this, and then it was back to the Blackhead range with a pair of friends. The three of us were treated to a wondrous blue-green-brown panorama of cloud shadows slipping across the mottled hills, while the mountains jumped, danced, ran,

and turned somersaults all around us, and young plant people burst
forth from the earth.

THE NATURE OF FLOW STATE

Thoreau's river metaphor brings to mind the popular term "flow,"
which refers to a mental state characterized by productivity, feelings
of control, and such deep absorption that the experience of time is
altered. Certain authors point to extreme athletes, like surfers or
BASE jumpers, as masters of this state. But the psychologist who
coined the term, Mihalyi Czikszentmihalyi, offers a simpler path.
Flow "appears at the boundary between boredom and anxiety," he
writes, "when the challenges are just balanced with the person's
capacity to act."

In my case, this boundary was an easy target. Hiking up these
peaks at a measured pace didn't subject me to anxiety, as would have
running in my injured state. Yet compared to office work, traveling
through the mountains was invigorating, both physically and
emotionally.

Of course, it helps to have mild spring weather.

The end of May drew near. I had three peaks left to do, one day to
do them, and now the forecast called for heavy rain.

I walked up Windham barefoot, but if I were going to get all
three done, I'd need to move faster, so the shoes went back on for
Kaaterskill High Peak, where ankle-deep water was flowing down the
trail. At least it wasn't sheets of ice at night. Reaching a terrace below
the summit, I decided to bushwhack straight to the top, thinking this
would be the quickest route, only to encounter a forbidding wall of
cliffs. I scrambled up on all fours over wet leaves and moss-covered
rocks, arrived at the base of a slab, circled around for a gap, reached
up to grasp a root, hoisted myself into a crevasse, and came face-
to-face with a tiny red flower shaped like a bleeding heart.

After reaching the summit, I made it back to the car, soaked to the
skin, and drove over to the base of Halcott. Bushwhacking 2,000 feet
up a steep and slippery mountain is not something to sneeze at. But
once again I became a balloon and floated to the top, and the Grid for
May was done.

A steep descent on slick, unstable terrain was surely a recipe for misery. But with May complete, there was no rush. It was one careful step after another, dropping first a foot, then a hundred, and then a thousand, until I'd slid down the slope like a raindrop rolling off a leaf.

At the base of the mountain, I found a handsome stream flowing through a rocky cleft. It cascaded over a ledge and pooled in a small basin before hurtling through a roadside channel—a journey that would take it into the Esopus Creek, through the Ashokan Reservoir, and then into a long aqueduct to New York City, and finally out to sea. It seemed to have no trouble finding its way.

At the base of Halcott Mountain. May 29, 2017.

CHAPTER 15

INTO AN ALIEN PLANETSCAPE

UNLIKE MAY, THE GRID FOR JUNE WAS ALMOST EMPTY. ONLY FIVE peaks were checked off in my spreadsheet, namely those from the Manitou's Revenge ultramarathon, which I'd run two years before. Unlike May, finishing the Grid for June this year wasn't feasible. For the part of me that loves to check off boxes, this was discouraging. For another part of me, however, there was the simple delight of being alive and outdoors during a beautiful time of year. This feeling propelled me back into the mountains whenever I could get away.

The more time I spent in the Catskills, the more I loved the multiplicity of sights and sounds and feelings. Every single climb was a new experience, for the colors in late spring were completely different from those of fall or winter. Each peak was unique, and I, too, was constantly changing.

SEEKING DIVERSITY, NOT SAMENESS

The contrast between the spring mountains and the sterile indoor environment where I passed my working hours could not have been greater. At the same time, I noticed a gulf was opening between me and my colleagues. I recall a business trip when four of us walked to dinner on a warm spring evening as the sun sank beneath a bank of gilt-edged clouds and shadows pooled beneath the trees. The restaurant had a lovely patio, but they didn't want to sit outside because there wasn't any air-conditioning.

I've always hated air-conditioning. The other day my mom and I recalled a disagreement we'd had when I was young. We were driving somewhere in the family's brand-new car, the first we'd ever had with air-conditioning. Yet I was adamant about rolling down the windows. My issue with air-conditioning is that it replaces diversity with sameness. Even on a sweltering summer night, I'd rather play the odds, hoping for a cooling breeze. I'd rather listen to the wind, the rustling leaves, the crickets and the katydids, a pack of coyotes yipping in the forest—not a droning fan. That people no longer feel comfortable in their natural environment, without machines to control the climate, seems so sad. I understand why this is so, but even as a teenager I had an instinctual distrust of comfort, an intuition that as a goal in life it led nowhere.

SPRINGTIME IN THE MOUNTAINS

The first weekend in June found me on the trail to Windham High Peak. With the solstice near at hand, the sun climbed into the center of the sky and poured its energy into the damp forest, churning the moisture into a light haze, making the air feel sticky and dense. Soon a cloud of gnats was bouncing around my head, and where the trail edged around a swamp, mosquitoes joined the party. I padded along barefoot, at a leisurely pace, enjoying the soft smooth surface of dirt and leaves, batting away the insects when they got too pesky (no repellent for this minimalist tramper).

But soon enough conditions changed. The sun peeked into a grove of spruce and pine, a breeze tiptoed through the treetops, the humidity dissipated, insects dispersed. And then conditions changed again with a cloud drifting overhead, dragging damp shadows in its wake. The contrast in conditions from one minute to the next was enchanting.

From the crest of the ridge, Blackhead and Black Dome came into hazy view, simmering in the spring sunshine as clouds bubbled up around them.

At the summit, mountain ash was blooming with dense mounds of tiny white flowers, while mountain maples sprouted pale flower spikes. Bees dashed among the flowers. Ants and spiders crept among stone flakes. I luxuriated in the feeling of sun-warmth on bare skin of face and chest and shoulders.

By this point the Grid had become a preoccupation, but the next weekend in June I had good reason to put it aside, as my family gathered in Chicago to celebrate Emeline's college graduation. We sat outdoors roasting in the sun (an awning for officiating academics but no shade for the audience), as her class walked across the stage to receive their diplomas. All of us were proud of her achievement, and no one was happier for her than her dad.

We returned from Chicago on Sunday evening. The next five days I spent working dutifully in my white-walled, climate-controlled, artificially illuminated office, with that slight whiff of toner emanating from the humming printer. Each day I emerged for lunch, visited the deli on the corner, and took a brief walk among the crowds, beneath the massive buildings, in search of sun, sky, and fluffy clouds, which I occasionally glimpsed in the distance, through gaps between the towers.

A GLIMPSE INTO THE FOUNDRY

When Friday evening finally came, I bolted for the mountains. Pulling into the trailhead two hours later, I parked and headed out into the dripping darkness as sultry air brushed against my shirtless chest and shoulders. Then a breeze shifted and cold drops cascaded from the foliage. At the fire tower that marks the summit of Balsam Lake Mountain, I turned off my light and took a few steps up the stairs. There was nothing to see but foggy darkness.

It'd been several years since I'd last traversed the backside of Balsam Lake Mountain. Now I found the trail surprisingly steep, rugged, and narrow, with dripping vegetation crowding in from the sides. Some species I recognized, like the ever-present hobblebush and a profusion of nettles and jewelweed. Some were unfamiliar, including tall sinister-looking plants with large, strangely patterned leaves and a cloying alien scent redolent of overgrown roadside ditches and other places where plant life rules. A few twists and turns later, the trail brought me to the lean-to. I spread out my sleeping bag and drifted off as the wind rushed through the canopy and raindrops beat against the ground. It was raining the next morning as I was getting ready to head out for Graham Mountain. But then the sun wrestled aside the clouds.

I'd worn shoes the night before to support the sore ankle, but they weren't really helping, so off they came. At first the trail seemed quite rocky and the mud was frigid. But with each step, the trail became a little softer and the air a little warmer. Soon I was ambling along in a cheerful mood.

From Graham's summit, I glanced over at Balsam Lake Mountain and spotted the fire tower I'd climbed the night before, poking over treetops, sunlight glinting on its cabin window. It was turning into a beautiful day. Small cloud-puffs came racing by, twisting and curling as they passed close overhead, sometimes dissolving into tendrils and then dissipating entirely. A wall of clouds was gathered in the north, and it was from this direction that the puffs were blowing in, like scouts dispatched in advance of a larger force. I wondered what kind of weather they presaged.

I returned from Graham, got back in the car, and drove over to the Barnum Road trailhead in the Blackhead Range, arriving around 4:00 p.m. Soon I was scrambling through a tumble of boulders, eventually reaching a local summit called Camel's Hump, where I stood upon a sunbaked sandstone slab, delightfully warm underfoot.

From here the trail turned smooth and grassy. I strolled along as butterflies fluttered through the air and alighted on small white flowers sprouting from berry canes. I snuck up close while they were busy feeding—spotted eastern tiger swallowtails, white admirals, an eastern comma. Lining the path were diminutive pixie cup lichens the size of needles with crimson fruiting bodies. Indeed, there were so many interesting creatures to observe, it was hard to stay focused on the trail.

Reaching the summit of Black Dome, I looked south, studying the mountain wall across which the Devil's Path wends its way. I noticed shadows lengthening across the gaps. *It's time to turn back for home*, I thought.

The path dipped into the shadows, rose back into the light, then descended again. Orange light began to percolate through the canopy. I hurried along, eager to reach the vantage point on Camel's

Hump before the sun was gone. The shadows beat me there, but the sandstone rock was still warm underfoot. When looking up, I saw orange-gold light flaring from behind the Catskills' western ramparts with remarkable intensity, as if supernatural flames were issuing from a foundry of the spirit world. As I stared, the light cast distant valleys and rolling farmlands in a bizarre orange-pink bubblegum hue, rendering the landscape unfamiliar, like an alien planet. Surely mere mortals weren't supposed to witness such marvels. Suddenly, as if on cue, a pitch-black cloudbank started sliding across the western sky, on a mission no doubt to screen the supernatural fires from observation by the likes of me.

A sudden thought came to me: The spirit world would surely have more than one cloudbank at its disposal. Glancing to the north, I spotted a second black mass on the move, this one riding above the orange-pink plains and bearing down straight toward me. Drops began to splash among the mountain ash and maple.

Time to go. I'd left my raingear in the car, so perhaps it would've made sense to pull my shoes out of the pack and move a little faster. But I was determined to stick to my purpose, which meant completing the trip barefoot, just as I'd started.

It didn't take long for the clouds to catch me. The rain intensified, and the path turned slick just as I reached the steep tumble of rocks I had ascended earlier. Suddenly it was dark.

My pace slowed to a crawl. The ache in my ankle flared up again. I started to fret: *How long will it take to make it back?* The anxiety connected to deeper fears: *How long will it take for the ankle to heal? Will I ever be able to run again?*

I tried to pull myself together: *Just stay focused on the task at hand, just put one foot after the other*, I thought. *And don't forget to breathe.* But the work was interminable. When the descent finally ended, the trail morphed into a rushing stream with sharp-edged stones lurking beneath the mud. Part of my mind remained firmly in control, while another part whimpered in dismay.

By the time I reached the car, I was quivering. My head was still reeling as I stopped on the way home for a late dinner. The next morning, though, I woke up wanting more.

Eastern tiger swallowtail.

CHAPTER 16

RACING THE SUN

I marched on through the Grid in my peculiar stubborn manner—sometimes enjoying the diversity of experiences, sometimes pushing myself unreasonably—and possibly learning some lessons about life that went beyond running, although it would be a long time before I would be able to articulate them.

So why was I so stubborn? Why not put on shoes when it rained?

Weight lifters train to failure, meaning they add weight until they can't complete the next repetition. I suppose training to failure is a principle of askesis, too. If you want to develop spiritually, you must add stress until your commitment, determination, and sense of purpose begin to fray.

PHYSICAL TRAINING, SPIRITUAL DEVELOPMENT

Walt Whitman was an advocate for physical training, which he thought should be a "regular and systematic thing through life." Writing under the pen name Mose Velsor, he argued that through exercise men could develop "perfect body, perfect blood," a healthy physique characterized by "herculean strength and suppleness," a disposition that is "strong, alert, vigorous." He saw physical and spiritual strength as intertwined, with the body serving as the foundation for the quality of "moral uprightness" and the ability to partake in "universal strength and joy."

Training is a concept in cultures outside the Western tradition, too. For the Yurok Tribe of northwest California, the traditional form of training, called *hohkep*, consists of sweating in hot lodges, fasting, thirsting, and going without sleep, after which they would venture into the wilderness, ideally at night and during stormy weather. According to the Yuroks, the purpose of this training is to gather spiritual power. To "build yourself" as a person. To achieve the freedom to "live out the purpose you came here for" instead of becoming someone else's "pet." Yuroks say that training is "all about making your mind strong."

Overcoming stress is the spirit behind ultrarunning, too, the essence of which is to move forward relentlessly, even when it hurts. In this regard, my Grid experience was starting to feel suspiciously like a race.

After bagging eleven peaks in June, the count at the start of July was 192, or 45 percent of the total Grid. From experience I knew that the halfway point of an ultramarathon is *not* the place to start celebrating. With respect to the Grid, I wasn't even there yet.

At times the huge quantity of remaining peaks made the Grid feel like a burden, as if it were my fate, like Sisyphus, to push a rock up a mountain only to see it roll back down again. But burdens are part of life, I reasoned to myself one day while taping up my sore ankle with the special tape in the way that Sue had showed me. The French philosopher Albert Camus wrote, "one must imagine Sisyphus happy."

Meanwhile, the six-week running moratorium passed. I told my doctor the ankle was feeling better.

"But we don't know what caused the problem," he observed.

"I was just trying to do a little too much," I replied nonchalantly.

He gave me a questioning look, but I left his office in a positive frame of mind, relieved to have finally turned the corner. The next day, however, the ankle ached while walking on a treadmill. Truthfully, it wasn't better. Some online research suggested that strained tendons are slow to heal. Of my own accord, I decided to extend the running moratorium for three more months. In the meantime, I'd keep moving at my barefoot pace, which was to say, slowly.

INSIGNIFICANCE IS LIBERATING

Despite my injured status, I was excited to kick off the Grid for July, this being such a wonderful time of year in the mountains. For the first weekend of the month, I planned to wrap up my work on Friday afternoon, get on the road, and find a peak to climb before dark. Plateau Mountain seemed like a good candidate since the trailhead wasn't too far away. If I got moving quickly, it might be possible to reach Orchard Point, the sandstone ledge that juts out above the valley, in time to witness the sun's last rays.

By the time I reached the trailhead, the valley was already filling with shadows. There was still an hour until sunset, but I faced a brutal 1,500-foot ascent. With daylight fleeting, sandals seemed like a good idea, and, ankle notwithstanding, I couldn't resist the temptation to charge uphill at an aggressive power-hiking pace. After a few minutes lunging along the trail, I saw sunlight dappling the foliage above me. There was still a chance to make Orchard Point before dark.

I was determined to outrun the sun. Breath short, heart racing, stomach churning, I hurtled along the path, mossy trees and lichen-splashed rocks flying past. A few more minutes of ragged effort and suddenly there were bright spots dotting the bushes around me. I'd caught up to the line of light, the margin between day and night.

But the race wasn't over, for now the trail leveled off, banked left, and slipped back into shadow. I labored along, ducking and weaving between tall plants with large, deeply serrated leaves.

The trail steepened on the final scramble to Orchard Point. I grasped for rocks and roots until finally I hauled myself up onto a broad ledge and lay there in the sunlight, gasping for air and feeling faintly nauseous.

Victory!

The evening sky was clear. Due west, Hunter's fire tower stood in silhouette against the burning orb, the tower stairs zigging up into the flames.

To the south lay Plateau's spurs, massive tentacles of rock coiling among the valleys. A distant spark flashed on the cabin window of Tremper Mountain's fire tower, almost eight miles off south by southwest.

Farther to the south, Wittenberg, Cornell, Friday, Rocky, Lone, and Peekamoose lined up in a row, the latter almost 20 miles distant, and off to the side was the stern profile of Slide Mountain, hulking and aloof. Even farther off, in distant southern plains, blood-tinged clouds boiled up into the atmosphere.

I sat on the rock at Orchard Point as flies buzzed about in the waning light, and reflected on this win. In relationship to the source of all energy, I felt like a fleeting spark, beyond infinitesimal. Yet this insignificance felt liberating. All my fears, frustrations, and disappointments—if I didn't matter, then neither did they.

I walked over to Plateau's summit and then returned to the car, ankle twinging on the descent.

Afterward I did some calculations. The 1.3-mile trail had taken me 42 minutes, for an average pace of 1.9 miles per hour. Based on the azimuth of the setting sun, the rotational speed of the Earth, the elevations, distances and angles between Orchard Point and Hunter Mountain, the shadows I was racing were moving 0.6 miles per hour. Shadows move on average with the speed of the Earth's rotation, or around 800 miles per hour at New York's latitude, which means they flash across flat terrain in a blink. When they encounter mountains, however, they slow down while climbing them, just like runners. But unlike us, once they reach the mountain's crest, they leap into space.

SEEING EGO IN ITS ABSENCE

Midway through July saw me on another Friday evening hike after work. This time it was Sugarloaf in the fog. From the summit, nothing was visible but grayness.

On the way down, I paused under an overhang and took a seat on a dry rock. Clicking off my light, I listened to raindrops pattering in the forest and made an effort to relax. At first it wasn't easy. After a moment, though, my thoughts turned to distant ancestors. I pictured them seeking shelter when the weather turned unfavorable and waiting patiently for conditions to improve. Perhaps waiting patiently is a skill that modern people like me have lost.

I scanned the dark forest. It was quiet. Strangely quiet. It gradually dawned on me that something was missing from this scene, and then

I realized what it was: my "ego." That's not to say my sense of self had disappeared, but absent was that part of my personality that is always comparing me to other people, goading me to aim higher, run faster, go farther, even if it meant taking unconscionable risks. My ego insists on my being better than other people. It cheers when I pass someone in a race. If other people are different from me— if they're not runners, or if they follow a different diet, wear different shoes, or have different political opinions—then my ego prods me to be judgmental and dismissive rather than trying to understand their point of view, because it cannot tolerate the possibility that I might be wrong.

It may be that in the modern world, where we have so many millions of interconnected peers, our egos have become irritated. Inflamed. That's my impression from the roar of social media, where the digital crowds of people make me cringe as they vent and shout and hurl insults back and forth. When I'm confronted with positions that differ from my own, I too feel the temptation to lash out. When walking in congested urban areas like New York City, sometimes I feel myself tensing up when thick crowds slow me down.

Maybe I'm more sensitive than others, but competition with peers is part of life, for us and other species, as even a casual glance at the crowded forest shows. Perhaps the ego is one way that Nature's found to crack the whip, prod us to compete, force us to be more productive, or if we can't, to take a risk and try something different. If so, ego may be a force for betterment, provided we can manage it.

I sat on my rock a few minutes longer, listening to the sound of raindrops striking leaves. Out here in the rain there was no one else around—no one to pass, no one to argue with or criticize, no one to be better than. For the moment, my mind was free of the endless calculations about how I compare to others, the frustrations with people who disagree, the tumult of the modern world where so many voices are always shouting.

I rose from my seat and wandered back along the silent trail.

MY FIRST TIME ON MOON HAW ROAD

With 17 peaks scratched off the list, July had turned out to be a productive month. Time allowed for one last trip, a new bushwhack route, another chance to learn.

My starting point would be a parking spot on the mysterious-sounding Moon Haw Road in the southern Catskills, which I'd never visited. On the last Saturday in July, with commitments during the day, it wasn't until the evening when I finally rolled to a stop at the end of Moon Haw Road. Above, twilight-colored clouds lingered, but the narrow valley was already dim, and the air was turning cool. The steep and densely wooded slopes on either side looked forbidding. Typically, I would study the map before undertaking an unfamiliar bushwhack—especially in the dark—but this time I'd forgotten to measure the distance for the route.

Feeling uncertain, I strapped on sandals, splashed across Wittenberg Brook, and started working my way up the side of the ridge. A faint trail led me on through a tunnel of mountain laurel. In some places the stems had been clipped. I muttered a thank you to whoever had cut them back.

It was fully dark now. I clicked on my light. Then the trail petered out, or I missed a turn and lost it. I panned the light around at tall laurel bushes with wavy, twisting branches. I'd wandered into a stiff and scratchy cage and now was trapped. There was no choice but to push on. I got scraped on the chest and slapped in the face and began wishing I wasn't here. Then I got poked in the eye, and my pride was severely injured.

The best strategy seemed to be to fight uphill in hopes of gaining easier passage higher up. The laurel resisted with scratchy determination, but I ducked and wriggled and squirmed until eventually I popped out onto the crest of the ridge, where the ground was indeed more open. I pressed on for another half mile before finding a spot to unroll my bag. Above me, hemlock trunks soared like cathedral columns, branches arching and interweaving into a dome, stars peeking through the gaps.

At first light, a hermit thrush was singing in ethereal, flute-like tones. Breath steaming, I pulled on a shirt, packed up, and this time headed out barefoot, enjoying the soft mix of leaf litter, club moss, and hemlock needles underfoot.

I clambered up a rock ledge about a half a mile later and found myself in a small clearing. There I found blueberry heather, yellow moss, boulders covered in toadskin lichen, and a solitary scrub oak tree—a scene reminiscent of the Shawangunk Mountains to the south.

Wittenberg lay to the west, and with the sun rising in the east, all I had to do was follow my shadow's lead to reach the mountain's shoulder. After another half a mile, I arrived at the base of a daunting climb: 1,260 feet over a third of a mile, equivalent to an average grade of 70 percent.

This was wild terrain, and, for me, a desperate scramble through rocks, roots, dirt, moss, and decaying leaves. Every move was tentative and needed a contingency plan—elbows dug in when a handhold gave way, knees backed up a slipping foot. Without shoes, I dug toes into the earth for grip and found my feet stretching as if elastic, a totally different experience from climbing in stiff boots.

I crawled upward, feeling with my hands and feet how the soil was warm in the sun and cool in the shade. A couple of spots required judgment but eventually glints of sky peeking through the canopy told me the summit was nearby. Then I heard voices. Pulling myself up onto a ledge, I found myself face to face with a small white dog. Looking up, I saw four college-aged kids packing up a tent and sleeping bags. After saying hello, I commented that camping over 3,500 feet was against the rules and state rangers could ticket them for this violation. Having done my duty on behalf of the community, I said goodbye and strolled over to the summit ledge of Wittenberg.

The sky was wonderfully clear. The late-July sun beamed down deliciously hot, and the air was cool and dry. Spread out below me was the long ridge I'd climbed from Moon Haw Road, including the knob with the solitary oak reminiscent of the Shawangunks. In the distance, the Ashokan Reservoir lay basking in the sun, a picture of indolence. Farther off, the Shawangunk Mountains dipped and curled, with Skytop Tower standing in the north and Monument Tower at High Point State Park in the distance no bigger than a pin. Even farther off to the south-southwest was a faint gash in that same ridge—the Delaware Water Gap, 72 miles away along an azimuth of 217 degrees.

The college kids joined me on the summit. I pointed out the towers. They introduced me to their dog, Snowy.

From Wittenberg, I took the trail to the Cornell Crack and then passed up and over the summit of Cornell, after which it was time to leave the trail and enter the thickets on the pathless ridge.

Hikers use a lot of gear to protect themselves from nature. When bushwhacking, most people wear trousers and long-sleeve shirts and sometimes eye shields, too. But today I stuck with my practice of going shirtless, as it keeps me cool, which helps me get by carrying less water. Plus, I love the feeling of the breeze flowing across my chest and shoulders. It's an unconventional uniform for the thickets, and one that requires some thoughtfulness. For inspiration, I've borrowed a mantra from SEAL Team Three, whose special operators are trained in the art of clearing rooms in urban combat: "Slow is smooth; smooth is fast." The point is to take it one step at a time and keep the mind from rushing ahead, thus avoiding mistakes (important when using live ammunition). My goal this morning was to slide through the thickets smoothly. If I didn't get speared by a broken branch, that'd be fast enough.

Off I went, weaving, slinking, tugging, snapping off branches where necessary, and accumulating a few scratches on shoulders and arms, but nothing serious. It appeared I might be following an emergent "social path" (an unofficial route that exists only because others passed this way before). The path was visible only in the absence of obstructions. It allowed me to move just fast enough to relax and enjoy the day.

As had become my practice, I'd brought no food on this trip. When hiking in a fasted state, sometimes I start thinking about the meal waiting for me afterward. A slice of pizza comes to mind, perhaps, or a frosty mug of beer. But today those kinds of rewards seemed unimportant. There was nowhere else I'd rather be than right here, right now.

In due course I arrived on Friday. I located the canister, a pale white plastic tube nailed to a tree, popped off the top, and fished a notebook and ballpoint pen out of a Ziploc bag. I wrote my name and the date. (The Catskills 3500 Club uses these logbooks to track visitors to the trailless summits.)

The wind had died. The only sound now was the whine of flies. I took a seat in the shade and scanned the surroundings, my sense of awareness expanding in all directions until I felt that I'd become a part and parcel of the place, until the currents of the mountain were circulating inside me, and the silence was crashing around the summit in waves.

From Friday it was time to drop back into the chasm, along an old rockslide on the mountain's eastern slope. This was another 70 percent grade, and the descent was an exercise in instability. There were rocks tilting and rotten logs collapsing underfoot, and so many leaves obstructed my face I couldn't see where to place my feet. At one point, my foot punched through leaves and into a rocky hole—a potential ankle-twisting or bone-breaking scenario. I got my hands and butt down to the ground quickly and avoided toppling over but wasn't happy to have made a careless move. So now I crab-walked and butt-slid, stepped over one branch and ducked under the next, found myself hanging from a fallen trunk, and began gradually to lose my cool until I was groaning with frustration. When a beech branch whipped me in the face, I bellowed with rage.

I suppose even the indigenous Mohicans who lived here in days gone by would have found this terrain somewhat vexing. As for myself, after years of running in shoes on roads and trails, evidently the habit of mindless rushing was difficult to unlearn, for here I was still struggling, even after a lot of practice. Who would've thought that moving slowly would be mentally so much harder than going fast.

Eventually the slope leveled out. A cool breeze rustled leaves high up in the canopy, and sunbeams flickered in the foliage. I started to feel calmer.

"Slow is smooth, smooth is fast" is a good mantra. The legendary ultrarunner Lisa Smith-Batchen, one of only a handful of people to have completed the Badwater Quad (and the only woman to do so), once told me, "Run slow to go fast."

Similarly, Emerson counseled people to "leave this military hurry and adopt the pace of Nature; her secret is patience."

During the long drive back to the city, I experienced a final bout of frustration, this time when stuck in heavy traffic. It was the same feeling as on the mountain. Suddenly I understood that patience is a necessary virtue no matter what environment you're moving through.

View of Ashokan Reservoir lazing in the sun, from the summit of Wittenberg. July 30, 2017.

CHAPTER 17

A SPEAR OF SUMMER GRASS

THE EARTH TURNED. THE SEASONS SAUNTERED. THE MOUNTAINS changed subtly and on each trip revealed a new facet of their inner nature.

As far as the Grid, August was a whole new month. For a change the spreadsheet column was almost filled, with only eight peaks remaining. This was a chance to slow down and appreciate the experience instead of rushing.

A FIRST ATTEMPT AT NATURAL NAVIGATION

This was also a chance to try something new. The term "natural navigation," coined by Australian aviator Harold Gatty, describes the art of finding your way through the woods without technology—i.e., without using a map, compass, or GPS. "In the process of evolution of our civilization," Gatty wrote, "we have lost something which was a matter of life and death to the primitive; that is, his highly developed powers of observation."

The more you stare at a compass needle or GPS, the less you look around. David Barrie, a fellow of the Royal Institute of Navigation, describes GPS as one of the greatest technological achievements of modern times. But then he comments on what the technology is doing to us, now that we've become dependent on it: "Though we may not realize it, we are fast becoming navigational idiots."

Natural navigation seemed consistent with other aspects of my increasingly minimalist practice, a way to travel through the mountains more instinctively and mindfully, a chance to rediscover latent capabilities, and possibly a more intense experience. In short, this was another intriguingly seductive challenge, impossible to resist.

I reached out to my friend Alan Davidson, whom I'd last seen on that desperate nighttime bushwhack up Slide Mountain. He was game to give this a try. We met up for an early breakfast and studied the map. It showed a broad ridge leading to the summit of Rusk, flanked by streams. We came up with a simple plan: Head uphill. And then an afterthought: To avoid veering off course, stay out of streambeds.

After breakfast, we drove to the Spruceton trailhead, took the gravel path for a mile, then turned into the woods at the familiar bend in the trail. At first there was an obvious social path where countless hikers had walked before. After a short distance, however, it faded out. We climbed uphill through open forest, keeping to the rising slope as per plan. It was a simple exercise. But missing was the sense of reassurance I got from the compass needle indicating direction or the dot on my phone showing our precise location. Without these tools, I felt uncertain. Vulnerable. Naked. There wasn't much to see besides leaf litter and trees. If we wandered off in the wrong direction, how long would it take us to recognize the mistake?

We stepped upon rocks and matted leaves, climbing steadily, and wondering if we were still on track. After a while, faint signs appeared: a rock knocked out of place, scuff marks in the soil, leaves on the ground looking slightly more compressed than those to the side, a fallen log with the bark scraped away where boot-shod hikers might have stepped. Nothing definite, but the more clues, the higher the probability that we were on a well-used route. Sure enough, a short distance later the social trail reappeared beneath our feet and led us directly to the canister on Rusk's summit.

So far, so good. After signing in on the notebook, we paused to orient ourselves. Our next objective, East Rusk, lay to the east. The sun was setting in the west, so we looked for where its rays tinged the clouds on the opposite horizon and headed off in that direction.

After a few cautious steps, we were met with a pleasant surprise—another social trail, this one unmistakable. It led us directly to the summit of East Rusk.

Alan and I congratulated ourselves for successfully completing our first natural navigation adventure, admittedly with the help of people who had gone before us.

ON THE INDESTRUCTIBILITY OF MIND BY TIME

Walt Whitman's *Song of Myself* opens, "I lean and loaf at my ease observing a spear of summer grass." It occurred to me that while I'd learned to identify some of the Catskill wildflowers, I didn't know any grasses. My last climb for August would be Windham High Peak, and as I began to plan the trip, I recalled that the path to the summit is lined with grass. There would be an opportunity to achieve three wildly disparate but strangely related goals in one outing: Bag a peak for the Grid, observe the grasses along the way, and ponder the meaning of Whitman's verses.

Odie and I arrived at the trailhead off Route 23 on a cool summer morning. Our first steps took us past a profusion of wildflowers—stalks of curly dock which had turned toasty brown, sprays of white daisy fleabane, bristly purple knapweed. Then we entered the forest.

When walking without shoes, I look down at where I'm stepping. This morning the ground was covered with small, round, pale green "drupes" (fruits with pits) about a quarter inch in diameter. These looked like basswood drupes, but at first glance there weren't any basswood trees to be seen. After a minute, through a gap in the canopy, I caught sight of a single heart-shaped basswood leaf, and the mystery was solved.

Farther along, the trail was covered with long green pine cones, some of which had been gnawed to the core, and then the trail passed into a grove of northern red oak, acorns underfoot, and, just as I remembered, there were tussocks of grass flowing across the forest floor. Upon examination, I discovered that some blades of grass were wide, while others were narrow—hardly a scientific revelation, but more than I'd ever bothered to notice before. Afterward I would manage to identify one species as bladder sedge and another as bottlebrush grass. Otherwise, there was so much variation in leaf and seed, the complexity was overwhelming.

Odie and I sauntered along the grassy trail, arriving at the top around noon. The first thing I noticed was a profusion of bright red berries. I was pretty sure some of these were cherries, so I took a tiny nibble . . . and found the taste quite astringent. Chokecherries! The hobblebush and mountain ash were also drooping with red berry clusters, but I left them alone, unsure if they were safe to eat.

I took a seat on an eastern-facing summit ledge and studied the view, but, once again, I was finding it hard to relax. That's the runner in me, I suppose, preferring always to be in motion. But after a bit, I let go and allowed myself to become a stationary object, until time itself seemed to flow around and past me.

Below the ledge, a pair of turkey vultures wheeled in languid circles. One hung in place nearly motionless. Two chipping sparrows flashed past, trilling in alarm. A moment later, a raptor came cruising in the currents.

At first glance the clouds seemed to be moving across the sky in a purposeful and deliberate manner, as unyielding as the prevailing wind. But when I stared closely and long enough, it turned out the clouds were tumbling, expanding, extending, breaking apart, coalescing.

Walt Whitman is regarded today as one of the great poets of the English language, on par with Shakespeare according to some critics, the "poet of Democracy" in the words of his friend John Burroughs. But during the nineteenth century, his lyrics were considered obscene. Even Emerson, who liked Whitman's work, advised him to tone it down.

The *Song of Myself* opens by questioning the concept of individual self:

> *I CELEBRATE myself, and sing myself,*
> *And what I assume you shall assume,*
> *For every atom belonging to me as good belongs to you.*

Whitman tells the stories of rich and poor, men and women, White and Black, his sense of self expanding to include not only peers, but the whole natural world, in which he takes a wild, sensuous delight. Since his sense of self incorporates all life, time loses its sting.

I exist as I am, that is enough,
If no other in the world be aware I sit content,
And if each and all be aware I sit content.
One world is aware and by far the largest to me, and
that is myself,
And whether I come to my own to-day or in ten
thousand or ten million years,
I can cheerfully take it now, or with equal cheerfulness I
can wait.
My foothold is tenon'd and mortis'd in granite,
I laugh at what you call dissolution,
And I know the amplitude of time

I pictured Whitman leaning on an elbow observing a blade of grass, while time slows down and almost stops. A scene unlike modern life, in which time feels like it's flying past so quickly that we'll never have the chance to achieve our goals.

Clocks play such an outsized role in modern life. We use them to synchronize actions so we can work together. We measure progress toward our goals down to the second, because you wouldn't bother to make an effort unless you felt that sense of urgency, that relentless pressure to achieve results in real time, when they matter. Corporate workers like me operate under time pressure constantly. So do runners. I thought back to Long Path and Badwater runs, to my best times at every distance, from one mile to one hundred, and how these results mattered so much to me. But then I wondered, at what point do we let clocks wield so much power over life that they come to rule us? At what point do we lose sight of John Muir's point—that our actions have a permanent impact on the world—that a day in the mountains might never end?

Other thinkers have questioned the modern perception of time and self. Erwin Schrödinger (1887–1961), Nobel Prize laureate and one of the fathers of quantum theory, criticized the moral attitude of modern science, which measures the motion of atomic particles, but has nothing to say about the self or subjective experience. "We do not belong to this material world that science constructs for us," he wrote. "We are not in it, we are outside. We are only spectators." Science creates the impression that reality is a "mechanical clockwork," in which effort, pain, and delight do not matter. Nor do ethics, beauty, and meaning. There is no theory that can explain why music delights us, or how an old song can move a person to tears. Schrödinger concluded that the field of quantum mechanics he helped develop, "strongly suggests the indestructibility of Mind by Time."

As I sat on Windham's summit ledge thinking about clocks and self and time, a small jet aircraft slipped above me, lanced out over the plains, punched into a cloudbank. A little while later, sunlight glinted upon the wings of a glider turning in lazy circles. Just the day before, while I was out trimming brush on a Shawangunk trail, a glider passed so closely overhead I could hear the whisper of air across its ailerons.

It was time to go. But I lingered. The sun slid out from behind a cloud. A bee landed on one of the few remaining flowers of a meadowsweet bush, as the wind rustled its small leaves.

Odie was asleep. On past trips, he would whine incessantly whenever we stopped, always anxious to get moving. Time had passed, and he was now 10 years old.

On the way down I glanced at my watch and saw we were running late. We hopped in the car and flew along the highway until mindless traffic snagged us.

CHAPTER 18

BRINGING FRIENDS AND FAMILY TO THE MOUNTAINS

I WANTED TO SHARE THE MOUNTAINS WITH OTHER PEOPLE. BUT IN my injured state, walking barefoot at a dawdling pace, I wasn't a suitable companion for my running friends.

On occasion I'd drop hints with Sue about the Catskills or remind her of family camping trips we used to take so many years ago. But she pointed out that some of those excursions had been longer and more arduous than advertised. When Emeline came home to visit, she preferred to explore alone.

So I was delighted when Philip stopped by on a break from school and expressed interest in a Catskills trip. Having joined the Army ROTC program at his college, he was eager to practice land navigation, still considered a critical skill for officers just as it had been for me 35 years before. Studying the map, I found a long winding ridge that led to Balsam Cap, which seemed like an interesting route, as well as another opportunity to practice the art of natural navigation.

A NATURAL NAVIGATION FAIL

One Saturday morning early in September, Philip and I arrived at the trailhead, where we met Alan Davidson, punctual as always, and another running friend named Tom DeSimone. Consistent with the natural navigation format for this hike, I was planning to build a "sun compass" from sticks, which would tell direction by the shadows cast. There was one complication, however. Heavy rain was forecasted, remnants of a hurricane drifting through the Hudson Valley. Undeterred, we headed out on the first leg of the route, straight up Breath Hill, which Tom explained is commonly referred to as "Out of Breath Hill," due to the 1,000 feet of elevation gain in the first half mile. I was soon struggling on all fours, face to face with wet moldy leaves and pungent soil.

Nearing the top, we pulled up for a moment. I peered into heavy cloud cover and announced with great enthusiasm, "That direction looks brighter, it must be east." No one disputed my judgment call, so we went that way. I was scanning ahead for the point where I expected the slope to turn sharply upward, when instead it dropped off. I knew it immediately—we were sunk. Out came our phones, which confirmed that not only were we in the wrong spot, but we'd somehow managed to go 180 degrees the wrong way. We stood around in the rain, clothes getting soaked, starting to feel chilled. After a brief discussion, we decided to abandon Balsam Cap and go after Peekamoose instead. Using compasses (all thoughts of navigating naturally now abandoned), we turned west and stumbled onto a broad ridge, this one relatively open and covered in endless waves of hay-scented fern. What a surprise, after struggling over rugged terrain all morning, to find ourselves for the moment moving as easily as the breeze.

Turning northwest, we passed through open forest, rose in elevation, and reached the fir-spruce thickets, which slowed us down. Steep cliffs loomed to the front, but we found a narrow ledge between big sandstone slabs and squirmed through. A few steps later there were blazes in sight, and the summit was only a few yards away.

This had been a natural navigation fail, but what fun to discover a new approach to Peekamoose, a mountain I'd climbed 10 times before but always on the trail.

MYSTERY BUS

The next weekend, Philip, Odie, and I were up at 5:00 a.m., in the car by 6:00 a.m., and at Peck Hollow a little before 7:30 a.m., aiming to complete a circuit of North Dome and Sherrill from the south for a change. This trip would also bag me Grid peaks number 221 and 222.

Philip led the way, practicing map and compass skills, while I lagged behind, checking the GPS from time to time to see if he was on track (he was), while Odie ran back and forth between us, determined to keep our small group together. We passed through a profusion of oak and hop hornbeam (acorns and hops scattered along the ground), suggesting this land had once been cleared for pasture. By 3,000 feet, these trees were gone, while the hobblebush crowded in and club moss spread across the forest floor. We passed through a fern glade ringed by fir trees and emerged onto the trail about 100 yards west of North Dome's summit. Not bad navigational work after traveling three miles through trackless mountain forest.

Next it was on to the familiar social trail that connects North Dome with Sherrill, a welcome break from branches in the face. We reached a ledge where Odie needed some assistance, so Philip lifted 50 pounds of muddy, squirming sinews and fluff and gently lowered him. We crossed a swampy area, traversed the saddle between North Dome and Sherrill, and then made the short climb to the top.

The plan was to return to Peck Hollow along another pathless ridge. Heading down from the summit, we were creeping through a waist-high patch of stinging nettles—trying not to brush against the leaves—when we spotted a large clearing. It was a cheerful scene, full of red bee balm and orange jewelweed, and in the middle there sat a yellow school bus. We could hardly have been more surprised if we'd chanced upon the Catbus from Hayao Miyazaki's popular anime film *My Neighbor Totoro*. Sitting at rest in this sunny clearing full of flowers, the bus looked peaceful and content. We noticed its seats had been removed and a bunk bed installed, so it was evidently being used as some kind of shelter.

How did the bus get here? We scratched our heads. It probably wasn't lifted in by helicopter. More likely it was towed, in which case, we reasoned, there should be a road. Sure enough, we found an ancient forest road not far off in surprisingly good shape. After hours of fighting through the brush, what a delight to scamper down the mountain!

A few days later, Philip was off seeing friends, so Odie was my sole companion on a warm late-summer evening jaunt up Panther Mountain. The focus would shift back to observation. What could we see and hear at night?

INSECT SYMPHONY

After parking, we scrambled up the familiar hill and took the familiar path of flat stones laid out to keep hikers out of mud. I strolled along feeling cheerful while Odie scouted ahead. A katydid called out from somewhere in the darkened forest, a raspy *klack-klack-klack*, like someone clipping away with a pair of rusty scissors. These green grasshopper-like insects are said to sing in choruses, with groups of males synchronizing their songs, or answering back and forth. Although for all the times I'd listened, I'd never discerned the pattern.

We passed by Giant Ledge and caught a whiff of campfire smoke and heard music and people talking. Woodland Valley lay far below, dark but for a handful of lights in the center, but we might have been sitting in a balcony above a mile-wide orchestra hall, for an insect symphony was rising from the depths, with a chorus of katydids clacking away with great passion against a background hum of crickets. To the north, one particularly loud katydid initiated a raspy call. A group in the middle jumped in. Then the song was taken up to the south, swirling around like a motif played first by strings and then the horns.

We headed on to Panther. At the summit we found stars shining straight above, but the eastern horizon was streaked with vaporous bands. For a moment, we paused in place. I ignored my watch, reasoning that the time was merely "now." And the summit was merely "here." Odie and I hung out in "here-now," as if we were aboard a tiny boat bobbing along in the great ocean of space-time. The wind stirred. It made a tearing sound as it sliced through fir needles: speeding up, slowing down, never ceasing. As I watched, a star turned into an airplane and banked to the south.

Eventually we got up and started back, at one point stepping over a solitary cricket crouched upon a rock. We paused again upon reaching Giant Ledge. Now the wind was blowing in intervals, like rolling waves; birch leaves fluttered against each other with a soft rustle, and then the air was still. The sounds of the insect symphony reached us intermittently between the wind waves, and the voices of the soloists rose above the accompaniment, sometimes klacking in threes, sometimes fours.

On the descent from Giant Ledge, the maple leaves lining the path began to draw my eye: Dark purple predominated, but mixed with brown and yellow, some with crimson flecks and green splotches in curious intricate patterns. When I focused on them, the colors became intense. To keep moving, I had to look away.

As we crossed the flat stones sitting in damp earth, here were two katydids singing, one on the right and one on the left. There was a point where both were audible simultaneously, as if they were indeed answering back and forth. At least it seemed so at first, but gradually their calls converged, and then they separated again.

It was past midnight by the time we reached the car. On the drive home, I was feeling tired (at one point I swerved to avoid a possum). Once back home, I heard a katydid singing in the tree outside our house, but instead of the characteristic three klacks (which are supposed to sound like its name "kat-y-did") or four klacks ("kat-y-didn't"), every measure in this song was two klacks. It stayed this way for a long time, although the interval between klacks was not constant. At least it stayed this way as long as my tired mind could listen.

I learned afterward that scientists have a new theory about katydids. Instead of coordinating songs with peers, male katydids are constantly trying to jump in first, as the earliest call seems to attract the attention of the females. Modulations in rhythm and number of klacks are an attempt to disrupt other males' songs. It's a game of one-upsmanship, and what some perceive as synchronization is in a sense accidental. Perhaps we should call it a mix of collaboration and competition, and, upon reflection, isn't our world much the same?

A FAMILY HIKE

I thought about Sue's complaint, that prior Catskills trips had sometimes been more than she'd bargained for. In the early days of our marriage, we'd done some great hikes together, but now I remembered that her knees sometimes bothered her. Perhaps as a young man fresh out of the Army, I'd been a little gung ho. It's one thing to lead soldiers who've been trained to gut it out and never quit. Or to run with friends who are passionate about ultramarathons. It takes more judgment to plan a trip for people who have different attitudes and capabilities. So now I reviewed the list of Catskill peaks, picked one that offered nice views and a reasonable trail without too many scrambles, and waited for some rain to clear, after which the mountains could not have been more beautiful. Maybe all this helped me make the case, for Sue finally agreed, for the first time in several years, to try a Catskill hike.

With Philip and Odie, we made a foursome. Three miles took us to the summit of Windham, where we hung out for a little while on a warm and sunny afternoon. Sue and Philip enjoyed the splendid views, Odie took a nap, and I studied a bright yellow caterpillar, which later I would identify as a definite tussock moth. Then a fuzzy gray caterpillar with a shiny black nose wandered by (hickory tussock moth) and crawled across my wrist.

On the way down I brought up the rear, limping, my ankle throbbing. Hiking two days in a row was evidently too much to ask of the strained tendon. But Sue had enjoyed herself, which made this trip a success.

The four us of went out a few days later and climbed West Kill. Once again Sue appreciated the experience. But that was enough for now. She returned to other interests, and Philip went back to school.

And I went back to my windowless office. Although the next weekend, Odie and I managed to escape to the Catskills again, where we joined up with a pair of veteran thru-hikers, Heather Houskeeper and Scott Weis, who were traveling on the Long Path.[5] We climbed Plateau, Sugarloaf, and Twin together. Impressed by his agility, Heather and Scott gave Odie a trail name: "Mountain Goat."

On the last day of September, Mountain Goat and I tackled Wittenberg. We passed crowds of hikers coming and going. Mountain Goat received many compliments for his grace (although I had to lift him up some of the steeper ledges).

Wittenberg was Grid peak number 225, leaving 195 to go.

---

5 For Heather's account of thru-hiking the Long Path, see her blog at https://thebotanicalhiker.blogspot.com/2017/08/thru-hiking-long-path.html and her book *Love and the Long Path*.

CHAPTER 19

LEARNING TO TOE THE LINE

AT WORK, I HAD A NEW OFFICE. IT HAD A VIEW, OF SORTS—OF AN aging building across the street and the deli on the corner where I often got my lunch. It was smaller than the prior unit, and the rent was about the same, which was how I rationalized the luxury. Meanwhile, the clock was ticking—two months until the sale of the company would close, at which point the next chapter of my corporate career would commence. Assuming I had found one.

I was sitting at my desk one day, with not a lot to do, when the phone rang. It was my boss. He wanted to talk about my next steps.

I broke down and confessed: I couldn't imagine working for the acquirer. They had a collegial culture. People sat around and talked politely, groping for consensus. I pictured myself dressed in pinstripe suit, tie, and clunky leather shoes. Wandering through a maze of carpeted corridors lit by dim fluorescent lights. Working on lengthy presentations for projects that would never happen. I felt like throwing up.

"That doesn't matter," my boss insisted. "You can take a role with them and stay in the game while looking for something else." Then he tossed out one of his favorite sayings, "It's easier to get a job when you have a job."

A few days later, I flew off for a visit with the acquirer. They put me up in a grand old hotel that had an odd tradition in which a procession of ducks was marched through the lobby at certain times of day. After breakfast I walked over to their headquarters, admired the artwork hanging in the lobby, then had a brief but pleasant conversation with the CEO, who was quite charming. Then I returned to New York and went back to waiting, feeling disappointed that I never saw the ducks.

MINDFULNESS AND THE SPIRIT OF EXACTITUDE

In our daily lives, we race through our activities feeling stressed and under pressure (the clocks are *always* ticking). And this can be a difficult attitude to shake. For all the time I was spending in the Catskills, it felt like often I was still rushing. There were so many times when I'd become frustrated and lose my cool when rough terrain kept me from moving as quickly as I wanted.

On a trip out East, John Muir paid a visit to John Burroughs, and the two men stayed up late into the night talking about Ralph Waldo Emerson, the hero of their youth. Muir had met Emerson in 1871, when the famous philosopher, then 68 years old, visited Yosemite. A much younger Muir (aged 33) screwed up his courage and introduced himself to the legend, and over the next few days, the two men talked at length. As Emerson was getting ready to depart, Muir invited him to camp out with him in a grove of giant sequoias. "You are yourself a Sequoia," Muir entreated. "Stop and get acquainted with your brethren."

Emerson advocated for self-reliance and nonconformity. He believed that inspiration, strength, and joy came from nature. One of his most famous passages encourages that mental state, which today we call "mindfulness."

> *Man postpones or remembers; he does not live in the present, but with reverted eye laments the past, or, heedless of the riches that surround him, stands on tiptoe to foresee the future. He cannot be happy and strong until he too lives with nature in the present, above time.*

Muir understood this point. He wrote that in Yosemite there is "no pain here, no dull empty hours, no fear of the past, no fear of the future."

In *Walden*, Thoreau put his own spin on Emerson's idea:

In any weather, at any hour of the day or night, I have been anxious to improve the nick of time, and notch it on my stick too; to stand on the meeting of two eternities, the past and future, which is precisely the present moment; to toe that line.

I'm guessing that Thoreau borrowed this terminology from his practice as a land surveyor, in which capacity he might have "toed the line" when marking out a boundary with compass, rod, and chain, his point being that to focus on the present moment requires the same attention to detail that it takes to plot a map. Put differently, mindfulness may require a spirit of precision.

Today we tend to talk about mindfulness in connection with relaxation or stress management techniques, like meditation or yoga. Maybe these are valid paths, too. But recall how Krishna counseled Arjun to "strive" to still the mind. Maybe mindfulness requires effort. Maybe it takes mental strength. Karate and Army training taught me to marshal my energy and focus, because in a fight, the stakes are high and mistakes can be devastating. I brought the same spirit to my corporate profession—when I briefed the board of directors on the estimated return from an acquisition, errors were not acceptable.

As I thought about Thoreau's metaphor, it occurred to me that there are many lines to toe in life. For race car drivers, the best line through a turn sets them up to exit at maximum speed. Marathon runners must follow the surveyor's tangent through the curves, otherwise they'll go farther than 26.2 miles. For bushwhackers, the best line typically takes you along the crest of a ridge (this minimizes climbing). Not all lines are visible. The optimal pace can be thought of as a line between moving too fast and too slow. There's a line between carrying too much gear and too little, as I'd learned the year before when I tried to challenge Keizer's record without bringing a tent or even a tarp.

With these thoughts in mind, I kicked off October with another visit to the Nine. This time, I approached the pathless thickets with a laser-like focus on navigation. From the lean-to on Table, I pushed out along the ridge toward Lone, reflecting on how I'd managed on every single trip before to *always* miss the saddle (and even blamed the mistake on unfriendly spirits). This time I stepped slowly and deliberately. I looked for flashes of sky flickering through the foliage. I kept inching forward until the glimmers of light were equal on either side, which suggested I'd reached the precise crest of the ridge. And a moment later, I stumbled onto a beautiful social trail. After *six* prior visits to this pathless ridgeline, I'd finally found the line! For the first time, I descended into the saddle perfectly instead of dropping too far downhill and having to claw my way back up. Then the social trail whisked me up to Lone.

Earlier I'd spotted a hiker in front of me. Now that I'd learned how to toe the lines along this pathless ridge, I wanted to demonstrate my newfound prowess! Determined to overtake him, I rushed on toward Rocky, overshot a turn, got tangled in the thickets, and never saw him again.

THE MIND IS AS TURBULENT AS THE WIND

The Catskills are typically mobbed on holiday weekends during peak foliage season. But today's forecast called for heavy rain, and no one else was at the trailhead for Windham when Odie and I arrived. The rain held off, though, and an easy saunter took us to the top. Standing on the familiar ledge, I watched the clouds come streaming in, passing by on the left and right and overhead, then converging again behind us. As we made our way back to the trailhead, the winds came thundering through the forest, whipping the birch trees back and forth, blowing so hard I had to hold my hat to keep it from flying off.

The winds gust around with such determination! But meteorologists describe winds as merely equilibrating the atmospheric pressure between different weather zones. We're taught in school that nature is a "blind watchmaker," devoid of purpose, without design. Which means that we, too, are the product of random forces.

So here's a question: Do winds toe their lines, the same as us?

In all my wanderings through the Catskills, maybe I was merely blowing around the mountains, equilibrating between my own set of internal pressures, my spirit no less turbulent than the wind. One way in which the Grid had begun to change me was that I no longer believed that I was or had to be more special than the rest of nature. I was happy enough in my role as spark, flickering for an instant in the breeze.

A HIKE POISED ON THE BOUNDARY OF THE SEASONS

It was midway through October and time for something new. I'd done the same eight-mile loop from Balsam Lake Mountain to Graham and back three times this year and once the year before. A long time ago I'd taken Philip, then five years old, out this way on a camping trip (I remember struggling with the stove—we had to use our toilet paper to get the fire started). Now, studying the map, I found a new route that bagged these peaks via the Hardenburgh Trail, which I'd never set foot upon before.

It was overcast at the Dry Brook Ridge parking area when Odie and I arrived. We headed out along the trail, an old forest road covered with rocks. When hiking barefoot, I've learned that speed depends on conditions. Where the rocks were thick, my pace was slow, while Odie ranged ahead.

We reached a junction, turned left, and headed out toward Graham, passing through a forest of beech, the foliage green or brown and in some places flecked with gold. The path was softer here, and I walked a little faster.

We arrived at Graham's summit to still conditions. Looking back toward Balsam Lake Mountain, I saw a single cloud hanging in the sky, a white mass tinged purple on the bottom, drifting slowly, expanding slightly, evidently in a languorous mood.

As I pulled out my phone to plot our next steps, a black-nosed hickory tussock caterpillar squirmed by. It was inching along in a two-step motion, first scrunching, then stretching, in a rhythm similar to barefoot hiking: slower, then quicker, slower, then quicker—overall a modest pace.

The day was warming up, so I stripped my shirt and tied it around my waist. We clawed our way through a tangle of berry canes and birch trees. I tugged branches aside, Odie scooted underneath, both of us searching for easy passage. The compass heading took us southeast, straight into the morning sun.

We dropped into the gulf between Graham and Doubletop and edged around a cliff. I kept one hand against the ground for balance as we descended a slick, rocky slope. The foliage sparkled and flashed around us, while Doubletop loomed ahead, a large skull-like mass with a cleft in the middle, as if it'd gotten a hatchet in the forehead.

The slope leveled off as we neared the saddle, a long groove in the ground between the two mountains. No water here today. I gave Odie a drink from my bottle, but carrying only a single liter, I'd wait a little longer for my turn.

We scrambled up and out of the saddle, both of us on all fours. Then the terrain leveled off, and the next half mile was an easy walk through waves of green and gold. On the final climb, Odie zigzagged upward, while I was back on hands and knees.

On the summit of Doubletop, the air was warm and still. I wanted to hang out in the sun-speckled shadows, smell the fir, feel the moss, study the lichens sprouting from decaying wood, get to know the hickory tussock caterpillar creeping by. Yet a glance at my watch showed that time was creeping, too. We had a long way to go to reach the Hardenburgh Trail, 1,000 feet below.

Another tricky descent. We got caught in a mess of cherry saplings tangled with bindweed, branches clawing against my arms, legs, and chest. We groped along what must have been animal trails when suddenly the ground rolled away and poured off into space. We backed off and worked around to the north, only to stumble into more cliffs. Compass in hand, I pushed southwest until we found a slope we could descend. Eventually the grade eased, and we were walking steadily, straight into the sun again, only now it was in the southwest.

The Hardenburgh Trail, when we finally reached it, was a marvelous discovery—velvety dirt shrouded in damp leaves, a luxurious surface for the barefoot tramper. I sauntered fluidly, ecstatic that the difficult descent was behind us. It was late afternoon now, and a gentle glow seeped through the foliage.

We walked along for four miles until Balsam Lake Mountain bulged above us, its rounded slopes glowing honey-brown in the fading light. The trail steepened. Odie darted ahead while I labored from rock to rock, breathing hard. To the west, a band of orange expanded across the horizon.

From the summit I got a signal on my phone and called Sue, alerting her that we'd be late. Then sandals went on to make the last few miles to the car at a faster pace.

It was a day poised on the boundary between summer and fall, not really in either season. If it hadn't been for the sun sliding slowly west, or the caterpillars inching along, time itself might have been on pause.

But time did not stay still. Soon it would be November, and the season for going light would be ending. Winter would bring new challenges, new lessons, and a whole new feeling to the Grid because the way I'd started thinking about nature—that it must always be a source of joy—is wrong.

CHAPTER 20

FACING THE WINTER PROBLEM

THE GRAY SKIES WERE TERRIBLE.

Back in January, I'd been so excited to start the Grid, I'd raced out in both day and night, enchanted by the mix of light and shadow, hunting for the distinctive tints of winter, hungry for new sensations.

But now the experience was different. In the face of cooling temperatures, coiling fog, and featureless depressing gray, my heart sank. My enthusiasm began to swirl away.

As someone who'd run through Death Valley in July, I found Catskills summers lovely and never sympathized with people who complained about the heat. As someone who'd long viewed winter with unease, I never understood how people could rave about snowshoeing. The Grid is not a vacation but rather requires you to check off every peak in every month, including whichever season you find least appealing. This format guarantees a diversity of experience, including the contrast between what you find enjoyable and distressing. And contrast is so important because it lets us differentiate and learn. Otherwise, life would be monotonous. Boring. And, eventually, desperate.

But I do so love the sun.

The first weekend in November, I was driving north into heavy clouds that smothered the ridge tops with plumes of gray. Soon rain was tapping against the windshield.

On the climb out of Devil's Tombstone, I encountered two hikers on their descent. Gesturing to my feet, one asked, "Is it meditative?"

"It can be, but often it's just aggravating," I replied, thinking to myself that you don't earn a sense of calm without first paying your dues to the rocks. Indeed, on this wet morning, the ground felt chilly and extra prickly.

I persevered and after an hour and a half reached the Devil's Acre lean-to, which offered a break from mist and wind. Sitting in the shelter, I noticed a robin on the branch of a mountain ash, feeding on a cluster of scarlet berries. Two companions were perched on either side, as if pulling security. A few seconds later, the birds rotated, and one of the sentinels got his turn at the berries. After a few rotations, the leader squawked, and the birds changed direction and circled around the other way.

After watching several of these rotations, I made my way over to Southwest Hunter, enjoying the soft dirt path. On my way back, I encountered a gentleman who introduced himself as Jim Bouton, the Catskill 3500 Club officer in charge of maintaining the canisters located on trailless peaks. When I mentioned the Grid, his eyes lit up, but then he put up a finger and counseled, "There's no rush." (Later I'd learn that Jim was the eighth person to complete the Catskill Grid, finishing on November 16, 2008.)

Noticing my feet, Jim mentioned a fellow nicknamed "Barfoot Phil," who'd climbed the Catskill peaks without shoes in the 1970s. I was intrigued to learn of Phil, having never met another barefoot hiker.

Then Jim explained the origin of the unofficial trail we were standing on. A hundred years or so ago it was the route for a horse-drawn railroad operated by Fenwick Lumber Company. Felled trees were taken to the lean-to area, where a coal-fired sawmill operated. The lumber was then sledded down into the valley through a narrow ravine. Jim asked if I'd noticed the coal slag littering the trail near the lean-to, which I had. Those sharp shards poked into the skin of my feet. We tried to imagine the scene back then, coal fires roaring, clouds of black smoke blanketing the denuded slopes.

Armed with directions from Jim, I took a shortcut through the woods and popped out on the trail near Hunter's gusty, fog-bound summit.

On the way back down, I was tempted to pick up the pace where the trail was soft. I wanted to run. But with my ankle tendon still in question, I resisted the urge. Instead, I took a shortcut through the woods and soon was weaving between trees, crashing downhill through fern glades, scattering flocks of robins, my feet sinking in damp dirt, wet leaves, club moss—and then a rock (ouch). After a bit I emerged back onto the trail, only to encounter a group of hikers toiling upward, bowed down with heavy packs, out of breath and seemingly out of sorts. Farther down I picked up a couple of empty water bottles lying on the trail.

Afterward, with help from Jim, I reached out to Barfoot Phil, inquiring how he got into the barefoot practice. He said that he'd heard about someone hiking barefoot in the Adirondacks, gave it a try, and liked feeling what his feet were doing: "I didn't care about mud or streams; I rarely slipped, something that happens more frequently in shoes; my steps were much quieter, and when alone I saw more wildlife. It is a good way to know the mountains that I have hiked in shoes all my life."

CONGRATULATIONS TO "TIGGER"

It was midway through the month. I dragged myself back out into the cold, wet, misty mountains. On Twin's eastern summit, I found crimson berry clusters still hanging from the mountain ash. I took a tiny nibble, and they tasted supremely tart, as if each berry contained a month's worth of vitamin C. I ate a handful, the sour taste perking me up. The tang was different from hobblebush berries, which remind me of fig jam, or wintergreen berries, which have a bland spearmint taste like toothpaste.

At Twin's western summit, a layer of stratus hung low, heavy with rain. To the north a watery glow seeped through the cloud cover, until an altostratus layer slid in above, shutting off the light.

Later that evening, I hiked the two miles to the Biscuit Brook lean-to and heated a cup of tea for dinner while the brook tumbled nearby and rain drummed on the roof.

The next morning the streams were swollen and rushing. With shoes on now, I tramped up the snow-dusted slope to Fir, while the winds barreled high above. Stepping over a yellow birch's serpentine root, my attention was drawn to the deep lemon bark flecked with orange; it took effort to drag my eyes away. Hiking in a fasted state seemed to make me more observant—maybe that's how our hunter-gatherer ancestors felt when out in the forest searching for food.

There was a surprise on Fir's summit. The last person to sign in on the canister logbook, nicknamed "Tigger," wrote that with this peak she'd finished her Grid. A final comment: "Woo-hoo!!"

I smiled for Tigger but felt a little glum. I was nowhere near finishing, and with winter almost here, it was time to face a discouraging reality.

THE WINTER PROBLEM

My progress in November had been modest, with 10 peaks bagged. This brought the total count for this grim month to 16, which meant there were 19 November peaks waiting for me in future years—a depressing thought. December was in terrible shape: The spreadsheet showed only three peaks complete, meaning 32 left to do. And it wasn't just November and December that were problem months. Until this year, I'd steered clear of the mountains in winter almost totally. Consequently, my spreadsheet had a gaping hole. In addition to November and December, an overwhelming number of climbs remained in January, February, March, and April. I'd started calling this the "Winter Problem."

I could have spread the Winter Problem over many years. This wasn't a race, after all, and there was no time limit to get it done. But the Grid had become important to me, and I was determined to complete it expeditiously, just like any other meaningful goal. Additionally, the need to climb so many peaks each month made the experience intense. Going out to the mountains in all conditions, and then again and again, this volume of activity was teaching me lessons about nature and myself that I might not have learned if I'd moved along at a leisurely pace or stuck to balmy weather. Lessons about my strengths and my limits. About how sometimes I hugged the line and exited the turns at high speed and how sometimes I lost traction and began to slide.

A FREE MAN, BUT INJURED

The sale of our company closed on the last day of November. Even after meeting with the acquirer's CEO, I remained unenthusiastic about them, and evidently, they felt the same about me. The first day of December found me without an offer, which is to say, a free man.

Here was my chance to take a break from the corporate grind and indoor lifestyle that I'd been complaining about. Here was my chance to go hike and run to my heart's content. But complicating things, my ankle still hadn't healed.

By this point I'd taken almost seven months off from running, and still there was no real progress. The tendon remained a chronic issue, even walking on a treadmill. After additional research, I'd sought out a nontraditional treatment called extracorporeal shockwave therapy, which is supposed to stimulate the healing process in stubborn, unhappy tendons. After five sessions over the course of a month, the doctor told me the therapy was complete, and now it was time to "spread my wings" and see what happened. A couple of brisk walks were encouraging, so I went for a short jog—and felt awful. My legs were burning from the first step. Then my groin started complaining. The next day, the ankle was stiff.

For my first Grid climb of December, I woke up with a headache. Stopping for some coffee along the way, I sat by a window in the coffee shop, staring at dust motes bobbing in the light. Stop fretting, I told myself, and make like one of those motes and float.

Back on the road, the forests whipped by, barren and colorless but for the shocking white jagged branches of sycamores growing creekside, which looked like they were mutely screaming.

I'd chosen Panther for today's outing and now charged uphill aggressively, even jogging a few steps on those flat sections of the trail, spreading my wings as the doctor ordered. By the time I reached the top, my ankle was throbbing. It was a mild day, so I took off my shoes and meandered back down at an easy walking pace, glancing out over Woodland Valley, whose empty forests shone with the ghostly pale green-silver sheen of greenshield and speckleback lichens spattered on the bark. I found plenty of mountain ash berries hanging in crimson clusters and couldn't resist helping myself to one bunch and then another. They tasted milder than before. Perhaps the recent frosts had softened them and removed some of the sour punch. Frost cycles may have a similar effect on people, it occurred to me. In other words, physical stress may make us milder. Drag yourself back and forth across rugged terrain for long enough, and the friction might smooth off some of your personality's rough edges.

The plan was to overnight at the McKenley Hollow lean-to, but it was still early, so I dropped pack, stuffed a flashlight in a pocket, and with shoes on now headed up the steep trail. Arriving at the top of Balsam, I paused in front of the cairn and extinguished the light. The moon was presiding to the east in a black velvet sky, with Venus hanging below and to the left, acting in the role of adjutant. So many times on Balsam's summit, I'd listened to the restless winds. But now the air was calm, so calm it seemed I'd reached the edge of the world, beyond which must lie perfect silence. I tried to still my mind but heard a faint persistent ringing, as if there were some kind of inner motion that could be stilled to a certain point but no further. *Strive to still the mind*, Krishna said. But while the heart still beats, I suspect that stillness can be only partial, or fleeting.

The moon beamed down, tracing twisted branch shapes upon the fallen leaves. Leaving my headlamp off, I took a tentative step along the trail, groping between sandstone blocks. My eyes adjusted slowly until I saw the moonlight was bright enough to walk by. Ghostlike, I slid along the shimmering trail for six full miles, headlamp off the whole time, sensing where to step even when the moon slipped behind the clouds.

Two days later, it was 40 degrees and raining lightly under heavy cloud cover, a day of perpetual twilight. Climbing Plateau this morning on the beastly ascent from Mink Hollow, the ice started about halfway up. I was carrying spikes but stubbornly refused to wear them, as if by force of will I could prevent the calendar from advancing, push off winter, keep the forests in autumnal mode forever. But ice had been forming in shallow puddles beneath the leaves, and a careless slip jolted my ankle, which started burning.

On to Sugarloaf, where the ice was everywhere, as if the mountain had bared its fangs and licked the trails with a silver tongue. From the summit, angry clouds chased me all the way back down, my ankle haranguing me with every step. Now my right knee was aching, too.

Plateau and Sugarloaf were too much. In addition to the ankle, my right knee had become a chronic problem as well. Back home, I hobbled up and down the stairs, feeling elderly and decrepit, wondering how many December peaks my body could handle and worrying about the Winter Problem.

That night I lay awake, battling with grim thoughts. Four years ago, I'd stood high in the Shawangunks, Odie by my side, gazed out at distant peaks glittering in bands of blue and white, and imagined myself running the 30 miles between here and there. The mountains warned me to stay away, but I didn't listen. Now I could barely walk.

LEARNING FROM THE ICEMAN

The next morning, I decided it was time to push back against winter. To regain my fighting spirit, I implemented certain practices recommended by Wim Hof, a Dutch fitness guru nicknamed "the Iceman," whose accomplishments include record-setting arctic runs barefoot and in shorts, swimming under frozen lakes, and sitting for hours in tubs of ice.

I'd first heard of the Iceman several years before, during a period when I was struggling with the cold in trivial ways. For example, returning from a run on a brisk fall day, my fingers were so cold I could hardly turn the key in the front door lock. Or leaving work on a winter evening, how I shivered in the dank wind, even on the short walk to the subway. I attributed these sensitivities to weak circulation, an inevitable consequence of the aging process. But then one winter day, I saw a middle-aged man running in New York's Central Park. He had dark skin, slick black hair, mirrored sunglasses—and no shirt. I was astonished.

Braving the cold, like going without food, must have been a necessary strength in earlier times. I read the account of a White man who worked as a doctor on a Sioux reservation. One winter day, when snow covered the ground, he encountered a Sioux man going about bare-chested. When the doctor asked how he withstood the cold, the man in turn asked the doctor whether he wore clothes on his face. "No," the doctor replied. "Well," said the Sioux, "I am face all over."

My friend Alan Davidson had been out of town on business travel, and on his return, we made plans to climb West Kill and Rusk. The thermometer read 25°F when I showed up at the trailhead wearing shoes, long pants, and a hat, but no shirt or gloves. Alan didn't seem fazed by my state of dress, as he'd heard of Wim Hof and was in any case familiar with my minimalist inclination. The miles flew by, as we had a lot of catching up to do. At one point, the conversation turned to social media. I wanted to know why Alan wasn't on Facebook. "If you're not paying for the product," he replied, "you *are* the product." This comment got my attention—evidently minimalism comes in different flavors.

A few days later, the car thermometer read 14°F at the trailhead to Balsam Lake Mountain, and the path was covered in a foot of fresh snow. Heading out in snowshoes, I immediately jammed my ankle on a hidden rock, which plunged me into a dismal mood.

Feeling rebellious, I stripped off shirt and sweater and soldiered on bare-chested through the grim forest, forearms turning red from the chill breeze. Once at the summit, I made a judgment call. With some difficulty, I got my pack open, fumbled around for shirt, sweater, and jacket, and got myself dressed again, frozen fingers barely working.

The weather turned a little milder for my next trip. It was partly sunny and 40°F at the base of Bearpen, where the trail was covered in muddy slush at first and then three or four inches of snow a little higher up. On a whim, I decided to try it barefoot, to see what my feet could tolerate. A hiker passed me on the way down, and thanks to him there were boot holes to step in, which spared the thin skin and exposed veins around my ankles from immersion in cold powder. My feet felt cold but did not turn numb. When the sun broke through, the trip turned into a bright ridge-top saunter through breezy gray forest and fields of purple canes, which once upon a time had sprouted such luscious berries.

Once back in the car, though, my spirits dropped. Next up was Doubletop and the bushwhack traverse to Big Indian, an intimidating prospect even in nice weather. With ankle tendon, groin, and knees all complaining, to say I was dreading this would have been an understatement. Back in shoes and spikes, I dragged myself two miles to the Shandaken lean-to. I tried to make a cup of tea for dinner, only to find my stove was out of fuel. I shivered through the night, feeling glum. The next morning, I woke up, scrubbed the mission, and trudged out.

After breakfast in town, though, I felt more energetic. It was 25°F at Slide's trailhead when I arrived. A pleasant walk took me up the mountain, and after warming up, off came sweater and shirt, and I strode forward bare-chested in the breeze.

I arrived at Slide's summit to an impressive scene: tall snow-clad fir trees standing watch over the memorial plaque to John Burroughs, handsome tree people dressed in their finest white robes, and above them through a break in the clouds, a circle of brilliant turquoise radiating calmness and serenity.

"The sun and blue sky are still there behind the clouds, unmindful of them," Burroughs wrote in one of his later books, part of a metaphor for how life must include both good and evil, health and sickness, light and darkness, growth and struggle. How remarkable to find the summit of his favorite mountain in agreement.

Slide was my last Grid climb for 2017. Thanks to the Iceman's inspiration, and through a terrific burst of effort, I'd climbed 22 mountains in December, bringing the count for the full year to 156—more than three times the volume of the year before. My Grid total now stood at 273, leaving 147 to go. The project was at a critical juncture. It was time to make decisions.

Blue sky behind the clouds. Summit of Slide Mountain, December 20, 2017.

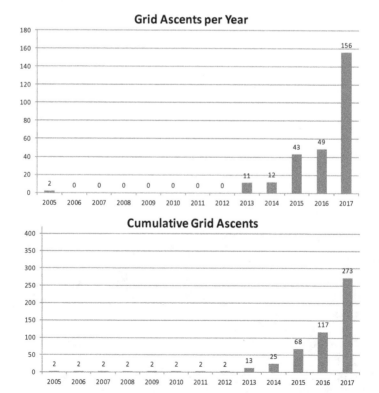

PART III
COMPLETING THE GRID

As I walked on eastward along the Tonto Platform, almost as naked as the other animals, I began to see everything around me as an intricate, interlocking web of life.

—*Colin Fletcher,* The Man Who Walked Through Time

In this manner the mind studies the way running barefoot—who can get a glimpse of it? The mind studies the way turning somersaults—all things tumble over with it.

—*Eihei Dogen, thirteenth-century Japanese Zen Master*

CHAPTER 21

BLACK TOES

HAVING LAUNCHED MYSELF SO AGGRESSIVELY THE YEAR BEFORE, the arc of this all-consuming project was becoming clear. I'd reached the apogee—the point of maximum intensity—and now it felt like the end was almost looming into sight.

Having come so far, to let the momentum wane would have been unthinkable. The Grid had become the single most important project in my life. Without it, I was washed-up. My notable runs were ancient history. Now I was injured. Frequently. Perhaps chronically. And every day I was getting older.

I *was* a runner. But who am I *now*?

The answer: one of the quietly desperate.

The Grid was a chance to reinvent myself, which is why I had to finish it expeditiously, while I still had the strength and time. Before something got in the way.

My first decision: I committed myself to completing the Grid in the current year. It wouldn't be easy. 147 climbs were a lot to do in a single year, and I could not afford to miss a single peak in its required month. Not to mention, almost half the remaining peaks (nearly 70) were concentrated in winter conditions: nine in January, 20 in February, 19 in March, and 20 in April. This was a huge load compared to the year before. Prior to that, I'd hardly set foot in the winter mountains. In my current condition, with aching knees, sore groin, and an ankle tendon that was still not fully healed, the Winter Problem would take extra time. And this calculation didn't include 30 climbs to do in November and December, which meant a total of *98* wintry peaks lay between me and project completion.

My second decision: I declared 2018 a sabbatical year from corporate work. Even without the Grid, it was time to take a break. Having labored steadily for over 30 years, somewhere along the way I'd lost the zeal. Not only was there so much time spent sedentary and indoors, but, if I was honest with myself, I'd reached a plateau in my career where my experience and skills did not support further advancement. Or if they did, the opportunities were not obvious. As a result, the sense of adventure had begun to fade.

In the back of my mind, I wondered what would happen when the Grid was done, my sabbatical was over, and it was time to return to the indoor world and try once more to be productive. Would I say goodbye to the mountains? Or would I find some way to bring the passion I'd found there into my indoor life?

Would the experience have taught me anything?

Would the new "I" have transcended what I used to be?

SOUTHWEST HUNTER IN THE SNOW

It was −1°F as Alan and I tramped along the shadowy shoulder of Route 214. A few steps later, we hopped over a guardrail, turned uphill, and began shuffling through three or four inches of fresh snow. To the south, we caught glimpses of Slide and Panther, bulwarks of the southern Catskills, tall and serious mountains. To the north, a long crescent ridge capped with spiky fir-spruce thickets swung in an arc from Hunter's shoulder to our destination, Southwest Hunter.

Steady as always, Alan took the lead breaking track, while I lagged behind, minding ankle and knees, pausing from time to time to strip off layers to keep from overheating—and getting distracted by the forest sights. This morning, it was a striped maple sapling that caught my eye, with one bud on the tip of the long red trident-shaped stem and two on the sides. A few steps later another sapling was clamoring for my attention, and then a whole thicket of striped maples started waving their branches and buds at me. To keep up with Alan, I had to turn away.

In due course, we reached the boreal zone and began weaving among the trunks of tall, healthy conifers. So far, it hadn't been necessary to refer to compass or GPS; we relied on the trusty "rule of up." But the summit did not appear. Southwest Hunter's summit is so broad and flat (almost a mile long), that "up" was imperceptible. Some compass work got us there, although it was a battle making our way through the wintry forest. Indeed, so much snow got dumped on my head that I couldn't see out my sunglasses. From the summit, we took the trail back for an easier descent.

A few days later, I pulled into the Fox Hollow trailhead, lugged a heavy pack out of the trunk, and headed out under relentless gray skies along a miserable, eroded trail running with muddy snowmelt.

I struggled along, burdened with a heavy pack full of winter gear and grumbling about the mud, when a figure materialized in front of me. I recognized the gray eyes and goatee. It was the speedy trail runner Mike Siudy, whom I'd last seen during my aborted Catskill run, on coincidentally the same day he completed his Grid.

Mike was carrying a handsaw to clear deadfall, some of which he explained was debris left over from Hurricane Irene in 2011. From the scores of toppled trees, it looked like a tornado had cut through. The conversation turned to peak-bagging. Having finished his first Grid, Mike was now working on a second one, with a lifetime Catskill peak count somewhere around 750.

After saying goodbye to Mike, I made my way to the Fox Hollow lean-to, where I dumped the heavy pack in a corner and then headed out to Panther, following the trail as it curled along the ridge. After a 10-mile round trip to the summit, I returned to the lean-to, heated some tea for dinner, and settled into an enormous arctic-weight sleeping bag my son Philip had given me for Christmas after hearing me complain how I always froze in my lightweight bag.

Just as I was turning in, a hiker showed up. Like me, Kal Ghosh was a corporate worker who fell in love with the Catskills after participating in the Escarpment Trail Run. We talked for a little while as I burrowed deeper into the arctic bag (later, Kal would tell me the temperature dropped to -3°F).

NATURAL NAVIGATION IN THE FROST

Ferocious cold was followed by a three-day thaw with temperatures bouncing into the 60s. Then a polar front plowed in again, pushing temperatures back to single digits.

That weekend Alan joined me for another exercise in natural navigation. This time the plan was to climb North Dome and Sherrill, returning by way of the valley of the Hagadone Brook. All of this off-trail.

We studied the map over breakfast, trying to commit the route to memory, then drove off to the trailhead, a small parking spot on Spruceton Road. Soon we were climbing through a grove of hemlocks, crunching through masses of stiff frozen leaves that just the day before were soaking wet. In some places, pools of snowmelt had iced over, but there were soggy spots, too. We carefully stepped around those, since wet feet would be unsafe with temperatures expected to stay in the single digits all day long.

We pushed south through a narrow tongue of State Forest. To the right, a handful of "no trespassing" signs. To the left, a line of yellow blazes painted on pine trees. Straight ahead the morning sun shone through the top of a yellow birch; it looked like the tangled ice-glazed branches were burning with silver flames.

Emerging onto an old forest road, we passed snowbanks sparkling and flashing and a frozen puddle crisscrossed with crystal needles. In some places, the needles had multiplied into large feathery flakes shaped like trees or ferns. We'd entered a world of hoarfrost.

Reaching North Dome's summit, we couldn't sign the logbook because the canister was frozen shut. We crunched and clumped along the social path, and when it petered out, we oriented ourselves to the west by keeping the late-morning sun to our left. After a short distance the slope dropped away, and there across the divide loomed Sherrill Mountain, glittering like a crystal palace.

The sudden transition from warm to cold had produced all sorts of odd effects. A dead birch vomited forth a plume of banana-colored ice (it looked like melted candle wax that froze in mid-ooze). Sandstone ledges were dripping with icicles, some clear, others pasty yellow or dirty orange. Everything had been wet, then froze. Each branch, twig, and bud was encased in a quarter inch of frost with a crust of rime ice on the north-facing edges.

We reached Sherrill, signed in at the canister, and dropped back into the saddle. So far, the natural navigation had been straightforward. From here, we planned to contour around the mountain's northern shoulder. This had looked like a good idea over breakfast, but now we found the terrain was steeply slanted. We stumbled across plunging streams flash-frozen into gray cascades, sidestepped over slickly varnished rocks, punched our way through ice-glazed hobblebush and beech, and suffered painful slaps from heavy ice-encased branches.

Behind us, Sherrill Mountain flashed and twinkled, while to the left a shadowed valley beckoned. But it seemed too soon to descend. The sun lit up a distant spur, and we groped our way in that direction until our afternoon shadows shifted to the front, indicating we'd finally turned back east. This was our cue. We dropped into the valley and crossed the Hagadone Brook on spray-crusted logs and rocks.

During the descent, my toes were getting jammed in the front of my shoes and squeezed by the pressure of rubber straps securing spikes on top of two pairs of thick wool socks. Now they were turning numb. Alan spotted our tracks from the morning, but just as quickly we lost them. I was starting to wonder whether this bushwhack would ever end when Alan saw the cars.

This was a natural navigation triumph, but sometimes there's a price to pay for success in winter. Once in the car, it was a huge relief to remove the spikes and wiggle my toes. But after a few minutes, my poor toes started stinging horribly. They ached all night. A week later blisters appeared and then turned black. It took several weeks for the skin to heal.

WISHING IT WERE SUMMER

The final ascent for January would be Kaaterskill High Peak, for the seventh time. There was the dreary snowmobile trail, the sketchy scramble, and a few moments standing on Hurricane Ledge, gazing out at the winter mountain landscape under midday sun, feeling faint warmth on bare chest and shoulders.

With this climb the Grid for January was complete. The Winter Problem had been whittled down to 59 peaks remaining (89 with November and December).

Descending the icy scramble, my spikes began to slip, which was unnerving since I'd heard that someone fell here once, broke an ankle, and had to be rescued by the rangers. I strapped on a brand-new pair of hiking crampons, and the longer fangs bit into the ice with authority. I crunched down the slick chute feeling more secure.

Once down at the base of the scramble, I changed back into spikes for the slushy walk back to the car, but the left spike kept slipping off my shoe.

Technology! It makes us so productive, and in the process, we become dependent. Then it fails and drives us nuts.

Eventually, I gave up trying to fix the strap and clumped along with one shoe spiked and one shoe bare, feeling vaguely ridiculous and wishing it were summer.

CHAPTER 22

A DAMNED CLOSE-RUN THING

Now it was time to wrestle with the worst of the Winter Problem. Twenty peaks in a single month would be a lot to do in the best of times, but as far as conditions, February is arguably the worst. Not to mention, it has the fewest days. The challenge was compounded by some travel during the first half of the month, which left only two weeks free. Then, sabbatical notwithstanding, I agreed to take on some project work when a banker introduced me to a company that was planning an IPO but whose management team needed help communicating their story. This meant a flurry of meetings and conference calls, which cut further into the calendar. Out of the two remaining weeks, only a handful of days were available for the Grid. There would be no margin for error.

I studied the map, trying to find the most efficient strategy to complete all 20 peaks. Be safe, I reminded myself. That was priority number one. But if I let even a single peak slip through my fingers, Grid completion would be pushed out at least a year, a possibility I couldn't tolerate. So I went back to the map again, trying to identify more efficient combinations of peaks or shorter routes, wondering whether I had the time and strength to pull this off.

A couple of days after my return, Amy Hanlon, whom I'd last seen a year ago on the nighttime bushwhack up Panther and Slide, invited a group of friends to join her on Windham, the last summit in her winter series (the Catskills 3500 Club offers special recognition to those who complete the 35 high peaks during winter). It was a brisk sunny day, and everyone was in high spirits. At the summit, we were treated to champagne and chocolate, while Amy, eyes flashing and all smiles, celebrated her achievement with a yoga headstand.

Nineteen peaks to go. I drew up plans to knock out the four eastern peaks of the Devil's Path, recalling how I'd run that route in January the year before, when the Grid was a brand-new project. To make life easier, I hiked into the Mink Hollow lean-to the evening before, positioning myself for an early start the next morning. But I woke up feeling lethargic. I completed Plateau and Sugarloaf but was too tired to continue.

SOME BREAKFAST MIGHT HELP

Ever since completing the 50-mile Rock The Ridge without food or water, I'd gotten into the habit of hiking in a fasted state, the goal being to keep my body in fat-burning mode. This practice followed years of work gradually weaning myself from sugar and processed carbohydrates (in my mid-40s I'd found that old habits like drinking Coke and eating donuts left me feeling ill). But during cold-weather conditions, a few more calories seemed like a sensible idea.

The next day, I showed up at Slide Mountain with a big breakfast in my belly. After reaching the summit, I made my way down the mountain's backside, with the new hiking crampons helping on the icy ladders. It was an unseasonably warm day, with the path to Cornell a stream of meltwater and the sandstone ledge on Wittenberg warm and dry. On the plains below, the Ashokan Reservoir lazed in the sunshine, while a row of almond-shaped lenticular clouds floated above the plains on the mountains' leeward side.

On the next trip, however, it was back to cold temperatures, snow flurries, and sullen skies. I dragged myself to Twin's cloud-bound summit and peered into a gray void. Later, at Indian Head, more grayness. It was like looking at a TV screen with no signal.

And then conditions seesawed once again. The next morning on the drive north the mountain peaks were poking through fog banks. I topped a rise and plunged into gray gloom as dark as dusk, with oncoming headlights shrinking to pinpricks. When I stopped for breakfast, the sun broke through, urging me to look up from my plate. The scene was exhilarating.

After breakfast, I returned to the car with a side of sausage for Odie, who'd waited there patiently. A short time later, we reached the trailhead, disembarked, and headed up toward Balsam Mountain. Here we crossed paths with a young man named Dakota Inman, who told us he was planning to hike not only Balsam, but also Eagle, Big Indian, and Fir, which was a longer route than what I'd planned. I wished him the best.

A little while later, to my surprise we ran into Mike Siudy and a friend. They too had encountered Dakota and thought he would benefit from some company. A few steps later Odie and I caught up with Dakota, only to find his determination wavering, as he didn't have much experience bushwhacking in the Catskills or the right type of navigational gear. We decided to join forces.

Now Dakota, Odie, and I were crunching through the slushy snow together, following the footprints left by Mike, who'd coincidentally started where we planned to end. Familiar landmarks passed by: Big Indian's summit, the saddle between Big Indian and Fir, the tangled wall of trees near the top of Fir where we were pelted with freezing rain, and then the steep descent into Burnham Hollow.

And then there were eight.

ZOMBIE DEATH MARCH UP WEST KILL MOUNTAIN

The next day, I woke with a sense of dread. The temperature was in the mid-30s, and it was raining—perfect conditions for hypothermia. I repeated my new standard operating procedure of a big breakfast for me and a side of sausage for Odie. A little while later we pulled into the Seager trailhead and started walking along Dry Brook. The stream was roaring with run-off. I had to haul Odie by his leash across a tributary rushing calf-deep with angry coffee-colored currents.

Past a bridge, an unmarked path took us upward through a grove of hemlocks, and then the slope moderated, and it was a long walk through beech and birch. Snow showed up around 3,000 feet, and by

3,400 feet, it'd turned into a crusty glaze. I had on spikes but wished I'd brought the crampons.

Frozen rain pattered in the forest, while the winds gusted on high. Tree branches were encased in ice, and the ground was littered with glassy fragments. We found our way through the frozen boreal zone, signed in at Doubletop's canister, and started back. Once below the snowline, the path felt soft underfoot, and being warmly dressed, I decided to take off my shoes and walk barefoot for the last mile and a half. When we reached the water-crossing, Odie picked his way across a log and then made a leap, while I slipped and fell in with a splash. It was hard not to laugh—once I got over the shock.

I'd planned a second peak for today, and arriving at the parking area on Spruceton Road, we found the trail to West Kill Mountain deep in slush. Still barefoot, I hustled along energetically and charged uphill until the trail became crusted over with ice and I was startled by a drop of blood. It was time for shoes, socks, and spikes.

The mist turned to rain. Odie looked bedraggled and uncharacteristically lagged behind. I helped him up some of the taller ledges, praised him when he jumped, and for encouragement called out the remaining mileage, figuring he'd appreciate the tone of voice even if he didn't understand the numbers.

0.88 miles to go!

We slogged along in slow motion. This trek had become an ordeal, reminiscent of the last miles in a long race, what ultrarunners call the "zombie death march." I watched Odie carefully. Maybe two days in a row was too much for a Labradoodle who was now ten and a half years old.

0.84 miles to go!

At our plodding rate, it took 35 minutes to finish that last mile, but the death march seemed to last forever. The return trek didn't pass much faster, until about a mile from the car, when Odie recognized the bridge across the West Kill and rushed ahead. That evening he was stretched out on the sofa, too tired to eat the roast beef I offered from my sandwich.

BACK TO THE PATHLESS RIDGE

The February Grid, if I could close it out this year, would be a damn close-run thing, so to speak, for now it was the last day of the month, and I'd saved the worst for last: six peaks on the pathless ridgeline with the awful spruce-fir thickets. In a last-minute brainstorm, I arranged for Smiley's Taxi to pick me up at the base of Peekamoose, where I left my car, and drop me off on Moon Haw Road, making this a one-way trip instead of a circuit. And then a lucky break—the forecast called for an unseasonably warm day with a high of 60°F. Even so, I woke up feeling apprehensive, unsure what to expect at elevation.

From Moon Haw Road, I toiled up the ridge to Friday, pausing on a rocky point that jutted into space. To the northeast, there stood Cornell and Wittenberg, bulging and hump-shaped, like a pair of standing waves. The Ashokan Reservoir lay to the southeast, basking in the sun. What a spectacular warm, clear day!

In due course, I was standing on top of Friday and studying my next objective, Balsam Cap, one mile to the south. On the descent into the saddle, a line of cliffs forced a detour to the west, after which I stumbled onto what appeared to be a faint social trail. Nothing obvious, no footprints or beaten path, just enough room to slip between the spindly trees.

On the way to Rocky, once again a line of cliffs forced me west. From the clearing on the mountain's shoulder came a glimpse of Slide, stately and aloof. Big, old trees moldering on the ground, saplings sprouting all around—a tangled mess.

At Lone, the ground was littered with crushed ice. Some footprints in the snow, the first I'd seen all day. A little later, I reached Table Mountain and stepped onto a blazed trail for the first time that day. From Table it was a short distance to Peekamoose—and the Grid for February was complete.

All that was left was the four-mile walk down to the trailhead where I'd left the car. Below 3,000 feet the path was dry, so I took off my shoes and padded along, the leaves, dirt, and stones feeling soft and smooth underfoot.

It had been a long bushwhack through challenging terrain during the toughest time of year, with not much room for mistakes. What a huge relief now, on this weirdly warm winter afternoon, to stroll along, mind empty.

In the west, a beam of copper-colored light appeared, forming a glowing triangle between a distant ridge and a low cloud ceiling. Three times rain blew in and sprinkled briefly as I sauntered down the trail, while the full moon watched from above my shoulder.

The simple joy of walking. This was my reward for bearing the aggravation of ice and snow and the anxiety of taking on a heavy burden. But the Winter Problem continued, for success in February meant nothing with respect to March.

View of Wittenberg and Cornell, from the shoulder of Friday Mountain. February 28, 2018.

CHAPTER 23

A GRUESOME SLOG

By the time I'd recovered from February and was ready to get to work on 19 peaks for March, two separate nor'easters had come roaring through and together dumped four feet of snow. I recall sitting by the kitchen window, watching heavy snowflakes tumble, and then the sound of thunder came rolling in.

The following Saturday it was snowing at the trailhead as I shouldered the heavy pack full of warm clothing and the large winter sleeping bag Philip gave me. Even with snowshoes, I sank in ankle-deep.

After plodding a short distance along the trail, it was time to head into the woods and up to Rusk, a climb I'd made a half-dozen times before. Tracks led toward the summit, but they must have been a few days old as the footsteps were half filled. With each step, my feet sank six inches into fresh powder.

I labored upward, stepping into the half-filled shoe-holes, my heavy pack an unwelcome burden. Despairing of the pace and lack of rhythm and fearing that I might lose my mind, I resorted to counting steps, 20 at a time, after which I paused and looked around. Then counted 20 more. The one-mile bushwhack to the summit took one hour and 45 minutes, for an average speed of 0.6 miles per hour. Surely Sisyphus moved faster than this.

The summit logbook showed seven people made it here two days ago, placing them after one storm and before the other. Without their tracks, this climb would have been unspeakable.

Clouds were raging past the summit, but I was in no mood to watch. I turned around and was slogging back down the slope when a fantastic vision appeared. Atop a distant peak stood a tall tower seemingly built of alabaster or white marble, gleaming in a cone of light that burned through the gloomy dusk. The eerie structure bobbed like a distant beacon as I crunched along. Eventually, with the help of map and compass, I identified it as the fire tower on Hunter Mountain's summit, which was incidentally my next objective. How odd, for all the times I'd descended Rusk, to see it for the first time from this angle and in these conditions. I took another step downhill, looked up one last time, and told myself this strange vision was a gift, that the mountains saw I needed some encouragement.

Once back on the trail, I turned uphill for the slog to Hunter. Now I was counting steps in sets of 100 instead of 20, glancing at my GPS watch in between each set and hoping to see some progress in mileage or elevation, no matter how minuscule the increment.

By the time I reached the top, the light was gone. The summit clearing had become a desolate place, ringed in with walls of boiling vapor, and the eerie white tower was now cloaked in shadow.

My pace quickened on the well-tramped trail to the Devil's Acre lean-to. Instead of counting steps, I was debating whether to bag Southwest Hunter tonight or wait until the morning. Without making a conscious decision, I found myself standing at the canister, where I saw that Mike Siudy and two friends had signed in on the logbook the day before. They did me a service by breaking trail.

Back at the lean-to, I rolled out the large sleeping bag. The floor was covered in a dusting of snow and dotted with paw-prints. Lying in my bag, I was wondering whether it would be prudent to stash my food somewhere out of reach, only to wake an hour later. But it wasn't the resident porcupine rummaging through my pack, just a pair of hikers arriving late.

The next morning was a downhill slog through a white trackless wasteland. I struggled past fir and spruce branches bowed down with loads of snow, which they dumped on my head as I brushed by. Moisture seeped down my neck and dampened the back of my shirt. Feeling grumpy, I stumbled down the mountain, crossed the West Kill Creek, and labored on toward West Kill Mountain. The mileage ticked by on my watch imperceptibly. Once again, the trek to West

Kill had become a zombie death march, although mercifully Odie wasn't here to share the suffering.

I was on the way back from the summit when I ran into a group of friends at Buck Ridge Lookout. We admired the wintry view and made plans to meet afterward at a nearby brewery. Thanks to the group, the trail was now well trampled and movement easier. As I made my way downhill, I noticed saplings so heavily burdened with snow, their slender trunks were bent over and upper branches plastered against the ground. Poor little creatures, it was hard to tell these waist-high blobs were trees. In passing, I gave them a shake. The snow fell away in clumps, and the youngsters rebounded. They probably didn't need my help, but maybe they appreciated it.

With four peaks complete, there were 15 still to go. March was becoming a veritable zombie death month. Then I recalled an indie song by Mura Masa and Slowthai, "Deal Wiv It," whose chorus goes "D-d-d-d-deal, deal, deal wiv it, f*ck, deal wiv it." This seemed apropos.

SNOWSHOEING IN SLOW MOTION

On the next trip, the Catskills foothills were sparkling in early-morning sunlight as I made the familiar drive north, but strangely the peaks had vanished. Suddenly, I was startled by large wet flakes hurtling through the air and splattering onto the windshield.

It was still snowing when I pulled into the Seager trailhead. Snowshoes strapped to boots, the heavy pack reluctantly shouldered, it was off to the Shandaken lean-to. I followed tracks for the first mile, but then they turned off a different way, and now I was facing four feet of fresh accumulation. Even with snowshoes, I was sinking to the knees. The second mile took one hour and 20 minutes. By the time I reached the lean-to, I was zapped.

The next morning, the big pack got stashed in a corner for the return. The saddle between Eagle and Big Indian lay only one mile away, but getting there was going to be a gruesome slog. Hopefully, I'd find a beaten track up top.

The first mile was indeed gruesome. With each step, my boots punched through six to 12 inches of fluffy powder, then crunched down deeper as I rotated my body forward. Where the trail was steep, I had to kick away in waist-deep snow until there was something to stand upon. To preserve sanity, it was back to counting steps. The single mile took two hours and three minutes, or less than 0.5 mph. This might have been the slowest pace I'd ever gone.

A wooden sign marked the trail junction on the saddle, but there was no track visible, nothing but sculpted white mounds. No one had been here recently, or if they had, fresh snow and wind had obliterated every sign. My plan was to bag both Big Indian and Eagle, the two peaks each lying one mile from the saddle, but now Big Indian was scratched, and my entire focus shifted to making Eagle.

At least it was more level up here, with only 500 feet in rise over the next mile. But the snow was knee-deep the whole way, and the muscles in my legs were starting to fatigue. To preserve my sanity, I counted steps again. A black-capped chickadee alighted on a nearby branch, gave me a dismissive glance, and warbled on at length. I counted more steps. The one-mile trip to Eagle's summit took well over two hours, although I didn't look at my watch. It seemed better not to know.

My boot prints led me back to the saddle. Both ankle and knees were aching now. With the sun out, the snow was turning wet and heavy and every step was unpredictable. I tried to edge around a rivulet, miscalculated, sank to my waist, floundered, and struggled to stand up. My snowshoes were coated with pounds of thick wet slush. I felt like howling.

Back at the lean-to, finally, it was time to buckle on the big pack for the last two miles. Unfortunately, the tracks from the day before were filled. By the time I reached the end, I was swimming with fatigue, anxiety, and frustration, and just about crying.

That was a lot of work for a single peak.

With Philip in town for spring break, I proposed a trip to the Devil's Path, reasoning the popular trail would surely be tramped down by now. After parking at Mink Hollow, we followed tracks up the hill. Where the path crossed a gully, Philip stumbled on a hidden root and fell into a snowbank. I reached a hand to help him up, my foot slipped, and I fell, too.

We reached the saddle, turned toward Sugarloaf, and looked around for a beaten track, but there were no signs of passage, nothing but a meringue-like coating spread thick everywhere. Initially this seemed even worse than Eagle because it was so steep. Each step had to be kicked out of waist-high snowbanks. When I leaned on a trekking pole for balance, it sank all the way to the grip.

The one-mile trip to the summit took one hour and 30 minutes. We stumbled a little farther, sinking into drifts, not sure whether to keep going or call it a day, when a dozen hikers came marching in from the opposite direction. They'd left behind a beautiful beaten track, as nice as a sidewalk, and this took us to Twin and back.

On the drive out, sunlight flooded the mountains, and for all the deep drifts we'd experienced on the slopes, the valley floors were almost clear. I reflected on the fickleness of March and considered the wide variability of my own experiences. Why should I be surprised that my feelings churn and blow—am I not much like a cloud, composed largely of water and animated by the sun?

WHY RUNNERS AND BIRCHES BOTH GET BENT

Why are runners so often injured, if running is such a natural activity?

My ankle was slowly healing, but it was by no means back to 100 percent, even though by this point it'd been nearly a year since the stress fracture and almost two years since the first signs of strain.

One evening, Sue and I were visiting friends. After dinner our hostess, Ann, played a recording of her favorite poem, Robert Frost's "Birches":

> *When I see birches bend to left and right*
> *Across the lines of straighter darker trees,*
> *I like to think some boy's been swinging them.*
> *But swinging doesn't bend them down to stay*
> *As ice-storms do.*

After the poem finished, I cleared my throat and interjected (wanting to set the record straight) that in the Catskills, it's not the birches that are bent over after winter storms, but rather the fir and spruce saplings, which I'd seen crushed to the ground under heavy loads of snow. Robert Frost lived in New Hampshire, I explained, where conditions might well be different.

Needless to say, on my next trip to the Catskills I was *astonished* to discover bent-over birches everywhere. Especially striking were the river birches, slender trees with black flecks in shiny white bark, bent over in graceful arches.

Better to bend than break. I'd seen plenty of trees with limbs fractured by the load of ice and trunks torn apart, whereas the pliant birches reminded me of runners bending over to touch their toes. Flexibility is such a helpful attribute, whether physical or mental. In the play *Antigone*, the king's son begs his father not to be so stubborn: "One can see the trees on the heavy riverbanks. Those that bend with the rushing current, survive, whereas those bent against it are torn, roots and all ... So, you, too, father, bend a little to the fury and try to change your mind."

But birches don't stay flexible. Being shade-intolerant, they can't survive by creeping about on the ground like vines. Rather they must race for the sun. To propel the crowns toward the light the trunks strengthen and eventually become stiff. Maybe flexibility is not a virtue but an attribute of rapid growth. After all, life is full of trade-offs, and maybe it's asking too much for trees or people to be both flexible and strong at the same time. Think of it this way: If nature could produce a tree strong enough to withstand the wildest storm, most likely it would grow too slowly to win the race for light.

It seems, with each succeeding generation, Mother Nature refines her calculations, balancing strength against speed. We see the results of her work in the forest as a whole, where some trees bend and others break, the fate of individuals being unimportant, so long as the population prospers. So it must be with runners, too. Some of us *must* fall by the wayside, otherwise Mother Nature would've made us too strong to be swift, or too cautious to compete.

As I look back at this period in my life, I was starting to appreciate that the individual is not separate from nature, but part of it—and subject to its logic.

ANOTHER TREKKING POLE BITES THE DUST

The next day, as I taped up the sore ankle in preparation for yet another winter climb, I reflected on how I had run hard while I could. And that it was, in any case, better to be bent than broken. Meanwhile, the calendar was hurtling toward month-end—with four days left in March and five peaks to go. Next up were Big Indian and Doubletop, and the daunting ridgeline bushwhack between the two. I woke up full of dread, but it didn't turn out as bad as feared. Sure, the snow got slushy as the day warmed, but heading downhill I took giant strides, sank a little here, slid a little there, the snow helpfully covering up rocks, branches, and other obstacles. What a surprise to find myself moving swiftly! From Big Indian, I plotted a shortcut through the woods, following a ridgeline down into the valley. Soon I was striding out through the thick snow—almost running!

On the drive out, I saw a pair of bald eagles wheeling in the sky. Screaming back and forth, they glided into a forest clearing, circled once, and flapped off.

It turned out that not every climb in March was pure misery. But now it was the last day of the month, and once again I'd saved the worst for last—in this case three peaks on the pathless ridge, namely Friday, Balsam Cap, and Rocky. I planned a route along the Neversink River, opting for a long but gradual ascent from the west, not wanting to mess with the steep eastern escarpment in deep snow.

March 31 might've been spring on paper, but it was a frosty morning in this north-facing valley, with heaps of crusty accumulation. The surface held my weight initially, but I reckoned it would be pretty sloppy by the time I was heading back.

I passed multitudes of bent-over birches, fought my way uphill, struggled through endless snowy thickets, bagged the three peaks, and just as feared, by the time I was on the way out, the spring sun had softened the snow into a soggy mess. Every step became a wet, heavy struggle. At one point, I leaned across a creek, put my weight on a trekking pole to lever myself across, and snapped the carbon shaft in two. These conditions were not unexpected; otherwise I might have lost my cool and started shouting.

A desolate place. Summit of Hunter Mountain, March 9, 2018.

CHAPTER 24

THAT SPECIAL SONG

LOOKING BACK ON THIS TIME, THE GRID WAS SUCH A PREOCCUPATION and the experience was so intense, it has tended to blot out other memories. Yet life was moving on. Freed for the moment from corporate work, I spent more time reading, writing, and volunteering. Sue went on a pilgrimage of her own, traveling with a friend to Asia, and came back full of stories. Emeline was working in Chicago as a freelance journalist. She wrote carefully researched articles about local issues with a focus on social justice. My ankle was healing finally. On Saint Patrick's Day, Sue, Philip, and I ran in a local 5K. It was my first-ever barefoot race. The course was smooth pavement, except for a scattering of gravel toward the end, and while my time wasn't anywhere near a personal best, I was pleased with my performance. Sue and Philip placed in the top of their respective age groups, making this a family triumph. Except for Odie, who would have loved to participate but had to wait in the car.

HELLO, INNER DAEMON

As for the Grid, I was looking forward to being done with the Winter Problem. After what I'd gone through in January, February, and March, I was starving for spring weather. But on the first drive north for April, there was the mountains' southern wall—shining deep white and flawless, like porcelain. Heart sinking, I watched the car's thermometer. By the time I'd reached the Biscuit Brook trailhead, it had settled at 23°F.

I headed out along the snowy path and stepped over a small creek after a mile. Ice glittered on the crusty rocks and sunbeams twinkled on the bottom of a pool, lending the scene a certain crystalline charm. But it failed to warm my heart. Besides the trickle of water, the woods were silent. The vegetation slumbered. The animals were hidden, the insects waiting to emerge. The migratory birds had not yet arrived. Everything was smothered in a dense white coating, monochrome and inert, which sucked the momentum from my every clumping step. My GPS watch read out a miserable 0.7 mph. The runner in me smoldered with resentment.

This winter environment was so *sterile*. There was so little to see, it felt like my old windowless office. But through the sterility, I caught a glimpse of the ridge where once upon a time Steve, Odie, and I hunted for the fall's first red maple. Off in the distance, there was Slide's stern profile, a purple frown under leaden sky. But these glimpses weren't enough to sustain me. At a faster pace, the sights would've flickered by quickly enough to create the impression of life, but as for pace, right now I might as well have been jogging in molasses.

I trudged along, frustration building—that feeling of becoming trapped—when a branch knocked the hat off my head. That was too much; I wailed in helpless rage.

Socrates was said to have a "daemon," which in Ancient Greek lore was variously described as an inferior deity, a local spirit, or the soul of a dead hero. In his case, the daemon acted like a guardian spirit, warning against risky courses of action. Now it occurred to me that I, too, might have a daemon, although mine seemed different. Instead of offering prudent counsel, it craved intensity, variety, and a sense of motion, and when there was nothing going on, it got furious.

I have not studied the scientific literature on daemons, but the idea came to me with such force that I took it as a prima facie valid explanation for my feelings. After further thought, I concluded that my daemon was the spirit of a long-dead scout or messenger who was frustrated he could no longer run.

I picked up my hat, plodded on to the summit, and got chased back down by a flurry of angry snowflakes. By the time I was back at the car, I felt winded. With Fir done there were still 18 April peaks left to do.

Next on the agenda was Panther. This being a popular trail, the surface had been compacted into a snowy sidewalk, which allowed me to power-hike along at a quicker pace. From vantage points on Giant Ledge, Woodland Valley spilled out below, and beyond it a convoluted maze of valleys. To the south, there was Slide once again, from this angle looking vaguely sphinxlike, while its neighbor Cornell leered with a crooked toothy sandstone grin.

From Panther's summit, finally, there was a vista with so many mountains billowing like waves, rising with convulsions in the earth's crust and falling away where rivulets carved the slopes. And something new appeared. Turning all the way to the left, I spotted St. Anne's Peak, North Dome, and Sherrill, roughly nine miles away to the northeast. For all the times I'd been to Panther (ten times), this was the first time I'd looked that way and seen those peaks.

As I was staring, low-lying mists came racing in from the north and obscured the scene. I kept watching, barely aware of my gloveless fingers turning cold, until after a few minutes the disturbance passed and the wind dragged away the haze. Mountain peaks snapped back into view with astonishing clarity. Individual trees popped back out in the depths of Woodland Valley.

I felt as if I'd been permitted to witness something special, and now I ought to hustle back and document these visions before they faded. The Greek philosopher Pindar wrote of the daemon that "it sleeps when the limbs are active," and now my daemon (if that's indeed the right term) seemed quiet, or perhaps it was feeling in sync with a quicker pace as I hurried down the trail. Spared of the whip, my conscious thoughts wandered freely, while my sore ankle complained on the steeper descents, and the part of me that thinks it's in charge tried to make sense of this circus while watching where to step.

BACK TO GOING LIGHT

I waited impatiently until halfway through the month for my first barefoot climb. After camping out at the McKenley Hollow lean-to, I was bushwhacking barefoot up Balsam Mountain along a new route, stepping on leaves still crinkly with frost. To make up for chilly soles I wore many layers of clothing.

White threads three or four inches long hanging from branches must have been the handiwork of local spiders, interrupted when super-cooled fog whistled through the forest and coated their work with rime. As I brushed past a tree, frozen threads fell to the ground with a lilting rustle.

By 3,400 feet, the rime had spread to beech and birch, beginning to coat fir needles, too. Patches of snow dotted the ground. Approaching the summit, I stepped cat-like across the crust, trying not to poke through. Then I danced along the icy trail to Eagle. (My poor feet hurt for the next week!)

A LONG LOOP TEACHES AN IMPORTANT LESSON

I was driving north once again, this time feeling highly confident of finding warm, brown slopes and dry trails. But cresting the rise on the Thruway, there was Plateau Mountain to the front, arms open to welcome, embrace, and crush me to pieces against its frosty white chest.

Back to shoes and spikes. The plan for today was a broad loop around the West Kill valley, starting with Rusk but from a new direction: I would bushwhack north up Evergreen Mountain, and then turn east and ridge-walk to Rusk's summit.

The initial climb was steep, but an inch or two of snow didn't faze me. Once on top of Evergreen, I looked south across the valley at St. Anne's Peak and North Dome Mountain and the steep notch between them. Through that notch I spied a tall and imposing ridge several miles further south, glimmering blue in a distant beam of light—unmistakably Panther Mountain. A few days ago, I'd stood right there, gloveless fingers turning cold, and looked this way exactly.

From Evergreen I turned to the right and walked eastward along the ridge toward Rusk. The forest was open, the passage easy, and I enjoyed the feeling of momentum. Nearing the summit, I entered the more densely crowded boreal zone. The trees here were strong and good-looking, like young athletes, and wearing such fine jewelry: clumps of beard lichen hanging a foot or longer, thin plates of hooded tube and hammered shield lichen filigreed upon the bark, pale green tufts and tendrils of ghost antler and boreal oakmoss sprouting from the twigs.

These little creatures impressed me with their innovativeness: They wrapped around the smallest twigs, some of them sprouting up, others hanging down, no doubt competing architectures designed to position them for the precious light. And so aggressive! On some trees they had spread over every square inch of exposed bark until they crowded against each other.

I sometimes wondered: When they bump into their neighbors, do lichens experience the vegetative equivalent of frustration? Or is it only humans who get angry with each other? Having spent some time recently on Twitter (now called X), I'd come away appalled by the insults and invective. You could attribute this rage to our egos, which lichens presumably lack. Or maybe our feuding is a part of nature, just as it is for other species whose members compete against each other. It occurred to me that from a distant-enough perspective, human conflict might appear as beautiful as the lichens' waves and swirls. To reach that vantage point, however, you'd have to make the effort to understand the point of view of other people, instead of merely disparaging them.

A little while later I reached Rusk's summit. So far, it'd been a pleasant five-mile saunter through the woods, and remarkably my legs, knees, and ankles were feeling better than they had in ages. On the descent, Hunter's fire tower hung off to the left, but this time it wasn't a fantastic marble tower floating in a cone of light. It looked just like another twig.

Once down on the trail, an easy stroll brought me to the base of West Kill Mountain, where the plan was to point straight into the woods and follow a bushwhack route to the summit. I crossed the West Kill stream, slipped off a rock and got one foot wet, stopped, wrung out the sock, and resumed the climb. My motivation, however, was starting to flag. Possibly I was running low on calories, having skipped breakfast (with conditions less desperate, I'd resumed 24-hour fasts). But the real problem, I think, was the unremitting grayness. There hadn't been a single flash of light all day. I was expecting spring, not a fight with winter that never ends.

An hour later, I popped out on the trail and a few more steps brought me to Buck Ridge Lookout. Here, finally, it was spring—at least to the south, where the brown plains of the Hudson River Valley lay toasting beneath a dome of robin's-egg blue. But in the north, where the Blackhead Range sat brooding sullenly, it was winter still. I watched as Blackhead Mountain shrugged the airflow over its lofty shoulders and sent a stream of dirty fog hurrying across the sky to shield the mountains from the sun. To keep them cold and barren a little longer.

Suddenly, to the east, a flash of white—a probing sunbeam lit up Hunter's fire tower. The beam shifted south across the snowy forest, but then a band of fog came racing in from the north and extinguished the light.

The play of light and fog was thrilling, but time was passing. There were still five miles to reach my car. I turned back into shadowed forest. It was an unpleasant surprise, after spending most of the day walking through untracked forest, to find myself back on a trail, which was to say a snowy-icy-crusty mess, full of "postholes" where people had stepped in slush that subsequently froze. After struggling all winter long, I'd hoped to resume that quick, confident, rhythmic gait that runners like me crave, but that was not going to happen today.

There was nothing to do but place each foot thoughtfully. Where the trail was especially rough, I groaned to myself and sometimes out loud, and where the footing was a little smoother, my thoughts and limbs flowed more easily.

I'd fallen into the habit of equating mountains with exhilaration, in contrast to the boring sterility of modern indoor life. But upon reflection, this wasn't quite right, for the mountains also inflict pain and misery—especially in winter—as this trek was now reminding me. I recalled Burroughs's point of view, that good and evil exist only in contrast with each other. Without struggle, failure, and disappointment, "life would be tasteless or insipid," he wrote. Indeed, there couldn't be life without pain and death, nor harmony without discord, light without shade, warmth without cold, development without struggle.

Well, here I was struggling. Yet in the back of my mind, an idea was forming, that my journey into the mountains would eventually circle around and bring me back to the city. That the purpose of this project was to *integrate* these two sides of my existence. So that I could return to corporate life, or whatever I might do next, with the engagement, intensity, and full range of feelings I experienced in nature—from the exhilaration of moving smoothly through the forest to the misery of stepping into frozen postholes.

On the drive home from the Catskills, the rain caught up to me. Back home in the city it tapped against the windows all night long. By morning it had become an oppressive roar, punctuated by ominous rumbles. Then the precipitation paused, while the wind came whipping down the street, rattling windows in their frames. A moment later, the sun broke through. I stepped outside and felt a breeze so warm and moist it seemed tropical, and birds were calling everywhere.

RETURN OF THE MIGRANT BIRDS

Halfway up the fire tower on Balsam Lake Mountain, the breeze touched my cheek. Through binoculars I picked out modest Bearpen, its steeper neighbor Vly, and the familiar gravel road leading to the saddle between them. Suddenly a marvelous warbling call rang out, a fast-paced, rollicking, burbling song full of ups and downs, like something played on a xylophone. I scanned the trees but saw nothing.

As I headed back down the trail—that same call again! I froze and peered through the binoculars once more, this time spotting a tiny olive bird atop a fir, half-screened by a branch, barely visible.

Standing on Twin's eastern summit later that day, I watched two black raptors with scimitar wings. One hung head down, motionless in the southeasterly flow. Then, folding wings, it dropped, caught the currents, and wheeled about. A moment later it flashed off toward Twin's western summit, half a mile away.

When I reached the western summit somewhat later, another hunter-killer was circling in the drafts, this one off-white with mottled markings. Through binoculars I watched it cock tail feathers and yaw. Then a broad-shouldered hawk soared out of the valley, its tail bands unmistakable.

As I hiked back down the trail, a dark-eyed junco sitting atop a tree issued a series of staccato chirps, dropped low to the ground, and darted off. I surprised another junco bathing in a puddle. It fluttered its wings vigorously, splashing drops about.

Down in the valley, I encountered a stout bird hopping along the ground: brown back, white chest with brown flecks, short beak, narrow tail, white ring around black eye. It was a hermit thrush, the first I had ever seen, although I'd heard the song so many times before, including right in this spot when I was finishing the Devil's Path Double.

Three days later, I was ravenous for sunlight and blue sky, but Deep Notch was socked in. I walked down the road on the way to Halcott and noticed for the first time how the pavement stank of tar and rubber. After a quick hop over the guardrail, I trudged uphill with binoculars at the ready, keen to identify that mysterious warbler whose call I heard the other day. But the forest was silent. During the climb to Halcott's summit, I saw and heard nothing. Perhaps the gray sky subdued the birds, just like me.

After signing in at the canister, I turned about for the descent. Looking out across the valley, I spotted my next destination: a spur leading to Sherrill Mountain. I altered course, aiming for the base.

Nearing the road again, I paused to admire a small waterfall when suddenly I heard it! That special warbling bird, somewhere in the canopy, its song all but drowned out by the splashing water.

I crossed the road (once again that acrid smell) before starting the climb. After passing an old stone wall, a few yards later I popped out underneath some power lines. Checking the map, I found I wasn't nearly as close to Sherrill as I thought. I realized with a sinking heart that this was going to be a long day.

The snow was just deep enough to slow my steps, there was just enough beech to keep me busy deflecting whiplike branches from smacking my face and chest. I moped along, frustrated with the slow pace, annoyed by the beech, dismayed by the gray sky and silence. The sun broke through the clouds for a moment, and to the south I caught a fleeting glimpse of green mountains marching before clouds hurried in to block the view.

The ground turned wet, my shoes were soaked, and my ankle began complaining as I fought through a knee-deep snowdrift. But I made it to Sherrill, and then a little while later to North Dome. The day's objectives were complete. Time to get out of here.

A friendly ridge carried me down into the valley, where the light snow cover was more helpful in clarifying the lay of the land. I descended into a grove of hemlocks and observed two robins flitting onto a branch and standing watch—serious and attentive birds—while a pair of downy woodpeckers darted in and got to work on the trunk.

Reaching the valley floor, I turned onto the road for the five-mile walk back to the car. I passed alongside pastures full of starlings, doves, sparrows, robins before coming upon a farmhouse. High in a tree was a bird so small I couldn't make out its features even with the binoculars, but it was singing that special song.

I recorded the song with my phone and later identified the mystery bird as a winter wren.

It was time for the last climb in April. I arrived in Woodland Valley to clouds of fog and headed out barefoot. My feet felt tender on the rocky trail, wet from last night's rain. A boot-shod hiker passed me. The trail leveled off, allowing me to run a few steps here and there, and when the grade steepened, I climbed vigorously. Above 3,200 feet, patches of snow appeared, and soon my feet were stinging. But I persevered, hopping from rocks to logs to stay off the ice. And then I caught that hiker and passed him.

The summit ledge of Wittenberg was warm and dry, and I settled back to watch exhalations of moisture rising into the air—the birth of a cloud.

On the descent, the snow and ice felt refreshing underfoot. I jogged a few steps before breaking into a run until the trail became too rocky. A black-and-white warbler flitted among the hemlock branches, and halfway back to the trailhead appeared another winter wren, bubbling away.

CHAPTER 25

A NEW RECORD FOR THE CATSKILLS

THE MIGRATORY BIRDS HAD RETURNED, HERALDING THE END OF THE Winter Problem (at least the first phase of it, as I wasn't yet thinking about the final 30 peaks in November and December). It was time to resume going light—and to go even lighter. In the coming months, I would push the envelope on minimalism until I was moving through the berry brambles and stinging nettles nearly naked.

At the same time, however, now that this grand project was grinding slowly toward completion, that question continued to nag me: What was I learning from all this effort? If I ended up behind a desk again, would the Grid have made a difference?

The clock was ticking: 332 peaks complete, 88 to go. Eight months remaining. Having made it this far, I was *1,000 percent* committed to finishing this year. This was, admittedly, an arbitrary, self-imposed deadline. But that's the way I operate—I like to take on big challenges and get them done.

Speaking of getting things done, the previous year I thought I'd completed the Grid for May, but later realized I'd taken my friend Dave up the eastern peak of Twin Mountain, when the official summit is the western one. After completing nearly 70 climbs in winter, a single peak for May seemed feasible. And when May 1 rolled around, the forecast called for clear skies and a high of 72°F. What a perfect day!

This ascent of Twin would follow a new route for me, and the first surprise was waiting just a mile in from the Roaring Kill trailhead at a point identified on the map as Dibble's Quarry: piles of bluestone slabs, in some places tumbling down the hill, elsewhere stacked into walls, columns, a fire pit, and four or five gracious seats, which looked like thrones. Taking my rightful seat, I surveyed Kaaterskill High Peak across the way and was surprised to see its upper slopes dusted white, which surprised me since the temperature was so pleasant. Near Kaaterskill's top I picked out Hurricane Ledge and recalled the first time visiting that peak with Odie three springs before: the icy slide on the summit's northern side, how I'd slipped and gotten mad. And that dicey nighttime climb with Alan, when my spikes bunched up around my heels and lost traction.

A broad-shouldered hawk flew up from the woods. Was it the same one I saw a few days earlier?

I rose from my bluestone throne, meandered a half a mile along the trail, and came upon a large pond with a chorus of creatures croaking enthusiastically: *GUNK, GUNK, GUNK.* Through binoculars, I made out a squadron of small, dark shapes with bulbous eyes spread out across the glassy surface, each green frog with its own small area of operations. Spring peepers were calling from the far shore. Eastern newts swam about in the shallows, both the bright orange juveniles called red efts and the older individuals who'd turned olive with yellow undersides.

A little while later I reached Twin's official summit, and the Grid for May was complete, this time for good.

ANOTHER LESSON IN PATIENCE

Finishing the Grid for May didn't preclude other visits to the Catskills that month, especially when the world was turning beautiful. A few days later, a glance at the map identified Ashokan High Point as a place I'd never been. So Odie and I piled into the car and off we went. There were so many interesting discoveries: a long thin creature with bright orange skin and black dots, which turned out to be a northern red salamander; vegetation reminiscent of the Shawangunks, including blueberry heather, mountain laurel, and scrub oaks with tender leaflets unfolding and long red flower strings unfurling from the buds; the contrasting scents of red spruce (sweet and citrusy), balsam fir (acidic, like a household cleaner), hemlock needles (sour resiny aroma), and white pine (smooth and subtle); and so many birds! Woodpeckers cackling in the distance, ovenbirds shouting *"teacher, teacher, teacher,"* black-throated blue warblers crying out *"cheep, Cheep, CHEEP!"*—not to mention prairie warblers, eastern towhees, and one red-eyed vireo.

At the top, we looked south at an ocean of blue mountain-waves. The spring sun beat down on us with force. Odie cooled off in a muddy puddle and emerged with stylish two-tone highlights.

Near the summit of Ashokan High Peak. May 18, 2018.

I'd come out here intending to try some barefoot running, but as we followed the trail further north, it was too rocky. Even at a walking pace, the gritty surface wore on my nerves, as did a surprising abundance of acorn caps, which poked into my feet and got stuck between my toes. Frustration began to build in me, like steam in the proverbial kettle. After picking my way down through a steep tumble of debris where the trail crossed back and forth across a dry streambed and then merged into it, I began to lose my cool. Odie came trotting back to see what was taking so long, at which point, I stopped, clenched my fists, and yelled "AAAARRRRGGGHHH!" And then felt better.

It's sometimes said that the barefoot practice teaches humility. You move at the pace the terrain allows, which is not necessarily the speed you'd like to go. For me, the frustration can become overwhelming, but I guess this is how a modern person learns nature's secret—a little bit of patience.

A LESSON IN CATSKILLS HISTORY FROM NIGHT DOG

Back in March, I'd met a veteran Catskill hiker named Ralph Ryndak, who was incidentally one of the volunteers supporting Ted "Cave Dog" Keizer on his record-setting run. Now Ralph had invited me to join him on a hike up Big Indian, with the goal of locating an unusually large specimen of yellow birch he'd found the year before.

As we walked in along Dry Brook, I listened to Ralph's stories about growing up in the Catskills. As a child he'd lived on Moon Haw Road, surrounded by those steep ridges. He first climbed Wittenberg at the age of nine, accompanied by his older brother, and then climbed it solo the next year. Soon after, he heard stories of a World War II bomber that had crashed in a storm. After five or six trips with friends up and down the mountain, they stumbled upon the wreckage.

Ralph's career kept him behind a desk, but every chance he got, he was out in the mountains hunting, hiking, climbing, and along the way gaining membership in the Catskill 3500 Club. On June 16, 2007, he became the sixth person to complete the Grid.

Teddy Keizer recruited Ralph as a volunteer for his Catskill thru-run after reading some of his trip reports online. Ralph went on to help Keizer with other adventures, too, including a record-setting run along the 273-mile Vermont Long Trail, where true to his nickname ("Night Dog"), Ralph accompanied Teddy at night carrying a heavy load of food, water, and extra clothing. Ralph also supported Keizer on a run in the Adirondacks, waiting patiently with resupplies on a stormy mountaintop, despite the risk of hypothermia. I could see why Keizer chose him for the Dog Team. This humble man was made of the right stuff.

From Ralph I heard the story of the first record thru-run of the Catskill high peaks. In 1978, Ralph's friends Jim Senecal and Joe

Hevesi, then 19 years old, stashed food resupplies in five locations and then headed out to thru-hike the Catskill high peaks. They went in true light mode with neither tents nor sleeping bags, just as I'd tried to do.

Their expedition got off to a rocky start when they found their first cache had been raided by raccoons—the critters spared only a can of sardines, a jar of applesauce, and half a carrot. Then they were hit by heavy rains that forced them to shelter in a culvert. Flashlight batteries ran low, limiting their ability to move at night. Nonetheless, they finished their quest in four days and 14 hours, which would stand as the unsupported record for 33 years until Jan Wellford and Cory DeLavalle came by in 2011 and beat their time by a single hour. Ralph showed me an old newspaper article in which Jim Senecal commented, "I could really notice the fatigue on my mind as well as in my arms and legs. I saw things darting away and then realized there was nothing there."

As Ralph and I searched for the big birch, our conversation turned to Mike Siudy. I'd heard rumors he was planning to challenge Keizer's record, which Ralph confirmed and then revealed that Mike would be launching his attempt in a matter of days. Using Ralph's green pen (his signature color) we left a message for Mike on the Big Indian canister logbook, wishing him great success. Then we headed for home, the big birch having eluded us.

CAVE DOG'S RECORD IS FINALLY TAKEN DOWN

And now another coincidence: Having offered to take some friends up Windham, it appeared that the date I'd chosen would coincide with the completion of Mike's run. If Mike stuck to plan, we might see him at the top.

Steve, the photographer, Kal (whom I'd met at the Panther lean-to), and I arrived at the trailhead at 9 a.m. and walked up to Windham. Sure enough, a few minutes later here came Mike power-hiking down the trail with a small team of friends, looking surprisingly fresh for someone who'd been on the move for two days straight. He thanked me for the message that Ralph and I left on Big Indian. And then he was off.

Steve turned back while Kal and I continued on to bag Blackhead, Black Dome, and Thomas Cole. It was a nice spring day to saunter along the ridge, but it was also that time of year when the black flies gather in swarms. Today they were ferocious. I rarely use insect repellent, but now in desperation I pulled a bottle from my pack and rubbed a drop on my arms and neck. I offered the bottle to Kal, but he declined. I was impressed. Underneath his mild-mannered exterior, Kal was evidently a hardcore minimalist. Later he'd tell me that he just doesn't like the smell of bug repellent (I think he was being modest).

As Kal and I were descending toward the trailhead, I noticed a red-and-yellow drooping cup-shaped flower growing next to the trail—the eastern red columbine. Then we said goodbye and drove off our separate ways. Imagine my surprise when back home I found a columbine growing right next to the front door, which I'd somehow never noticed.

No doubt the world is full of connections, once you learn to open your eyes and look around.

Eastern columbine.

CHAPTER 26

A NEW RECORD FOR THE LONG PATH

MIKE SIUDY BROKE KEIZER'S RECORD BY A DECISIVE MARGIN, finishing the circuit of the 35 high peaks in 57 hours. I felt a little wistful, for this was what I'd once hoped to achieve.

Two years ago, on my ill-fated run, I'd encountered Mike on Balsam Lake Mountain, coincidentally, just as he was completing his Grid. I'd thought he might well be the best candidate to take on Keizer's record. That was a good call. And then I also had that small epiphany that what matters is the achievement, not the personal identity of the achiever. That was also right, for I now felt proud for Mike and inspired by what he had done.

I turned my attention back to my own work, of which there was plenty. June was another nearly empty month, with 19 cells to fill in my spreadsheet. I got the Grid off to a fast start with a 24-hour operation on the pathless ridge, bagging Table, Peekamoose, Lone, Rocky, Balsam Cap, and Friday, and walking back through the Neversink Valley in a drenching rain that left me so chilled I put my shoes back on.

Then I talked Kal into some barefoot hiking, which wasn't hard to do. In another strange coincidence, it turned out he was an accomplished barefoot runner, having completed a marathon without shoes in a time that I could only dream of. We headed up the familiar gravel road to Bearpen, hiking briskly and mixing in some jogging. From the summit, I pointed out the Upper Minekill and Schoharie Reservoirs, and Windham High Peak, explaining to Kal that the Long Path passes those three points and mentioning that a pair of young runners, Will Fortin of New York City and his friend Dustin Smith of Boston, were out there, somewhere, trying to break the record I'd set five years ago.

We were trotting down the hill, when along came Mike Siudy, out for an easy hike with his wife and their dog, just one more in a series of chance encounters.

MEETING WILL AND DUSTIN

Meanwhile those young runners were making speedy progress on the Long Path. The next day, I pulled up the track from their personal locator beacon and saw they'd entered the Catskills and were heading down from North-South Lake toward the base of Kaaterskill High Peak. An idea occurred to me. I could drive up there, meet them on the trail, and then scratch Kaaterskill off the list for June.

In due course, I arrived at the Platte Clove parking area only to find the scene gray, misty, dank—the surly side of June. I cracked the car door open and reluctantly set a tender, naked foot upon the cold, muddy, rocky road that heads up the mountain.

At 2,500 feet, a signal got through to my phone and updated the runners' track. They were just ahead. And a moment later, they came shuffling down the trail, moving purposefully and carrying on a spirited conversation. I shouted a greeting, and they pulled up in surprise.

They told me they'd gotten a cold start that morning (45°F and raining) but otherwise were feeling good and hoping to reach the hamlet of Phoenicia by evening. I reminded them to be mindful of slippery rocks on the Devil's Path, but they'd been there before and were undaunted. We chatted for another minute, but the clock was ticking on their record attempt, and I didn't want to hold them up, so I wished them the best and sent them on their way.

I felt wistful once again, part of me flattered that my record had attracted such strong contenders, but another part hoping that it might somehow withstand their challenge and last a little longer.

In any case, it was time for my ninth ascent of Kaaterskill High Peak. I struggled along the soupy trail and made my way through long stretches of mud and pools of standing water. Strangely, Will and Dustin didn't seem fazed by this atrocious trail.

Once through the mud, however, the scramble to the summit felt easy. I charged uphill, pulled myself up three or four sandstone ledges, and soon was striding across the summit to Hurricane Ledge, where I found a scene quite different from prior visits. Today was a drama of clouds in motion. In the west, there was a smooth gray layer moving in high above the Devil's Path. In the east, a low-lying mass of white fog was working its way up the valley, emitting lazy tendrils. Suddenly the white mass erupted and a column of vapor shot upward a thousand feet. I stared in fascination, trying to understand the celestial fluid dynamics in play. Had the easterly gray flow sucked up the white fog in its wake?

On my next trip, it was back to Balsam and Eagle, with a secondary goal to spot new birds. All the usual suspects were calling, but not a single bird revealed itself. The binoculars hung across my neck unused the whole time, except when I discovered I'd left them behind at Balsam and had to run back a mile to retrieve them.

If the birds wouldn't cooperate, at least the spring plant people were easy to see: Canada mayflower, foam flower, star flowers, aniseroot, Solomon's plume, Virginia waterleaf, hooked crowfoot, a few boreal lilies in the shadows, and some chicken of the woods—a sulfurous yellow-orange shelf fungus—growing from the base of a tree. By this point in the Grid, identifying new species had become a preoccupation. On each trip, I'd take countless pictures, then once back home, pore through websites and guidebooks and sometimes reach out to knowledgeable friends to help identify them.

Later when I checked the spreadsheet, I found this was my twelfth climb for Balsam and Eagle. As far as the Grid was concerned, they were done. How sad . . . I'd grown so fond of them.

WILL AND DUSTIN REACH NEW YORK CITY

Meanwhile, Will and Dustin were making steady progress. A small community of Long Path enthusiasts followed and cheered for them online. On the final night, their pace slowed down considerably. Everyone watched with bated breath. As Will would later explain, after so many miles with limited rest, the "sleep monsters" had caught them and were messing with their minds. They slowed, but they did not stop. The next morning, I met them at the trail's southern terminus and became the first person to shake their hands and congratulate them on a marvelous performance setting a new record for the Long Path of 8 days 14 hours. Then I gave them a lift to Will's apartment for some much-needed rest.

It was sad to see my record fall, but I was pleased that my experience had inspired these young runners. Together we'd changed the world in a small but meaningful manner by showing what determined people can achieve.

CAUGHT IN THE NETTLES' KILL ZONE

Halfway through June, my goal was Halcott, but it was going to be at a torturously slow pace. A new and worrisome pain manifested in my left foot, not the ankle tendon, but at the base of the fifth metatarsal. It happened while I was running intervals at the track.

Odie took point while I brought up the rear using trekking poles to keep some weight off the injured foot. Bird calls rang out from the canopy. I pulled out binoculars and motioned Odie to be still, but he kept rustling around, anxious to be moving, exhibiting the runner's restlessness.

"You're scaring off the birds," I growled. He looked up at me with a dutiful expression but continued circling.

On the move again, it was a steep hike up before the slope leveled off, bringing us into contact with the day's first field of stinging nettles. I tiptoed through the hostile plants, swinging my poles about and whacking at the stems. For all their toxin-filled bristles, nettles are weak watery plants without a lot of backbone. They crumpled under my blows.

We gained the crest. Odie scouted ahead and found a faint passage through the fronds and canes, as if someone had recently trekked through this way. After a quarter mile, the bent vegetation coalesced into a social path, shepherding us to the summit.

For the descent, I chose a slightly different route, aiming to shave some distance off our journey. The slope turned steep. Odie bounded ahead while I tottered downhill on shaky rocks, still trying to keep weight off the sore foot. What a relief when the terrain leveled off. We were tramping along cheerfully when suddenly a dark-eyed junco dashed out from beneath our feet with one wing held off to the side, as if broken. Looking down, I spotted a small nest in a patch of blue cohosh, and inside two tiny orange featherless creatures squirming around, no bigger than jellybeans. What a clever mom, trying to distract us! "Stay away, you killer," I barked at Odie unnecessarily. He ran past without seeing them.

Nearing the valley floor, we found ourselves back in nettle country. With some irritation I discovered a compass error had taken us off course, resulting in an unwelcome extra quarter mile of moving through these unfriendly plants. I spotted a large fallen tree ahead, clambered on top, and teetered across this makeshift bridge as far as it went. Then there was no choice but to drop back to the ground. Resigned to my fate, I began whacking away for dear life, searching for some way out of the kill zone as waist-high nettles stung my naked feet and ankles and started poking through my pants. Odie came back to check and inadvertently blocked my swinging poles. "Get out of my way!" I shouted in desperation, the tops of my feet on fire.

Eventually we escaped. I stumbled upon a sprig of jewelweed, whose sap helped soothe the irritation. After 15 minutes, the sting was gone, but my embarrassment at having lost my cool and yelled at Odie remained. Worse than the nettles' sting, I reflected, was my own anxiety.

WE CANNOT SEPARATE OURSELVES FROM NATURE

Late June is the time for Manitou's Revenge, the 53-mile Catskill ultramarathon I'd run three years earlier. This year I was a volunteer helping at an aid station. I spent Friday stashing water jugs before heading off to bag Panther for the twelfth and final time.

By the time I reached the summit, the light had gone. I found a rock to sit upon, took a deep breath, and surveyed a ring of darkened peaks beneath squid-ink sky. After contemplating this scene, a random thought bubbled up: There's a voice inside my head that's always talking. This raises a question: If I'm the one talking, then who's doing the listening? Conversely, if I'm the one listening, then who posed this question? Upon further reflection, it seemed that the real "I" must be big, big enough to contain both talker and listener, and therefore big enough to contain everything I perceived, including the ring of darkened mountains in front of me.

I turned this idea around. Staring at mountains seemed at first no different from watching them on TV. Here I am and there they are, subject separated from object, just like we're taught in school. But out here, there is no TV. The "screen" is inside my head; it's a part of me. What I perceive as mountains must therefore be an *interaction* between outer world and inner. Put differently, subject and object are mixed together.

I don't consider myself an animist, but the mountains have always seemed so alive and full of meaning. This must be because my perceptions of the outer world are infused with my own energy and life. Which is why Schrödinger criticized science for "cutting out" the subjective sense of self. And why John Muir saw plants (and birds and insects, too) as people. "The whole wilderness seems to be alive and familiar, full of humanity," he wrote. "The very stones seem talkative, sympathetic, brotherly. No wonder when we consider that we all have the same Father and Mother."

Or as Burroughs put it, writing about saints and devotees who went into the wilderness to find God, "of course they took God with them, and the silence and detachment enabled them to hear the still, small voice of their own souls, as one hears the ticking of his own watch in the stillness of the night."

My "I" is not that which is stipulated on my driver's license. Rather I am the natural world, and everything contained therein, and my experience thereof.

We cannot separate ourselves from nature, Burroughs wrote, "any more than we can jump off the planet."

REDISCOVERING THE MAGIC OF CHILDHOOD

It had taken a lot of work, but the June Grid was nearly done. A few days before month's end, I climbed the path to the Devil's Acre lean-to, unrolled my bag, and drifted off to the sound of steady rainfall. I woke up in the middle of the night. The rain was over, but a monstrous wind was booming in the mountain and thrashing forest limbs.

The wind subsided the next morning. I rose, packed, and headed out to Southwest Hunter. Through the foliage I caught a peek of Hunter Mountain, fog rolling across its shoulder. Then a flash of sun broke through, and it became a clear breezy morning, although quite cool. Where sunbeams penetrated the canopy, I caught sight of my breath steaming.

I returned from Southwest Hunter, headed on to Hunter, and reached the horse trail leading down the mountain. A year ago, the gravel surface was too painful for walking barefoot, but this morning I sauntered along, stepping slowly where steep or rocky, striding out where the path was smooth. Perhaps it was tougher feet or better form or the right mindset, or perhaps it was such a beautiful cool clear day that anything was possible.

Around the next bend, a ragged-looking coyote trotting along looked up, spotted me, then vanished. A moment later, a ruffed grouse scurried across the trail, heading the opposite way. Had I interrupted something?

The next weekend was the last in June, and the last two peaks to climb were North Dome and Sherrill. On the way up Sherrill, I passed a patch of cow parsnip mixed with nettles (a vexing combination that can burn and sting), blue cohosh heavy with green drupes, wood sorrel with white and purple blossoms, tall meadow rue beginning to flower, and Indian hellebores yellowing away.

On the way down from North Dome, I discovered a diminutive waterfall where the stream splits in two, pours 10 feet down a ledge, and pools in a red-brown basin that reflects the tint of shale and fallen pine needles. I crossed a narrow wooden bridge over the creek and then cut through a field of timothy grass dotted with yarrow and red clover. Walking back to the car on pavement warming underfoot, I passed staghorn sumac with fuzzy yellow-green flower spikes and eastern tiger swallowtails fluttering about.

It was well after dark when I finally pulled into the driveway back home. A sweet, musky scent hung in the air, redolent of wild rose, honeysuckle, and autumn olive. The moon was hovering in the east, shimmering behind a sheet of haze, the shape and color of a tangerine. A warm dry breeze tussled an ancient maple, and suddenly I remembered how as a child, the summer evening wind rustling through the foliage had always seemed so magical. Here I was 50 years later, having finally figured out that nature is full of sentience and feeling.

Author, Will Fortin, and Dustin Smith on the shoulder
of Kaaterskill High Peak. June 4, 2018.

CHAPTER 27

AN UNCONVENTIONAL UNIFORM FOR SUMMER BUSHWHACKING

THE FORECAST FOR THE FIRST WEEKEND IN JULY CALLED FOR A HIGH of 96°F and plenty of humidity—such wonderful weather, such luscious conditions! This was the perfect time to drop gear, go light, and push the envelope on minimalism and simplicity.

This was also the time to savor the experience, for soon enough my sabbatical year would be over, and I'd be back at work in an office somewhere, unless I came up with a different plan. Recently, I'd gotten a phone call from a private equity partner who'd invested in my former firm. He wanted to talk about a different company in which he had a stake, one which had just gone public, where the share price had inexplicably fallen. He thought I was just the man to help them shape their story.

A few days later, I met the company's CEO for lunch in a posh Manhattan hotel. He was wearing a dark suit, a tasteful tie, and white earbuds and had a hungry look. The talk turned to basketball, which he'd played in college. I mentioned running. He told me to switch to indoor cycling because it was easier on the knees, said he'd set up a bike in his garage and spent hours there pedaling away at high intensity. I bit my tongue and nodded. For the right opportunity, I was prepared in principle to postpone the Grid, although it would have been a difficult decision. When he asked when I could start, I hemmed and hawed. To my relief, the conversation went nowhere.

The morning of July 1 was already steamy, the eastern sky the color of a peach, when I met Steve Aaron at the trailhead for Kaaterskill High Peak, which was on both our lists: number 13 for him and 360 for me. After parking on Clum Hill Road, we hoofed up to the abandoned Cortina Mountain Ski Area and passed beneath a rusted chairlift then through a forest gate. Steve took photos of distant peaks while I bent down to study a clump of dark green bulrush with spiky ball flowers turning brown. I spotted a patch of partridge berry crawling along the ground, sporting small white cross-shaped flowers growing in pairs (in due course, small red berries would appear with tiny twin navels where the flowers once were). A few steps later, I heard a splash, then another. These were leopard frogs, bright green with black spots. I bent down to scoop one up, but the squirming creature wriggled out of my grasp and splashed off in the muddy water.

From time to time a breeze rolled through the forest, but mostly the day was sticky and still. We reached the base of the scramble to the top, and here we found an oddly shaped birch tree guarding the approach, its trunk dipping down then turning up like the trap on a sink drain. It might've been a Native American marker tree, as it was their practice to bend saplings into these shapes to mark their routes, although most likely they had left this area long before this tree first sprouted.

We began the steep ascent. I went ahead. Halfway up, I heard a rustling in the trees. Thinking it was a bear I froze, only to discover it was Steve, smiling sheepishly (he had wandered a few feet off the trail).

Later that evening after Steve had headed for home, I hiked up Fir, nodding to the massive triple-trunked black cherry that I'd passed so many times before, and then it was on to the saddle below Big Indian, where I unrolled my sleeping bag for the night. This evening the wind was blowing steadily, cool air after warm day reminiscent of trade winds at the beach but smelling of damp earth instead of salt. Above me, a dome of beech leaves created a mosaic of green and gold, interstices filling with dim blue light. Then everything went dark.

The next morning, I woke to a hermit thrush singing loudly. After a cup of tea for breakfast, it was off to Big Indian, following the crest as it curled northwest. I navigated to Doubletop through beech saplings and hobblebush, past stands of fir, a small peat bog. Eventually I caught a glimpse of the summit through a gap in the foliage just a few leaves wide, a tiny corner of the spiky fir-clad ridge, while on either side holes between the leaves let in glimmers of clear sky where the summit's shoulders dropped away. From such clues, I formed an idea of the peak's location and then found my way there through the vast, tangled forest without referring to compass or GPS.

STUBBING TOES ON RUSK

A few days later, it was time to hit Bearpen and Vly for the eleventh and tenth times, respectively, and then off to Rusk for climb number 10.

It was another glorious summer day, hot and humid, temperatures in the '90s, which meant another steamy morning, the mountains indistinct in the haze and melting into the air. Today's goal was to mix in some running, so I charged up the hill to Bearpen, reflecting on how once upon a time this gravelly road felt so painful I almost couldn't walk it, but now here I was trotting along barefoot and feeling fine.

I jogged all the way back down to the saddle, and next I power-hiked and scrambled up to Vly. On the descent, I encountered three hikers coming up the trail, who introduced themselves as Tom, Steve, and Rick. Tom was close to completing his first Grid, Steve was close to completing his second Grid, and Rick was working on his third.

Later on, I'd run into Rick again, who by this point was nearly done with Grid three (35 x 12 x 3 = 1,260 ascents). Why so many Catskill peaks? It was the social aspect, he explained. Rick had begun feeding off his friends' enthusiasm and enjoyed helping them achieve their climbing goals. But three Grids, he thought, would be enough, there being many other adventures.

Inspired by this chance encounter, I trotted back down the mountain, loving the warm, damp, sweaty air, feeling exultant.

Next up was Rusk. I drove to the parking area at the end of Spruceton Road through a spray of rain. Exiting the car, the air was heavy and full of flies and gnats. I broke off a spruce branch and swished it around to keep the pests at bay. The familiar gravel path was painful, but there was only half a mile until it was time to step into the woods. Still full of energy, I started out aggressively, wanting to *run*—but almost immediately I stubbed a toe. A few strides later, this happened *again*, and now I was howling in pain. It was always the left foot where things went wrong for me, and then I stubbed a toe on the right foot even worse. There was nothing to do but shut my mouth, stop cursing, step slowly, pay attention. And then I stubbed the right foot again.

If there are many lines to toe in life, finding the line *between* the rocks would be among the most important.

Once at the summit of Rusk, I hung out for a bit and tried to pull myself together. A faint breeze stirred the canopy. A single large cumulus cloud drifted across the sky, as if towed on a line.

I crept back down the mountain, wincing with every step, feeling like an idiot.

MINIMALISM REQUIRES MINDFULNESS

A friend once remarked on the fact that I was running shirtless on a brisk winter day and carrying neither food nor water. He wanted to know why, if I was such a "minimalist," was I using a GPS? To which I replied that I didn't want to get lost. In other words, the point of minimalism is not to eliminate *all* technology, nor to produce an authentic paleo lifestyle in all respects. Rather, the minimalist subtracts one piece of equipment at a time, in order to measure the trade-off between benefits and costs. This attitude springs from skepticism about conventional wisdom and the suspicion that the modern world may have taken some wrong turns here and there, especially in the uncritical acceptance of new technologies. Harvard University evolutionary scientist Daniel Lieberman uses the term "dysevolution" to refer to the costly side effects of modern life that leave people worse off than our ancestors in certain ways. For example, the chronic ailments that result from wearing shoes, sitting in front of computers all day, getting insufficient exercise, and eating highly processed food. In my opinion, the worst side effect of modern life is a timid mindset that accepts dependence as the price to pay for comfort.

But if you're going to challenge conventional wisdom, you'd better pay attention. I thought of my poor banged-up toes and then recalled the trip to Halcott where I'd lost my cool in the nettles and yelled at Odie. It was the same problem in both cases—a failure to move with care and thoughtfulness. If you carry less gear, you need to be more mindful.

So now I came up with a special plan to practice mindfulness. The goal would be to travel through the forest's worst obstacles not only barefoot and shirtless, but also wearing shorts instead of trousers, this being the final step short of going buck naked.

NEARLY NAKED AMONG THE NETTLES

Kal Ghosh was looking for another adventure in the Catskills, and after a little hesitation at the unconventional mission profile, he agreed to come along.

We met up that Saturday at a parking spot on Spruceton Road and pointed ourselves toward Sherrill, but we started out veering slightly to the east, eager to take advantage of easy passage through an open field. What a shame, I thought to myself, to miss that pretty little creek, the one that tumbles over a ledge and pools in a basin of red shale and pine needles. That we were moving along the eastern side of this creek, instead of the western, didn't seem consequential.

A little later, though, something didn't feel right. This was supposed to be a natural navigation ascent, but I stole a peek at the GPS—only to discover that we weren't on Sherrill, but rather its neighbor, North Dome.

Oh, that little creek! The map showed it draining from a saddle between the two peaks. By taking the fields to the east instead of crossing into the woods in the west, we'd pointed ourselves ever so slightly off course, and from there the rule of up took over. This was a natural navigation fail, but also a valuable lesson in paying attention.

No harm done. We'd simply complete the loop in the opposite direction.

Ninety minutes later, we reached North Dome and signed in, noticing from the canister logbook that someone named Jake had been here earlier that morning. Then we took the social trail over to

Sherrill, where we found Jake sitting on a rock eating crackers. After introducing ourselves, Jake mentioned he was headed down the same way we were going and asked if he could get a ride back to his car, which was parked a mile or so farther down the road from ours. We were happy to accommodate him, but I warned him we'd be slow.

So far this morning we'd enjoyed quick progress, but now we struggled through fir-spruce thickets, groped our way through hobblebush, dodged beech branches, swished through waist-high ferns, stumbled on lurking tilting rocks, and, after following a level contour around the mountain's shoulder, plunged downhill straight into the dreaded nettles, at first growing dispersed among other plants, and then forming dense bands. Here was the chance to prove our mettle. Marshaling all our mindfulness, we steered for gaps between the nettles or tried to step among them where they were only ankle-high. We looked for places to wade through ferns and other plants and hopped across rocks and logs, anything to avoid brushing against the toxin-filled needles. It was very slow work, like moving through a minefield. Poor Jake should've walked to his car, it would've been much faster.

Our journey became somewhat desperate at times, and we suffered a few stings, but the irritation faded after a few minutes, as did the angst.

Eventually we made it back to the car and gave Jake a lift to his vehicle. Then Kal and I headed into Phoenicia for an early dinner.

Now it was time for phase two of this unconventional operation. We convoyed out to Moon Haw Road, where after a steep scramble, we reached a grove of hemlocks, our campsite for the night.

The next morning, we were awakened by a hermit thrush. Kal was charmed by the song, and while I too appreciated the bird, 5:00 a.m. is not my favorite time of day, and this thrush was quite boisterous. Without breakfast to slow us down or even a cup of tea (I brought the stove but forgot the pot), we were soon on the move, following the social trail up the ridge.

Today's challenge was to navigate through the fir-spruce thickets without getting scratched to pieces, and the art of this would be to follow the social trails gradually emerging in the area. An unmarked path took us to Balsam Cap, but on the way to Rocky it petered out, abandoning us among a crowd of spindly saplings. I veered south, probing for the route I'd stumbled upon during a prior visit, but no success. Until on the way back the southern route suddenly revealed itself. Not that any path was visible per se, but nonetheless it felt like I was being shepherded around the worst obstacles, while Kal, who was searching for easier passage a little to the north, got caught in a tangled mess. And then on the way down, it was Kal's turn to find the easy way, while I got stuck at the top of a cliff wishing I had a rope.

Back at the base, Kal said goodbye as he had to be at work the next day, while I headed out for phase three of this operation: Halcott Mountain, which, if I survived, would finish the Grid for July. I had barely enough energy to keep moving.

After parking on Shaft Road, I darted across the highway, lunged across a bone-dry streambed, and started groping up the steep embankment. Halcott has distinguished itself among its Catskill peers by attracting an especially dense concentration of blackberry canes. The young shoots aren't too bad, still green and pliable, although they might give you a nip as you brush by. It's the old monsters that cause problems, the thick purple canes bristling with shark teeth. I got trapped in a particularly virulent patch and began to regret my choice of uniform (still shirtless, shoeless, and in shorts). I reached out, grasped the stems delicately between the thorns, teased the canes apart, and tried to keep the small daggers from dragging across bare shoulders, chest, stomach, thighs, and calves as I squeezed through.

At this rate, the summit was a long time coming. By the time I reached the top two and one-half hours later, my resolve had wilted. Shoes went back on for the descent, and made quite a difference. Now I was practically running—only to find a quarter mile later it was the wrong direction. After catching this error, I navigated back across the ridge, finding my line down the slope by glimpses of alpenglow on the trees overhead and the ridge on the far side of the valley. I stomped upon the berry canes from above, crushing the stems and grinding them into the dirt with unrepentant glee.

The fast pace lasted until I regained the nettles. Mindful of exposed skin, I grabbed a fallen branch and whacked away, like a sword-wielding knight, until the branch broke in two, and now I held a dagger as I faced off against these waist-high foes. I tossed the stick away in disgust. After struggling through two or three bands of hostile vegetation, I was unscathed but for a sting on one calf, but thoroughly fatigued.

Reaching the hemlock grove in the dark, I rolled out my bag and called it a day. The next morning at 5:00 a.m. the cacophony returned, featuring another rowdy thrush, accompanied by an eastern peewee squealing *PEEEE-A-WEEE*. I heated my cup of tea (having remembered the pot this time) and stumbled back to the car.

Overall, the mission was a success, with six peaks bagged despite thickets, nettles, and berry canes. As far as gear, I was almost as naked as the other forest animals. The experience was a good reminder that there is often safe passage through even the worst obstacles, so long as you're patient and pay attention. It would also be fair to say I came away with renewed appreciation for shoes and trousers.

CHAPTER 28

BACK TO WORK

With the Grid already complete for August, I took a trip out West to visit places I'd never seen: Arches, Canyonlands, Capitol Reef, Bryce Canyon, Cedar Breaks National Monument, Zion, the Grand Canyon, and John Muir's temple of the wilderness, Yosemite National Park, where "every rock seems to glow with life." To avoid the crowds in Yosemite Valley, I walked in from a remote trailhead to the top of Yosemite Falls and peered unsteadily at the valley floor, 2,000 feet below.

Many years ago, John Muir stood right here. Seeking a closer view of the falls, he took off shoes and stockings and worked his way onto a granite ledge overlooking the torrent. There he spotted a three-inch niche of rock that would get him even closer. It looked quite dangerous. "I therefore concluded not to venture farther," he wrote, "but did nonetheless."

In contrast, I was content to study the falls from the safety of the trail, gripping a metal railing bolted to the granite so hard I might have bent it.

On my return, another big Catskills month was waiting, with 20 peaks for September and commitments on the calendar that would limit available time. So it was back to that fast-paced operational tempo where each trip started with a planning phase—identifying peaks, evaluating routes, establishing objectives, assessing risks, selecting gear—before making the drive north to the trailhead and finally the climb itself. I found it ironic that to experience the simple joy of nature seemed to require the same kind of organizational skills

I'd learned in the Army and practiced at work. But who's to say these skills aren't natural?

This morning the familiar drive north was a study in contrasts. Passing through the Shawangunk Mountains, I found the landscape in a wild mood, with goldenrod and loose strife painting the fields in hallucinogenic yellow-purple stripes, while crickets chirped and cicadas wailed in grand cacophony. When I reached the Catskills, however, the mountains seemed so serious. The sprawling green forests were silent, dark, and somber.

Steve Aaron met me at the Biscuit Brook trailhead. It was a cool, misty day, the trailside rocks beaded up with moisture, the leaves dripping. It was that time of year when tiny orb spiders were busy spinning webs, and as you groped your way through the woods, you collected thin strands on hat and shoulders and continuously brushed them off.

We walked in along the trail and once past the lean-to turned into the woods, with Steve leading us toward Fir's summit, following the tracks of prior visitors, including mine. I introduced Steve to some of the locals, including the triple-trunked cherry halfway up the hill. From Fir it was on to Big Indian, which was Catskills peak 16 for Steve and 372 for me.

We rested on the summit for a moment while Steve unwrapped a sandwich. With nothing to eat, I sat patiently on a rock and watched an inchworm descend along a strand of silk and hang motionless by my ear. It dropped level with my knee, paused for a moment, eventually reached the ground, and moved out. Then a smooth-skinned green caterpillar with a stripe on its back crawled by (prominent moth, probably).

Steve finished his lunch, and we headed back on the five-mile walk to the cars, at one point crossing an unnamed stream where the water rushed over a blood-red sandstone slab spotted with olive-colored moss. Steve, who is sometimes curious about my barefoot practice, asked if it was refreshing to splash across the stream. But I was thinking of the end of summer, the return of fall, and winter on the way. "No," I replied, "it's just cold."

After saying goodbye to Steve, I headed out that evening to Balsam Lake Mountain, walking the three miles in the dark on a path that seemed rockier than when I was here last. I was feeling slow and tired, but from time to time a faint breeze stirred the trees, and this motion was comforting, a reminder that nothing is static, everything is in flux. If my pace wasn't fast, the environment was in motion around me. There was enough relative displacement to sustain the feeling of forward progress.

The next morning it was on to Graham, where I crossed paths with a tiny toadlet as it hopped off into the leaf litter. Then I saw another one, and soon it seemed that dozens of these small creatures were darting across the path, and no doubt thousands or millions more were on the run throughout the forest. I wondered, was this the time of year when the moms give birth? And then a handsome caterpillar with black spikes sticking out of yellow fuzzy fur crawled over to introduce itself, an American dagger moth.

The last peak for the day was Vly. After driving over to the trailhead, I made the quick march up the familiar gravel road and then the scramble to the summit. A quiet pattering echoed in the canopy. A single drop hit my cheek. I saw in the canister notebook that three other Grid aspirants had signed in with their peak counts: 347, 348, and 379. I was now at 375. For a moment it felt like a race, and I wanted so fiercely to leave these competitors behind! But then I reflected; how quickly you can reach the finish depends on which months you need to fill, so running faster wouldn't matter. If all went well, the finish for me would be in December.

I hung out at the summit for a moment until thunder rumbled somewhere in the west. On the way back down, the mist cleared, the humidity dropped, a dry breeze filtered through the canopy, and the sun peeked out. Suddenly rain was crashing against the foliage. A moment later the sun was shining once again, even while the rain kept pouring. Then the rain faded. Flux, change, contrast, diversity—how I crave this in my life!

CLIMBING FRIDAY WITH RALPH AND KELLY

One week later, I met Ralph Ryndak and his friend Kelly on Moon Haw Road. Ralph mentioned this would be the *fiftieth time* he'd been up Friday. It would be my tenth.

Moon Haw Road was named for Chiefs Moon and Haw, Ralph explained, who conveyed the land to settlers in colonial times. Ralph theorized that the trail we were following had been used by Native Americans for trade between the Esopus and Neversink river valleys, the route through the mountains being considerably shorter than going around. Settlers might have used it, too, judging from an iron ox shoe he'd found along the path.

It helps to have a veteran guide. Ralph set a steady pace, and after a little more than two hours we were standing on Friday's summit, where we signed the logbook with his signature green felt pen. Ralph gestured to the surrounding forest and asked, "Isn't this the best therapy for your mind?"

I agreed. But taking it as a rhetorical question, I didn't reply out loud.

AUTUMN FOG IN THE MOUNTAINS

Fall is the foggiest time of year in New York. The average monthly temperature drops by seven degrees in September, while the average humidity rises by three percentage points. Yet the winds are calm, conditions conducive for the formation and persistence of fog.

On my next drive north into the mountains, I found fog blanketing the ground and obscuring the forests. To the north, there was a momentary break in the mist, and Kaaterskill High Peak popped into view.

Higher in the mountains, the air was clear. I saw long filaments of cirrus flowing through the upper atmosphere, the patterns reminiscent of braided streams or the motion of wild ponies cantering across the steppes.

I headed out for Blackhead at a slow-paced barefoot jog. I reached a northern vantage and looked out at remnants of radiation fog, which forms at night as the ground cools, now dissipating in the sun. Then fresh sheets of mist blew in and closed off the view. Past the summit, jogging where the path was level then dropping into Lockwood Gap, I passed so many familiar points, this being my twelfth and, for the Grid, final visit to the Blackhead Range. I sat for a moment on the ledge on Black Dome's shoulder and listened to the southerly wind pouring through the gap until I nodded off.

On the way back, dense clouds blew in from the south. The light faded, and my shadow grew indistinct. But there was much to study along the trail: maturing puffballs ready to burst in gray-green clouds of silky spores, wood asters and whorled asters and asters with blue and purple-tinged petals, snakeroot with tiny white flowers and lumpy black berries, tiger's eye and suede bolete fungus, and so many hickory tussock caterpillars squirming around on important missions.

Summer was ending, fall was nearing, the warmth was subsiding, the cold was approaching. Time was passing for me, too. Whether I'd run ultramarathons again was open to question, but it was such great fun trotting barefoot on these trails, even if at a pace barely faster than walking shod. Even if there were nothing else than this simple joy, the Grid would have been worthwhile.

WHY BAREFOOT?

People often ask, Why? One answer is that it's the natural way to move and should therefore pose less risk of injury than running in shoes. But the real answer is, "It's more fun." There's the sensation of light-footedness. The sensory connection with the environment. The feeling of adventure. Of course, it's not the case that every step is fun, but what I've found is that the joy of barefooting emerges from the intensity of the experience, and the intensity relates to the contrast between difficult surfaces (like gravel) and delightful ones (like moss). Shoes shield us from gravel, but when you step on moss, there is no pleasure. That's the trade-off implicit in many kinds of technology—you may go faster, but the experience becomes narrow and monotonous.

Take technology to the extreme, and one day perhaps we'll rocket through the forests in cyborg bodies. Wouldn't it be cool to never sweat or get out of breath? And why put yourself at risk when you could pilot a drone through the mountains from the safety of your sofa? You'd see the same wilderness, just streaming past through camera eyes. Even simpler, skip the drone, let someone else gather imagery, and explore the mountains in computer simulations (no risk of crashing an expensive device into a tree). Better yet, just admire the images on social media when they catch your eye, for this requires no concentration or effort.

Ecce homo—is this who we've become?

DO WE RUN TOO FAST?

Midway through September, with injuries having finally healed, I headed back to the track for a progression workout, the miles starting slow and gradually accelerating, until I was circling the blue oval at speed—posture tall, knees bent, calves relaxed—reveling in the wild exhilaration that comes from running without shoes. The new procedures (the color-coded entries in my training log) must have helped. After two years struggling with injuries, my log now showed all green.

So many runners are injured every year (upward of 90 percent by some accounts). Some of this risk is inescapable, as injuries happen to all living things. But the minimalist in me wonders how much of this is a case of Lieberman's dysevolution. Consider that we wear shoes to protect our tender soles, smooth out roads and trails to clear the way, carry food and water to keep us fully energized, and then there's the impatience that comes from living in a world full of clocks and the egotistical irritation from comparing ourselves with so many peers. Could it be that we injure ourselves by running faster than is natural?

CLOSING OUT THE SEPTEMBER GRID, ONE PEAK AT A TIME

It was time to climb Kaaterskill High Peak for the eleventh time. On previous visits, I'd wondered about a small tree with pink fruits growing on Hurricane Ledge. I reached out to Catskill forest expert Mike Kudish, who thought it might be a crab apple. He explained that many years ago, there was a dwelling on the summit; maybe someone tossed away a core. Now I took a tiny nibble of one of these pink fruits. Mike was right.

Over to West Kill, I encountered a golden-green patch of knight's plume moss flourishing on a rock, orange jelly fungus spotting a fir tree, a blob of scrambled eggs slime mold clinging to a yellow birch trunk, hickory tussock caterpillars in motion. From Buck Ridge Lookout, dirty yellow light in the west, clouds massing in the south with ragged gray underbellies. A little while later, raindrops probed the canopy. The descent turned dark, wet, and steep. It might've been pure misery, but I remained steady and resolute.

To finish the Grid for September, I volunteered at a Catskill trail race called Cat's Tail Marathon. My job was to stand at an aid station and write down the bib numbers of the passing runners. Suitable duty for someone with a career in financial analysis and a background in accounting.

As the race began to wind down, I turned in the clipboard and hustled off for a slippery 14-mile round trip that would bag me Wittenberg, Cornell, and Slide, the final three peaks for my September Grid. I'd forgotten to bring a light, so I kept my shoes on to ensure I'd get back before dark.

It was a sunny fall weekend, and the trails were crowded. A few runners were still on the course, trailed by the "sweeps" whose job is to keep an eye on the stragglers and make sure all participants are accounted for. Crowds of day hikers were hanging out on the summits, talking, lazing about, checking phones. Through the trees, glimpses of backpackers setting up and wisps of campfire smoke. As I made my way through the Woodland Valley Campground, I saw a father chasing his young son in circles around their tent.

All these people were experiencing the mountains in different ways. Once upon a time I might have looked disdainfully upon those who were moving slowly or out of breath. Or been critical of those who seemed unprepared. Or outraged by those who camped in illegal spots or left trash behind. But now it seemed to me that all of us were answering the same call. I'm sure John Muir would have approved of every one of them (maybe not those who littered).

John Muir in the High Sierra. Credit: Helen Lukens Gaunt, 1903.

CHAPTER 29

A LOST GOOSE

With the October Grid already complete, I was eager for a break. Instead of hiking, I did barefoot speedwork at the track and ran a five-mile road race and a half-marathon. After so much time spent injured, it felt like I was finally on the comeback trail. And barefoot racing was such a thrill, combining that special feeling of light-footedness with intense concentration (better pay attention to where you step!).

Midway through the month, I was reviewing my files, hoping to find a November climb I'd done at some point in the distant past but failed to document, which would reduce the load I faced next month. However, what I found instead—to my surprise and consternation—was an error in the spreadsheet. There were five peaks listed incorrectly for *October*, when photos and GPS tracks confirmed they'd actually taken place in *September*. Of course, sloppy record-keeping is always an embarrassment. Then I realized, with a shock, the October Grid was *not* complete.

CLIMBING SOUTHWEST HUNTER WITH MY INNER DAEMON

This time, on the familiar drive north, it was the dead leaves that caught my eye, tumbling through the air or swirling in circles. No fall colors this year to speak of. Sure, there were some sour red patches in the maples, but mixed in with green, as if the trees were loath to let their leaves turn color. And understandably so, for those leaves had provided so much energy for growth. What a shame to let these assets go and have them be dispersed by mindless winds.

Upon my arrival at the Diamond Notch trailhead, the car thermometer read 32°F. Not what I'd hoped for, but I stuffed my shoes in my pack anyhow and bundled up in extra layers. It was a slow start, with tilting rocks hidden under fallen leaves and cold soles sensitive to every bump and edge. Alongside the path ran a stream, its gently flowing currents mocking my halting pace and clumsy progress.

The trail passed a talus field of broken sandstone plates. This was not a good place to start climbing, so I continued walking, crossed up and over the saddle, and arrived a few steps later at a lean-to where a group of hikers was packing up. Strolling past in bare feet, I wished them good morning nonchalantly before stepping into the brush and beginning the climb toward Southwest Hunter's summit. Soon I was on all fours, grunting with exertion. The leaf litter was dense, damp, and dotted with spots of frost, and as my feet began to feel the cold, the grunts turned into growls of displeasure. Memories came to mind of that early barefoot adventure on Bearpen Mountain, when cold feet drove me out of the woods and back onto the trail. But now, while my feet weren't happy in the leaves, they didn't seem yet at risk. And there was no trail here to retreat to.

The slope turned steeper and more cluttered, forcing me to pick my way across tumbled rocks and snake through hobblebush and beech. A branch snagged my pack and hung me up, and the growls turned to groans of aggravation. This pace wasn't fast enough to generate body heat, and now the cold was affecting my feet, which were starting to go numb.

I crept past a sandstone block the size of a small truck, which must have broken off and skidded down the hill some 12,000 years ago, when the Laurentide ice sheet was retreating. Up ahead I saw a steep band of ledges, which looked like the block's point of origin, and a jumbled broken chaos at their base. Crawling through this mess was slow work. Soon I was howling with frustration because I couldn't move fast enough to keep my feet warm, yet I absolutely refused to put on shoes.

Emerson saw man as a "jet of flame." The Norwegian painter Edvard Munch had a similar impression of the human condition, writing in his diary, "We are flames which pour out of the earth." This while painting his modern masterpiece, *The Scream.*

Someone watching me storm along would have wondered what was up. Friends and colleagues would have been surprised, because they see me as thoughtful and mild-mannered. But they don't know about my inner daemon, the presumptive spirit of a long-dead scout, the one who always wants me on the move.

To some extent, I sympathize with the daemon's attitude, as no doubt he's disappointed he can no longer run. It may well be the case that the daemon's frustration is triggered by my disappointments— the injuries, screw-ups, disagreements, and various failures I've experienced. The scars that still hurt. And maybe, too, the daemon is provoked by my deepest fears of aging and decline, of slowing down and losing all those capabilities I worked so hard to develop, of losing passion and intensity, of losing everything.

It may well be that my daemon's frustration runs deeper than just my personal experience. Perhaps the daemon channels the accumulated fears and disappointments of a thousand generations of former scouts. Maybe it represents the frustration that all living beings must feel (in their different ways) when they fail to achieve important goals. If so, the daemon is merely another manifestation of the energy of life.

Meanwhile warning lights were flashing in my mind. The frost was getting deeper, the wind was picking up, and my feet were now more seriously at risk. I groaned and howled along—making almost as much noise as the wind—until suddenly I popped out on the broad flat mountaintop. Here I saw the sky winking through the trees on either side and felt my soles treading upon a strange mix of spongy needles and frozen moss. I strode a little faster and more quietly. My feet began to thaw.

I reached the canister, signed in, descended to the familiar Fenwick Lumber Railroad Trail and jogged off toward Hunter Mountain. Turning the corner past the lean-to, I slowed to a walk, when suddenly a hiker in a yellow jacket overtook me. Pleased with the quicker progress, the daemon had gone to sleep, and now my ego woke up and goaded me on, since it cheers like a small child when I pass people. I jogged all the way to Hunter, leaping across rocks, crunching through frozen mud, dodging columnar needle ice, all while trying to catch the hiker in the yellow jacket. But I never saw him again.

That was enough barefoot running for today, I decided, taking note of temperature, terrain, and muscular fatigue. I slowed to a barefoot walk. On the long descent from Hunter Mountain, the frozen mud gradually softened. The sun broke out once or twice, and those flashes of light felt so nourishing.

On the way back to Diamond Notch, I caught sight of a butterfly wing lying on the trail. Such a delicate mechanism with its stripes of orange, black, white—a reminder that the season has passed for these sparks of life.

I followed the trail back to the lean-to where I'd started the desperate climb, and then it was up and over the saddle, past a shallow groove in the ground, the starting point for the two creeks that roll down out of the notch on either side. Twelve thousand years ago, this groove would have been a thousand feet higher up, and the water would have been sawing through those sandstone ledges near the top where the truck-sized sandstone block broke loose.

The winds rocketed overhead as I descended from the realm of cold and ice, feeling like a pilgrim nearing home after a journey of many years. Slide, Cornell, and Wittenberg stood in the south, shimmering like sapphires, chanting of a promised land of calm and warmth.

BLOWN OFF COURSE

Two days later, I ventured out to West Kill Mountain, where halfway up the ridge I encountered a brant goose resting on a ledge. It was a large bird with a slick black head and neck and mottled brown body— not a species you'd expect to find at elevation. I tiptoed to within three or four feet of the mournful-looking creature before it flapped off down the trail.

Jim Bouton, the Catskill 3500 Club officer in charge of canisters whom I'd met on the way to Hunter the year before, told me he'd once encountered a flock of brant geese sheltering in the bushes between Doubletop and Graham. They'd gotten blown off course during a storm, he surmised. He didn't think they made it out. Nor would this one, probably.

And now, as I prepared for the final Grid hike of October, a nor'easter was inbound, with computer models projecting freezing temperatures on the summits, winds of 45 mph, and a heavy mix of snow and rain: perfect hypothermia conditions and increasing the risk of slipping on ice or getting caught under falling branches.

Not surprisingly, the Spruceton Road parking area was deserted when I arrived. Sitting in the car, sipping the last drops of coffee from a Styrofoam cup, I stared at a young beech whose green leaves were flapping furiously. The wind accelerated until the whole tree was rocking back and forth. Then the flow subsided, and the branches began to undulate with a gentle motion, like kelp leaves waving underwater.

Heading out along the trail, the winds roaring, a loud crack rang out somewhere. Turning into the forest undeterred, I marched underneath a fallen ash that marked the start of the social trail. Cottonwood leaves dotted the ground, heart-shaped, with ragged edges and still shining dark green, as if stripped from the trees prematurely.

In these conditions, the social trail was difficult to follow. With tread marks covered by layers of fallen leaves, it had become a ghost-path, visible only in the absence of obstruction. I groped my way up into a small col at 3,000 feet. The terrain steepened further. I zigzagged upward, stepping carefully on frost-slicked rocks. I passed a yellow birch with four stout trunks, which looked like a gnarled fist raised in protest against the heavens. Then I was up top slipping through frozen hobblebush and berry canes, pushing past crumpled blackened ferns while stepping through a scattering of icy debris. The wind tore through the trees with a sound like ripping paper. A huge wave of air crashed across the summit. Before it had tumbled past, another wave broke, and then it was still.

On the way down, sticking to my tracks where visible and checking the compass when in doubt, I recognized waypoints from the ascent: a grove of baby spruce, a dead sapling cracked and bent over in an arch, a flat rock that tilted up out of the ground when I stepped upon an edge. Here was a stout black cherry tree rising like a column to a height of 20 feet, at which point it had been decapitated—the rest of the trunk flung downslope, the fracture exposing fresh orange-brown wood ringed with yellow.

I passed through a cloud of green leaves tossing randomly in the mist. Tall slender maples were whipping back and forth, as if desperate to shake off their remaining foliage, which had now become an icy liability.

On to Plateau for the very last climb of the month. Once again it was cottonwood leaves that caught my eye, trees I'd never noticed growing so far above the valley (or were they some kind of aspen?). Here the young beeches were ice-coated, bent over, upper branches plastered to the frozen ground. It was silent until I reached the top. Then the wind sprang out from the forest and came hurtling across the ridge. A dead tree was waving violently, its broken top describing jerky ovals. I put on spikes to move faster in case I had to dodge falling branches.

I was thoroughly damp and chilled when I arrived back at the car, but overall, this had been a steady execution. Exactly what I was supposed to do.

As an aside, after I posted a picture of that brant goose online, a team of enthusiasts raced out to West Kill Mountain and rescued the bird. They took it to a wildlife rehabilitation center and gave it a name—Mooki Schmaltz.[6]

The rescue of the brant goose was good news. But the bird's close call was a reminder of the mountains' capricious nature, which puts even seasoned operators at risk. With October complete (this time for good), the count stood at 391, with 29 to go. Now winter was moving in for real, on silent haunches with claws unsheathed.

---

6 The name refers to Red Sox right fielder Mooki Betts and the Yiddish term for clarified poultry fat. The bird was later released back to the wild. See references for more information.

Mooki Schmaltz being rescued. Credit: Yanina Levchinsky-Grimmond.

CHAPTER 30

THE NINE, THE SIX, AND THE ONE

SOMETHING DIDN'T FEEL RIGHT.

As November drew near, one of my typical ambitious plans came together, involving multiple summits, long distances, an overnighter. I kept hashing through the routes, feeling increasingly uneasy. It took some time to clarify my thoughts before I could articulate the concerns: There was a race in a couple days that I wanted to run hard, a few twinges out of the left ankle that ought to be respected, and with my sabbatical year almost over, it was time to get serious about finding work.

Part of me would've liked to keep running in the mountains, as there was so much more to learn. There were flowers, birds, mushrooms, and insects to identify. There were patterns to appreciate in the rocks and streams and clouds. For every mountain, there were still a myriad novel bushwhack routes to reach the top. I'd already created the spreadsheet for a second Grid, populated with a handful of climbs redundant with the first. But would a second Grid be productive? Would family and friends support this project, or would they think I'd lost my mind?

THE WORLD DEMANDS PRODUCTIVITY

So long as we have energy, we must put it to work. Even John Muir settled down. He raised a family, wrote extensively, advocated for conservation, and managed the family orchard. He may not have cared about money much, but with a family to support he worked assiduously and was thrifty to the point of self-denial. In 1873 a friend visited him at his orchard and found him supervising the cherry harvest.

"Why, look at me," Muir said, "and take warning. I'm a horrible example. I, who have breathed the mountain air—who have really lived a life of freedom—condemned to penal servitude with these miserable little bald-heads!" (holding up a bunch of cherries). "Boxing them up; putting them in prison! And for money! Man! I'm like to die of the shame of it." Then he lapsed into his native Scots, "Gin it were na for my bairnies I'd rin awa' frae a' this tribble an' hale ye back north wi' me."[7]

When Muir died, his estate was valued at $240,000, which is more than $4 million in today's dollars, making him a successful small businessman on top of everything else he did.

It was October 31, and instead of hiking to a lean-to, I was sitting at home by the fire, ruminating about my career. In the last few weeks, I'd started talking with a company that needed someone with my skills. I liked the CEO, who'd built an impressive organization but seemed a humble man. The position was essentially the same as my prior job. Part of me hungered for a more important job, where I could play a bigger leadership role and have a more decisive impact. However, a bigger opportunity wasn't going to just fall into my lap. I'd recently met with a friend who'd made this kind of transition. He's a very organized fellow. His job hunt had entailed over 200 separate meetings. Furthermore, to succeed in this new role, he'd given up his passion for triathlons and switched instead to yoga.

The flames danced in the fireplace as I pondered this fork in my path. Eventually the fire died out, and I went to bed.

The next morning, after a good night's sleep, I drove off for the Catskills in positive spirits. At the trailhead for Balsam Lake Mountain, the register book fell open to a series of entries from April, and there was my name written on the page, as if my ghost were staring up at me.

---

7 "If it weren't for my berries, I'd run away from all this trouble and haul you back north with me."

Last time here, the rocky washed-out trail slowed me down, but today my bare feet twisted around the stones and rolled over them with hardly a complaint. If the pace wasn't fast, it was steady and comfortable, as so many familiar points streamed by.

The air was still, the leaves were wet, and dense mist limited visibility to just a few yards. But there were many small things to see: flickers of cinnamon sprouting on the deadfall (crowded parchment and crimped gill fungus); thin brown stems poking up through damp leaves (beech drops growing parasitically from beech tree roots); hooded tube lichen with soredia clustered in a froth on the wavy margins of pale green lobes.

This morning, I studied the rocks. Red clay and mudstone were everywhere. In one spot there were paper-thin flakes of red shale. Toward the top, the trail was lined with gray sand, pebbles, and pieces of conglomerate so coarse-grained they crumbled apart in my fingers.

Those 10 miles were so joyful and interesting, but the next morning I woke up feeling nervous—17 peaks still to go.

THE LAST OF AUTUMN

Once again, I was in the car racing north, this time headed for Peck Hollow and planning to repeat the circuit of North Dome and Sherrill I'd done with Philip the year before. It was another dark, overcast day, with temperatures in the low 40s. Soon I was climbing up through hemlocks and into oak, passing large sandstone ledges with thin cross-bedded layers, getting a few glimpses of the neighboring ridgeline before the mist closed in. Then it started to rain. My naked feet were wet and cold, and the crowds of saplings were irritating, but I pushed through. Around 3,000 feet the oak faded out, and I found myself in a grove of beech with shriveled leaves still sallow green, as if the leaf flesh had perished before the color had the chance to change.

Reaching North Dome without map or compass, I signed in, noticing from the logbook that Jim Bouton had been here the day before. Then it was on to Sherrill along the familiar social trail. A golden-crowned kinglet skittered along the forest floor, the yellow stripe on its head standing out in the mist. On Sherrill, I picked up two red kerchiefs someone had left behind and a deflated mylar balloon, which must have floated up from somewhere in the civilized world. Down Sherrill's backside, past the mystery bus looming in the mist, I was now skipping down that marvelous forest road with such wonderful momentum! But the final leg had me dropping down a steep slanted rocky slope, and this resulted (predictably) in a little grumbling (I refused to put shoes back on) and a couple of growls, especially now that I was thoroughly wet and cold. I kept it together (barely), discovered the thin wavy varnished plates of golden curtain fungus and an antique teakettle half-buried beneath a fallen ash.

On the dark, rainy drive home, the oaks were glowing in subtle colors: cordovan, cinnamon, port. By the side of the road, a splash of yellow—a solitary maple sprouting like a dandelion.

Four days later on the next drive north, the sun was flickering fitfully, but soon enough dirty gray layers unfurled across the sky and crushed the light. The roadside foliage was thick with oak, the colors latent in the landscape yet still nourishing to the eye, while here and there scarlet saplings glowed like embers in the ashes.

On the way up Bearpen, I stepped upon blue-green sandstone fragments stained dusty red. A brief shower of frozen rain caught me on the trail, the pellets bouncing off my shell. On the return, I stole through an open forest with trunks covered in a tapestry of tawny moss. Blue mountains sauntered under dead gray sky. High above, the wind raged about at random.

On the way to Vly, another shower of frozen rain clattered against the trees. During the descent, I got a clear view of the rounded shoulder and smooth brow of modest Bearpen. Not one of the Catskills' flashy peaks, it is not particularly high, boasts no scrambles or boreal fir-spruce thickets, has a summit that is broad and indistinct, and a graded gravel road leads all the way to the top. Yet, from this angle, the mountain had an air of quiet contentment, as if it were satisfied with its modest profile and did not aspire to be more than what it was.

Heavy drops began to strike against the forest floor as I marched back to the car. On the drive out, gold flashes in the hills—larches singing the end of fall.

The next day an errand took me into New York City, and then there was a meeting in New Jersey, and now the GPS was taking me through rush hour traffic on a complicated, unfamiliar route. I felt my inner daemon begin to stir. *Calm yourself, daemon! Think of this as just another obstacle on the way to our next peak.*

It's interesting how I never recognized my daemon until I started spending so much time outdoors. Feelings of frustration, and some of the underlying disappointments that trigger them, are surely natural. But those feelings are difficult to express around other people without creating a toxic situation. With friends and family, I choose my words with care and often bite my tongue. And the daemon stays out of sight. But the feelings don't go away. Instead, they pool in the basement of my mind, become a part of that malaise I associate with the indoor world. Whereas it's so much simpler in the forest. If I step on an unfriendly rock, I can clench my fists and shout so loud the birds fly off, and then I feel much better.

A CELEBRATORY CLIMB

Dick Vincent, founder and director of the Escarpment Trail Run, is a local celebrity and arguably the father of Catskills trail running. On Saturday, November 10, he planned to complete the 35 by climbing Doubletop. A group assembled to accompany him and celebrate his accomplishment, including Amy Hanlon, Mike Siudy, and many other friends. With his 35-mm slung over one shoulder, Steve Aaron was there in the capacity of official photographer for the expedition.

On the journey up, we got caught in a brief whiteout, and soon an inch of crunchy powder had accumulated underfoot. But a steady pace saw us through. Drinks and party favors were passed around at the top, while Dick posed for a ceremonial photo, dressed now in cape and crown.

From here I said goodbye to the group, which was returning the way it came, while I headed east toward Big Indian across the intervening saddle. Crunchy snow, flashes of sun, and so many familiar cheerful sights, like a sandstone boulder coated with droopy rock tripe lichen the size of dinner plates. Passing precisely through the saddle, I steered a little north to bypass the band of ledges that guards the ridge. I oriented myself east again by checking that the sun, which hung in the south, was on my right-hand side. I looked for lines of moderate grade, stayed below the beech-fir boundary until flickers of light through the tangled branches indicated the crest was just above. My navigation was perfect.

Halfway through the month now, there were 11 peaks left, including the daunting bushwhack loop that comprises the Nine. Once again, an ambitious plan—to complete the Nine in a single circuit. Once again, a coastal nor'easter inbound, projections pointing to a foot of snow. It was bad enough in New York City, where a couple of inches knocked down branches and brought traffic to a halt. So I had to hatch a new plan to break up the Nine into smaller pieces.

First, I knocked off Slide in snowshoes. A day later the path to Wittenberg was well-tramped, allowing me to get by with spikes. After warming up, I stripped off shirt and jacket and enjoyed bracing air across my naked chest and shoulders, following the path as it hugged a spur and then circled around the mountain's southern shoulder. Glancing behind me, I was startled by an iconic Catskill landscape: Panther standing prominently in the center while the surrounding peaks were cast in cobalt blue, the color of a Chinese vase or Persian tile, as if a blue jay of titanic size had risen from the valley and spread its massive wings across the sky.

The trail scrambled up Wittenberg's eastern knife-edged ridge and eventually reached the summit ledge. On the way to Cornell, fir and spruce crowded the trail and showered my bare shoulders with bits of snow. The Cornell Crack was choked, the rocks above ice-varnished; getting up was an ordeal. The trail ended at Cornell. No one had been between here and Slide since the recent snow.

I turned about and jogged all the way back. After five hours shirtless in subfreezing temperatures, my forearms had turned a dull red. It was a minor challenge for my cold fingers to sign out at the register and turn the key in the car door lock. But I made it home.

GOODBYE, INNER DAEMON

Midway through the month, I was driving north through the Shawangunks, alongside fields draped with advection fog, which is produced by warm air blowing over snow-covered ground. By the time I reached the highway, the world had turned opaque. An hour later I arrived in Deep Notch.

With a foot of fresh snow, today was going to be Halcott in slow motion. Looking about the empty forests, for the first time I recognized that two spurs descend from Halcott's summit, with a creek draining from between them. Keeping to the northern spur, I labored uphill through the powder. It was agonizingly slow. My inner daemon began to seethe.

I suppose everyone has some kind of daemon. I don't know how other people manage theirs, but I decided I'd heard enough complaining. Indeed, I was beyond fed up with its churlish attitude. I felt like shouting, *JUST SHUT THE F*** UP*. Instead, I inquired, in a voice dripping with sarcasm, "What *precisely* would you like me to do?"

There was no answer.

Evidently it had nothing constructive to suggest.

And that was, incidentally, the last time I've heard from it.

Signing in at the canister, I found that Mike Siudy had left a message in the logbook. Halcott was his nine-hundredth Catskill peak, "but who's counting?"

AN ILL-CONCEIVED OPERATION

With Slide, Wittenberg, and Cornell complete, the Nine had been whittled down to the Six, and this was all that was left for the November Grid. I drew up plans to do them all at once and invited Alan Davidson to join me. Then, on a whim I offered up an aggressive option—we could climb Balsam Cap from Breath Hill, the route we'd meant to follow during our natural navigation failure in the rain the year before. A couple of days later, computer projections indicated 7 to 10 inches of fresh snow were on the way, and the aggressive option began to seem a little questionable.

In any case, I was looking forward to catching up with Alan as we rendezvoused at the trailhead. But deep snow and steep grade required total concentration. Hardly a word passed between us as we struggled upward.

It was a long way to Balsam Cap. We climbed "out of breath hill" first and almost made the same mistake we did the time before (but today we checked the compass and GPS frequently). Then we crossed a small saddle to Hill 2035 and next ascended Hill 3088, where we started to hit thick stands of snow-crusted fir and spruce. We fought our way to Hill 3446, and yet we were still a couple hundred feet below the top. On the map this route had looked so alluring as it curled along a sinuous line of cliffs. But on foot we saw nothing but snow-covered branches crisscrossing our field of vision and a maze of snowy trees.

I'd warned Alan that upon reaching Balsam Cap, I'd face a difficult decision. The plan required a detour north for Friday Mountain before we'd turn south to bag the other four peaks, but there'd be a strong temptation to skip that detour if conditions were unfavorable. On the other hand, if we skipped it, I'd need to make another trip for Friday, and the month was almost over.

As we slogged through deep snow, I began having problems. My Gore-Tex shell was leaking, my legs were damp, feet wet, gloves soaked, hands cold. It occurred to me that here I was on top of a mountain in the middle of nowhere, with little else in my pack besides a tarp.

Friday would have been a bad idea, but how I dreaded making another trip to this desperate ridgeline. "Strive to still the mind" was Krishna's advice to Arjuna, but that's hard to do when your mind's screaming, *Your plan is really bad!*

Conditions were so difficult that there was no real choice. Abandoning any thought of Friday, we banked south and plunged down the ridge toward Rocky, and it became an afternoon of ups and downs. I grumbled when a huge fallen tree forced a workaround, groaned with irritation when a stand of saplings barred the way, yelped in dismay when a snowshoe caught a rock and I toppled over in the snow. But in between these aggravations, there were strange little gifts: A sideways glance revealed a passage through the tangles, behind the saplings a small clearing let us move a little faster, a smooth line appeared across a rugged slope, and then a helpful chute appeared between big slabs.

It was dark by the time we finally reached Table and stepped back onto a blazed trail. I noticed one of my spikes had come unclipped and was now lost. Struggling to close my shell, I ripped the zipper off. My gloves were sopping wet, and my fingertips had lost sensation; they felt disturbingly as if they were swathed in cotton.

We had bushwhacked almost 10 miles through some of the Catskills' most difficult terrain in atrocious conditions. But now that we were finally headed back to the cars, time no longer mattered. I strolled along feeling mellow, holding fists in armpits to keep my fingers warm. Alan, who'd been steady as a rock all day, now raced ahead, as if eager to escape. It was the first time I'd ever seen him in a rush.

Back at the cars, I apologized to Alan for involving him in such an ill-conceived operation. Later, he'd tell me that after several weeks on the road, this trek was more arduous than he'd expected.

BACK TO FRIDAY, NO ROOM FOR ERROR

The next day I had a headache and my fingertips felt prickly, as if I'd been handling sandpaper.

The November Grid was done, except for Friday. But there were only two days remaining in the month to get this last peak done. Otherwise, completion of the Grid would be pushed out for a full year, the thought of which was beyond unbearable. Yet the outlook seemed fraught, as this climb would represent the intersection of me—feeling weak and battered following the misadventure with Alan and intimidated by tough conditions—and unsympathetic nature.

Hoping for some support, I reached out to Ralph Ryndak to see if he could guide me. He knew Friday so well that once when rangers were searching for a missing hiker, he made an off-the-cuff suggestion, and that's where they found the body. But he wasn't available to accompany me.

To increase the odds of completing Friday solo and surviving, I drew upon the organizational skills I'd honed during my military-corporate career. To start with, I drafted a five-page operation order which included risk assessment, mitigating strategies, time schedule, route plan, and equipment list. I studied the map, memorized headings, distances, and elevations for each leg of the route, and identified escape routes in case I got into trouble. Then I laid out, inspected, and tested all my gear.[8]

November 29 dawned with a spooky red glow. At the Moon Haw trailhead, the snow was soft and deep. I headed out at a measured pace while the wind gusted violently, whipping treetops and kicking up white clouds. The climb went as smoothly as could be hoped for, although the ramp was hard to find in the snowy tangles. On the final scramble, I hoisted myself up a ledge, snowshoes flailing against the rocks, then had to squirm underneath a dense spray of fir branches. I kept muttering to myself that this isn't what runners are supposed to do. By the time I reached the canister, I was exhausted.

On the descent, though, my spirits improved when I came face-to-face with a young porcupine sitting in a fir tree chewing on a clump of needles.

Four hundred and ten Grid-qualifying ascents were complete. There were 10 to go, and two days until December.

---

8 The operation order is in Appendix D.

CHAPTER 31

THE FINAL ASCENT

So MANY PEAKS, SO MANY EXPERIENCES. WHEN I REFLECTED ON THE enormity of what I'd undertaken, images of the mountains streamed through my thoughts in faster and faster succession, until I felt as if I'd passed through a portal to an alien world and was now gliding across a darkened landscape under flickering neon skies.

There were 10 climbs left to complete the Grid, but at the same time, life was morphing. I'd made my decision: I took the job with the company whose CEO I liked. I'd discussed this decision with Sue, and she thought it was the right move. Even if the role didn't offer the authority I sought, it would be a chance to sharpen my skills while still leaving some time in my life for mountains.

INSIDE THE SCENE AND PART OF IT

The new job brought my sabbatical to a close one year and two days after it began. Monday, December 3, would be my first day at work, so I hustled to get the December Grid kicked off on Saturday the first. With so much going on, my intention was to execute the final peaks with ruthless efficiency—nothing long, nothing complicated, and nothing new. But an idea popped into my head of climbing Big Indian from Burnham Hollow, which was a novel bushwhack route too interesting to ignore. So there I was on Saturday morning, moving stealthily past some homes in a gated community, checking my phone map frequently, and staying out of sight.

Once on the far side of a creek, a forest road made for faster progress, and soon the homes were behind me. I paused for a moment and looked to the south, where a valley lay in shadow, flanked by massive mountain walls. Up above, brilliant sunlight frothed against the ice-glazed forest. It poured through a notch, arced across the valley, splashed in the snow by my feet. That notch was the saddle between Fir and Big Indian. Six or seven times I'd passed that way, and once I'd camped there, always wondering what lay down below. Now for the first time, I was down below looking up.

I followed the forest road deeper into the valley until it petered out. It was time to buckle on snowshoes and make a choice, as the map showed two potential routes up to the frosted ridge. I studied the tiny wiggling contour lines on my phone, then looked up at a massive spur soaring out of shadows. The terrain seemed impossibly steep. So I went that way.

It was hard work. I kicked one step into the snow after another, pulled myself up one small ledge after another, until my heart was racing from the effort and I had to pause to let my breathing settle down. Then it was up and over a steep knob and out of shadows and into sun-warmed snow that was turning soft and heavy. There was an equation to solve, whose inputs were steep terrain and heavy snow. The solution: a very slow pace. This was fine with me because I knew that, in a sense, this climb would never end, which implied that I had all the time in the world. I became a ghost and floated up the spur and materialized on the summit of Big Indian, the last mile having taken three full hours.

Now I began descending into the saddle between Big Indian and Fir. I pushed through a snowy matrix, a tangle of stems scraping against my shell. An inch of snow lay on every branch, while hanging from the underside of every twig were quarter-inch tendrils of rime ice inclining to the east. Sunlight flooded the forest and flashed upon crystal grains uncountable.

Five years ago, almost to the day, I'd stood high in the Shawangunk Mountains, braved the wind-blast, looked north, and contemplated a distant mountain wall shimmering in bands of blue and white. I thought I heard a call emanating from those peaks, although it sounded more like a warning to stay away than an invitation to come higher. Now, five years later, here I was inside that scene, becoming a part of it. And those colors have taken on for me a special meaning.

White is the color of ice but it also signifies the pure flame with which our passions burn, while blue, the color of water, connotes regret for what we tried but could not do.

RUNNING AS ATTITUDE

It was exciting to take on a new mission. During the first two weeks at work, I ran around trying to figure everything out, then lay awake at night, mind racing. The job entailed frequent travel, which would mean less time in the mountains, although it occurred to me that it made no real difference where I was, so long as there was a chance to make a difference.

One morning, I was driving to the office through endless corporate sprawl, rows of boxlike structures ringed with sidewalks that no one ever seemed to walk upon. Strangely, this scene reminded me of the alluvial fans that wash down from the mountains in Death Valley. Both landscapes share an air of random emptiness and inhospitality. I'd endured the desert, and I would manage myself through this sprawl, too. I wondered, could running and corporate work be considered the same activity, just taking place on different kinds of paths?

I've never minded running through the night (although the second sleepless night in a row gets difficult due to hallucinations), whereas I find working all night at a desk much harder. But I've had colleagues who thought nothing of it. You could say they were running with their brains, if not their legs. You could say that running isn't so much a gait as an attitude, a sense of purpose, a willingness to undergo discomfort and take on risk. "Now bid me run, and I will strive with things impossible, yea, get the better of them," exclaimed Ligurius, when Brutus approached him with a risky proposition.

That weekend I ran a half-marathon. The asphalt was cracked and gritty, necessitating a tentative pace, but as my bare soles became accustomed to the surface, I ran a little faster and began to pass other runners. Mindful of my ankle, I kept to a responsible pace. But with the finish line in sight, a young man tried to overtake me, rousing my competitive spirit. Ever so gently, I nudged the throttle forward . . . and then I tapped the afterburner—and *wow*, what a thrill, dropping him decisively, despite bare feet on rough pavement and so many extra years! But there was a price to pay. After crossing the finish line, I limped off the course, poor ankle throbbing.

"As we age, speed is the number one cause of injury," warns Olympian Jeff Galloway, who is perhaps the running world's best-known coach and ambassador, and who continues to run marathons well into his 70s. He warns about older runners who listen to their egos. Did he have someone like me in mind?

I wonder if it's even possible to control your ego. Consider the fact that I am generally quite constructive when posting on social media, which is to say I generally bite my tongue instead of hurling insults. What this means, of course, is that I've learned to manage my ego more effectively than most other people—which, come to think of it, seems like pretty convincing evidence of my moral and intellectual superiority. (You see, the ego is a slippery customer. You may think you're managing it, but possibly that's just how it wanted you to feel.)

In any case, it would be a mistake to reject the ego, were that even possible, for it's a source of enormous energy. Meaningful, notable, distinctive, and worthwhile tasks often contain a touch of egotistical pride, and there's nothing wrong with this provided you manage the ego's contribution. Don't let it drive you off the proverbial cliff. Don't let it become your inner Lady Macbeth and talk you into bad ideas. For aging runners, it's not a question of giving up on speed, but rather finding the *optimal* speed, the pace that balances goals and risks. Think of it as just another line to toe, but one that shifts with the years.

THE PHILOSOPHY OF TRYING HARDER

Sometimes I'd think to myself that instead of trying harder maybe I should try running *smarter*. But there's a catch; it's hard to be smart. Indeed, it often seems that most everything worthwhile is hard. So spend your energy on raw physical power (think muscular torque and wheezing breath as heart rate maxes out), direct it into calculations (strategy and planning, just like at work), or structure your thought processes (monitor function of body and mind as you manage through discomfort). Light up the moment with an all-out effort. Spend your energy thoughtfully. Precisely. Mindfully. But whatever you do, spend it. Because you can't store the energy of life, and you can't take it with you when you leave.

Try. Hard. Try. Harder.

And you may find, from time to time, that you are rewarded with a moment of stillness.

GOODBYE, PATHLESS RIDGE

My new job took me out of town on a business trip, and by the time I returned, it was halfway through the month with eight peaks left to complete the December Grid. Eights peaks left to finally put to bed this mountain-sized project that had taken over my life. Once again, I'd somehow saved the most difficult for last, for next up were the six peaks on the desperate pathless ridge, the ones Alan and I had tangled with just three weeks earlier. Once again, computer models were projecting difficult conditions: five inches of snow at elevation. Saturday morning, I stared out the window at steady rain and felt, once again, a sense of dread.

This time, however, the Six went smoothly. Along with me were Aaron Anaya, who'd joined me three years ago on the Winter Eight, and Dakota Inman, whom Odie and I'd met on Eagle. Starting from Moon Haw, the unmarked trail to Friday was tramped down and crusty. Offering solid walking with good traction, it took us up the ridge along a catwalk I'd missed the time before, brought us straight onto the ramp, and then weaved up to the canister along the easiest lines.

From Friday, the trail shepherded us on to Balsam Cap before fading out. As we donned snowshoes, I reminded Dakota and Aaron that "slow is smooth, smooth is fast," and then the forest opened and let us through. It was remarkable—it was a gift.

Dakota was delighted. An experienced Adirondacks hiker, he was still new to the Catskills and appreciated the company. Aaron was happy, too, as he was working on the four seasons challenge, a precursor to the Grid, which entails climbing the 35 high peaks in each of spring, summer, fall, and winter.

On Lone Mountain, we found a message written in the canister logbook: "Happy birthday to me, happy birthday to me, happy birthday to meee—I'm done with Grid three!" Later on, Jim Bouton, who'd once counseled me that "there's no rush," would confess that finishing his third Grid on his birthday sounded like something he might do.

And now there were two peaks remaining.

GOODBYE, DOUBLETOP

The morning of December 21, 2018, Odie sensed something was afoot. He was running around in circles barking, then jumped into the car unbidden. Today was another of those unseasonably warm winter days with temperatures in the 50s and one to three inches of rain in the forecast, possibly heavier at elevation. You'd think by now these climbs would be routine, but there was nothing casual in my attitude. Odie would come another time.

On the drive north, the Esopus Creek was swollen, choppy, turbid, the waters colored bright red-brown like the wilted knotweed along the banks. The Catskills are composed largely of "red beds," as the geologists call them, full of clay and sand that washed down from the Taconic Mountains three hundred million years ago and the source this morning of the fine red silt suspended in the Esopus's angry currents. From here the red waters would drain into the Hudson and Delaware Rivers and empty thence into the Atlantic, where the Catskills' final mark may well be faint red swirls on the lightless ocean floor.

Leaving Odie behind was the right call because today the Dry Brook was raging out of control. In one spot the trail was flooded knee-deep, and the two tributaries that cross the path were rushing too hard to wade through, forcing me to detour upstream and commando crawl across a fallen tree. After that, it was a slow, steady, snowy walk to the top, where I signed in on the canister logbook with my name and the number 419, and then wandered down the ridge, orienting myself by glimpses of the surrounding mountains and sounds of rushing water on either side. Such a kindly gentle ridge, such a nice way to say goodbye.

THE GRID AS PERSONAL TRANSCENDENCE

Driving home that evening, I reflected on how I'd followed a lot of footsteps—those of Muir and his contemporaries, the older philosophers who'd inspired them, and my fellow runners, hikers, and Catskill lovers. But eventually the footprints faded out, and I headed in a direction unique to me. Here I was now driving in darkness, as the wipers flicked back and forth in metronomic rhythm.

Emerson wrote that the pursuit of life should not be "by any known or accustomed way; you shall not discern the footprints of any other; you shall not see the face of man; you shall not hear any name;—the way, the thought, the good shall be wholly strange and new."

I mulled over this experience, and specifically how my practice of running had morphed so radically while working on the Grid. I started out as a conventional-minded runner, and by the end I'd gone so minimalist I was nearly as naked as the animals (in the summer, anyhow). This transformation was partly due to age and injury, which forced a slower pace, but it also seemed to me that it was a natural outcome of spending so much time outdoors. When I looked upon the mountains, I felt excitement, exhilaration, wonder, awe, and curiosity. And the small things in this wild world—the moss and lichen, the butterflies, the colors vibrating in a faded leaf, the sour taste of a mountain ash berry, the scent of a sprig of spruce, the way the water in a stream poured over the rocks and pooled—these sensations gripped me so intensely. By following where feelings and sensations led, I'd let the mountains become my teachers. Or as Walt Whitman put it, "Now I see the secret of the making of the best persons, / It is to grow in the open air and to eat and sleep with the earth."

The word transcend comes from the Latin "trans," across, and "scendere," to climb. In a sense, the word means to cross the next mountain range. It's not hard to picture our distant ancestors staring at a range of peaks, wondering what they would find in the next valley. Assuming they could find a pass through the intervening stony wasteland.

In a more general sense, self-transcendence is the idea that we could become tomorrow, in some way, better, stronger, happier than we are today. Or as my boss used to joke when talking about the typical corporate year-end performance review process, how everyone's evaluation was essentially the same: "Do better now."

Emerson, Whitman, Thoreau, Burroughs, Muir, and a handful of other philosophers are remembered today as the American transcendentalists. They believed that nature was the path to transcending ego and time. The path to stillness. Mindfulness. Full mind-body engagement, which is how we're supposed to operate. They believed that nature was the antidote to dysevolution in all its morbid forms—sickness, weakness, depression, distraction, and loss of agency and purpose. Thoreau saw the downside of civilization in the "quiet desperation" of his sedentary contemporaries, while Emerson railed against conformity, timidity, anxiety, and toxic egotism. And Whitman was blunt, warning students, clerks, and those employed in sedentary and mental employments that "all study, and no developed physique, is death."

The transcendentalists are still remembered, but the popular narrative has moved on. *Transhumanism* embodies a very different mindset, the hope that we will overcome our limitations by merging with technology. But will this work? When we spend our lives sheltering indoors, hunched over devices, not only sedentary but nearly motionless, will we lose a portion of that natural strength, both physical and spiritual, which makes us fully human?

To achieve happiness, flow psychologist Csikszentmihalyi writes that people must learn to "impose structure on conscious thought processes," that is, to "achieve mastery over consciousness itself."

When we are left alone, with no demands on attention, the basic disorder of the mind reveals itself. With nothing to do, it begins to follow random patterns, usually stopping to consider something painful or disturbing. Unless a person knows how to give order to his or her thoughts, attention will be attracted to whatever is most problematic at the moment; it will focus on some real or imaginary pain, on recent grudges or long-term frustrations. Entropy is the normal state of consciousness, a condition that is neither useful nor enjoyable.

Pam Reed, the ultrarunner who cautioned about extreme running, makes a similar point. In her mind, "I'm not really running 100 miles, I'm running 1 mile 100 times." She characterizes this state of mind as a form of "self-hypnosis," which takes real mental toughness and self-discipline to achieve. She often sees young runners struggling because they can't find the patience or perspective, they get intimidated by the distance, or they get bored and turn negative— and their feet stop moving.

Csikszentmihalyi and Reed speak from different disciplines, but their messages share much in common with the transcendentalists: The good life requires a strong mind. Which is our birthright, passed down from ancestors who lived before modern technology. To access this strength and the energy that comes with it, I would echo Muir, with a small edit—when the mountains call, we must run.

Let nature inspire you. Let the mountains teach you. Learn to run like John Muir did, when the spirit seized him, just as he did as a child, recalling, "to improve our speed and wind, we often took long runs into the country." In Yosemite, he ran "in the moonlight with firm strides; for the sun-love made me strong." He ran down a talus pile "without any haggling, puttering hesitation, boldly jumping from boulder to boulder with even speed." On the Alaskan shore when a wild storm came blowing in, he ran out "against the rain-laden gale," only to see the minister's little dog, Stickeen, at his heels; then together "we ran ahead joyfully over smooth, level ice" and then he ran "anxiously" upon encountering a crevasse.

TALLYING UP THE COSTS, REGRETS, AND BENEFITS

No reckoning of my Grid would be complete without tallying the cost, for the project took an enormous effort. My records show I ran and walked 1,975 miles, the equivalent of nearly 75 marathons. I climbed an estimated 500,000 feet, equivalent to almost 50 trips from base camp to the summit of Mt. Everest. According to my spreadsheet, the climbs took place on 189 unique dates, the equivalent of spending six full months in the field. And think about the opportunity cost—I could have spent this time at work getting more projects done and positioning myself for a bigger leadership role with more impact, or doing good things in the community, or with my family.

But I have no regrets. This was my pilgrimage. This was my chance to take myself offline and learn. To level up in ways that might not matter for other people, but which are central to who I am, such as discovering my ego and appreciating its limitations. Coming face-to-face with the source of my peculiar form of energy. Developing a new relationship with time. Coming to recognize the joy of life is found in everything.

I have no regrets because I was trying to cram a lifetime's worth of nature into a narrow window.

THE FINAL COUNTDOWN

The final climb seems no more or less special than the preceding ones, and thus I see no need for celebration. When running ultramarathons, I came to realize the goal was not to reach the next aid station, but to make it to the finish line, and I often cruised through the aid stations without stopping. When I was racing frequently, I understood my purpose was not to finish one race, but to keep on racing, and therefore the finish line was merely a point where the focus shifted temporarily to recovery. Similarly, the final Grid climb is merely one more step along the way.

However, the final climb is a special occasion to include friends. And I can't resist coming up with a unique adventurous minimalistic twist. As it turns out, number 420 will be Kaaterskill High Peak, so why not climb it at night, follow a novel bushwhack route, and take advantage of the full moon to complete the ascent without lights?

The day before, I check my watch. T minus 22 hours and counting.

The next day at 1:00 p.m., I begin gathering gear: compass, lights, spikes, snowshoes, crampons, Gore-Tex shell, lightweight boots, and the big pack with sleeping bag and tent (a conservative loadout, just in case).

1:30 p.m.: Final map checks. After reviewing the route on both laptop and phone, I write down azimuth, distance, and elevation for each leg. Out the window, the sky looks clear.

3:30 p.m.: Arriving in the mountains—thick stratus layer overhead.

4:00 p.m.: The group assembles at the trailhead. I'm honored that Mike Siudy is here, delighted to see Amy Hanlon again, pleased to meet some new friends, too. Jim Bouton couldn't make it but sent a message with a report on trail conditions. No one's carrying snowshoes, so I leave mine in the car.

Mike suggests a variation to the route based on a past visit, during which he found an unmarked trail. I approve his proposal (how could I not?) and brief the group on the plan to move without artificial illumination. Sunset is at 4:35 p.m. Evening nautical twilight ends at 5:35 p.m. Moonrise will be at 5:50 p.m. to the east-northeast. When operating under conditions of limited visibility, it's best to look at things out of the corner of your eyes, instead of straight on.

We peer up at thick cloud cover, wondering whether enough moonlight will seep through to let us see. Somewhere out there, the sun is sinking.

The abandoned ski area, the forest gate, the snowmobile trail, all this is waiting for us. And then we'll step into the woods, and who knows? Perhaps we'll experience something new.

I'm thinking about the route and anticipating obstacles, yet in a corner of my mind, I'm also wondering—after the Grid, what next?

Someone cracks a joke. Laughing, we saunter into the dusk.

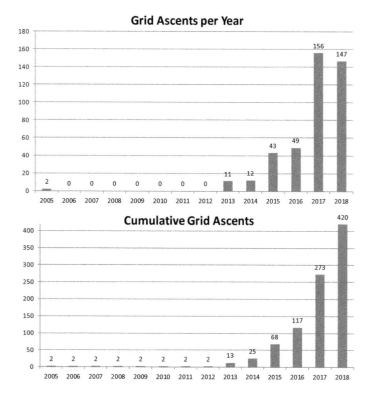

APPENDIX A

THE GRID

THE GRID IS A PEAK-BAGGING CHALLENGE THAT REQUIRES ASPIRANTS to climb each designated high peak in a given mountain range in every calendar month. As of April 22, 2025, 71 people have completed the Catskills Grid, according to the Catskills Mountain Club, including a handful who have finished it two or more times.[9] The first known Catskill Grid was completed in 1980, by Samuel Steen and Richard Davis, during a time when 34 mountains were recognized as high peaks (Southwest Hunter was added to the list in 1990). Steen observed that "the more you get out and into the woods, the more chance you have to see things." He also commented that having the Grid as a goal gave him extra motivation.[10]

---

9 Instructions for completing the Catskill Grid and the list of completions is available at https://www.catskillmountainclub.org/the-catskills-4-seasons-140-the-catskills-grid-420.

10 The story of the first Catskills Grid is recounted in Edwina Henderson, "Though 'Over the Hill,' 2 Climbers Reach Their Peaks," *The Sunday Freeman*, June 1, 1980, p. 23, accessed at https://hikersanonymous.org/#catskill-420-grid.

	JAN	FEB	MAR	APR	MAY	JUN	JUL	AUG	SEP	OCT	NOV	DEC
Peekamoose	1/18/15	2/28/18	3/12/17	4/23/16	5/9/15	6/1/18	7/8/17	8/28/13	9/6/15	10/7/17	11/27/18	12/16/18
Table	1/17/16	2/28/18	3/12/17	4/23/16	5/9/15	6/1/18	7/8/17	8/28/13	9/3/17	10/7/17	11/27/18	12/16/18
Lone	1/17/16	2/28/18	3/12/17	4/24/16	5/9/15	6/1/18	7/8/17	8/3/14	9/1/15	10/7/17	11/27/18	12/16/18
Rocky	1/17/16	2/28/18	3/31/18	4/24/16	5/9/15	6/1/18	7/8/18	8/3/14	9/9/18	10/7/17	11/27/18	12/16/18
Balsam Cap	1/17/16	2/28/18	3/31/18	4/24/16	5/9/15	6/1/18	7/8/18	8/25/16	9/9/18	10/7/17	11/27/18	12/16/18
Friday	1/17/16	2/28/18	3/31/18	4/24/16	5/9/15	6/1/18	7/30/17	8/25/16	9/9/18	10/7/17	11/29/18	12/16/18
Cornell	1/17/16	2/20/18	3/26/17	4/28/18	5/9/15	6/3/17	7/24/16	8/29/13	9/29/18	10/30/16	11/18/18	12/22/17
Wittenberg	1/14/17	2/20/18	3/26/17	4/28/18	5/9/15	6/3/17	7/24/16	8/29/13	9/30/17	10/30/16	11/18/18	12/22/17
Slide	1/17/16	2/20/18	3/26/17	4/24/16	5/7/16	6/3/17	7/24/16	8/29/13	9/29/18	10/30/16	11/17/18	12/20/17
Panther	1/13/18	2/12/16	3/26/17	4/8/18	5/30/15	6/22/18	7/2/17	8/25/16	9/2/14	10/10/15	11/18/17	12/2/17
Fir	1/28/17	2/24/18	3/26/16	4/8/18	5/30/15	6/29/17	7/1/18	8/25/16	9/2/18	10/22/17	11/19/17	12/1/18
Big Indian	1/28/17	2/24/18	3/28/18	4/1/16	5/23/15	6/29/17	7/2/18	8/26/16	9/2/18	10/22/17	11/10/18	12/1/18
Doubletop	1/28/17	2/25/18	3/28/18	4/1/16	5/23/15	6/29/17	7/2/18	8/31/14	9/23/18	10/14/17	11/10/18	12/21/18
Graham	1/3/18	2/18/17	3/12/16	4/23/18	5/23/15	6/24/17	7/12/17	8/26/16	9/3/18	10/14/17	11/1/18	12/14/17
Balsam Lake	1/3/18	2/18/17	3/12/16	4/23/18	5/23/15	6/23/17	7/12/17	8/26/16	9/2/18	10/14/17	11/1/18	12/14/17
Eagle	1/28/17	2/24/18	3/15/18	4/15/18	5/31/15	6/7/18	7/4/17	8/31/14	9/1/17	10/4/15	11/3/17	12/2/17
Balsam	1/28/17	2/24/18	3/19/16	4/15/18	5/31/15	6/7/18	7/4/17	8/26/16	9/1/17	10/4/15	11/3/17	12/2/17
Halcott	1/5/17	2/26/17	3/25/16	4/26/18	5/29/17	6/15/18	7/8/18	8/26/16	9/27/14	10/29/17	11/19/18	12/28/17

	JAN	FEB	MAR	APR	MAY	JUN	JUL	AUG	SEP	OCT	NOV	DEC
Bearpen	1/2/18	2/4/17	3/23/18	4/10/18	5/22/17	6/3/18	7/5/18	8/26/16	9/27/14	10/17/15	11/9/18	12/19/17
Vly	1/2/18	2/4/17	3/25/16	4/10/18	5/21/17	6/3/18	7/5/18	8/26/16	9/3/18	10/23/17	11/9/18	12/3/17
Sherrill	1/14/18	2/11/17	3/4/17	4/26/18	5/14/16	6/29/18	7/7/18	8/26/16	9/10/17	10/25/14	11/5/18	12/28/17
North Dome	1/14/18	2/11/17	3/4/17	4/26/18	5/23/17	6/29/18	7/7/18	8/26/16	9/10/17	10/25/14	11/5/18	12/27/15
West Kill	1/15/17	2/25/18	3/10/18	4/20/18	5/23/17	6/17/18	7/1/17	8/25/16	9/26/15	10/23/18	11/8/14	12/9/17
Rusk	1/29/17	2/18/17	3/9/18	4/20/18	5/24/17	6/29/18	7/5/18	8/4/17	9/26/15	10/27/18	11/8/14	12/9/17
Hunter	1/7/18	2/18/17	3/9/18	4/9/17	5/24/17	6/25/18	7/2/17	8/4/17	9/12/15	10/21/18	11/5/17	12/25/16
Southwest Hunter	1/7/18	2/19/17	3/9/18	4/9/17	5/24/17	6/25/18	7/2/17	8/5/17	9/12/15	10/21/18	11/8/14	12/25/16
Plateau	1/7/17	2/19/18	3/31/17	4/28/18	5/14/17	6/20/15	7/3/17	8/29/13	9/26/15	10/27/18	11/19/18	12/5/17
Sugarloaf	1/7/17	2/19/18	3/17/18	4/23/18	5/14/17	6/20/15	7/14/17	8/29/13	9/24/17	10/28/17	11/1/15	12/5/17
Twin	1/7/17	2/22/18	3/17/18	4/24/18	5/1/18	6/20/15	7/9/17	8/29/13	9/24/17	10/25/15	11/1/15	12/31/17
Indian Head	1/7/17	2/22/18	3/26/18	4/24/18	5/21/17	6/20/15	7/9/17	8/29/13	9/7/18	10/25/15	11/18/17	12/31/17
Kaaterskill High Peak	1/21/18	2/11/17	3/23/18	4/25/15	5/29/17	6/4/18	7/1/18	8/14/17	9/27/18	10/30/17	11/1/15	12/22/18
Thomas Cole	1/16/16	2/25/17	3/11/17	4/15/17	5/27/17	6/24/17	7/15/17	8/5/17	9/17/18	10/11/15	11/12/17	12/17/17
Black Dome	1/16/16	2/25/17	3/11/17	4/15/17	5/27/17	6/24/17	7/15/17	8/5/17	9/17/18	10/11/15	11/12/17	12/17/17
Blackhead	1/16/16	2/25/17	3/11/17	4/15/17	5/27/17	6/20/15	7/30/05	8/29/13	9/17/18	10/11/15	11/12/17	12/17/17
Windham	1/14/17	2/17/18	3/25/18	4/14/17	5/29/17	6/18/17	7/30/05	8/30/13	9/4/17	10/9/17	11/1/15	12/3/17

APPENDIX B

LIST OF SPECIES OBSERVED IN THE CATSKILLS

TREES

American basswood	*Tilia americana*
American beech	*Fagus grandifolia*
American sycamore	*Platanus occidentalis*
Ash	*Fraxinus* spp.
Balsam fir	*Abies balsamea*
Black birch	*Betula lenta*
Black cherry	*Prunus serotina*
Black locust	*Robinia pseudoacacia*
Chokecherry	*Prunus virginiana*
Crab apple	*Malus* spp.
Eastern cottonwood	*Populus deltoides*
Eastern hemlock	*Tsuga canadensis*
Eastern red cedar	*Juniperus virginiana*
Eastern white pine	*Pinus strobus*
European larch	*Larix decidua*
Hop hornbeam	*Ostrya virginiana*

TREES

Mountain ash	*Sorbus americana*
Mountain maple	*Acer spicatum*
Northern catalpa	*Catalpa speciosa*
Northern red oak	*Quercus rubra*
Norway spruce	*Picea abies*
Paper birch	*Betula papyrifera*
Pitch pine	*Pinus rigida*
Red maple	*Acer rubrum*
Red spruce	*Picea rubens*
River birch	*Betula nigra*
Serviceberry	*Amelanchier* spp.
Shagbark hickory	*Carya ovata*
Staghorn sumac	*Rhus typhina*
Striped maple	*Acer pensylvanicum*
Sugar maple	*Acer saccharum*
Trembling aspen	*Populus tremuloides*
Willow	*Salix* spp.
Witch hazel	*Hamamelis virginiana*
Yellow birch	*Betula alleghaniensis*

HERBACEOUS PLANTS

Aniseroot	*Osmorhiza longistylis*
Bee balm	*Monarda didyma*
Beech drop	*Epifagus virginiana*
Bird's foot trefoils	*Lotus* spp.
Bleeding heart	*Dicentra spectabilis*
Blue bugle	*Ajuga genevensis*
Blue cohosh	*Caulophyllum thalictroides*

HERBACEOUS PLANTS

Blue-bead lily	*Clintonia borealis*
Blue-eyed grass	*Sisyrinchium angustifolium*
Bluestem goldenrod	*Solidago caesia*
Broad-leaved dock	*Rumex obtusifolius*
Broad-leaved goldenrod	*Solidago flexicaulis*
Bull thistle	*Cirsium vulgare*
Burdock	*Arctium minus*
Burning bush	*Euonymus alatus*
Calico aster	*Symphyotrichum lateriflorum*
Canada mayflower	*Maianthemum canadense*
Canada violet	*Viola canadensis*
Canada wood betony	*Pedicularis canadensis*
Canada yew	*Taxus canadensis*
Carolina horsenettle	*Solanum carolinense*
Catchweed bedstraw	*Galium aparine*
Cinquefoil	*Potentilla* spp.
Coltsfoot	*Tussilago farfara*
Common blackberry	*Rubus allegheniensis*
Common blue violet	*Viola sororia*
Common selfheal	*Prunella vulgaris*
Common tansy	*Tanacetum vulgare*
Common woodsorrel	*Oxalis acetosella*
Common yarrow	*Achillea millefolium*
Cow parsley	*Anthriscus sylvestris*
Cow parsnip	*Heracleum maximum*
Creeping dogwood	*Cornus canadensis*
Curly dock	*Rumex crispus*
Daisy fleabane	*Erigeron annuus*
Dame's rocket	*Hesperis matronalis*

HERBACEOUS PLANTS

Dandelion	*Taraxacum* spp.
Dogbanes	*Apocynum* spp.
Dutchman's breeches	*Dicentra cucullaria*
Dwarf ginseng	*Panax trifolius*
Eastern red columbine	*Aquilegia canadensis*
Foamflower	*Tiarella cordifolia*
Forsythia	*Forsythia* spp.
Fringed loosestrife	*Lysimachia cilata*
Fringed bindweed	*Fallopia cilinodis*
Garlic mustard	*Alliaria petiolata*
Germander speedwell	*Veronica chamaedrys*
Golden Alexanders	*Zizia aurea*
Goutweed	*Aegopodium podagraria*
Gray goldenrod	*Solidago nemoralis*
Great mullein	*Verbascum thapsus*
Great rhododendron	*Rhododendron maximum*
Herb robert	*Geranium robertianum*
Hobblebush	*Viburnum lantanoides*
Honeysuckle	*Lonicera* spp.
Hooked crowfoot	*Ranunculus recurvatus*
Indian hellebore	*Veratrum viride*
Indian pipe	*Monotropa uniflora*
Jack-in-the-pulpit	*Arisaema triphyllum*
Japanese barberry	*Berberis thunbergii*
Japanese knotweed	*Polygonum cuspidatum*
Knapweed	*Centaurea maculosa*
Lilac	*Syringa vulgaris*
Lowbush blueberry	*Vaccinium angustifolium*
Mayapple	*Podophyllum peltatum*

HERBACEOUS PLANTS

Meadow buttercup	*Ranunculus acris*
Meadowsweet	*Filipendula ulmaria*
Mountain laurel	*Kalmia latifolia*
New England aster	*Symphyotrichum novae-angliae*
Orange hawkweed	*Hieracium aurantiacum*
Orange jewelweed	*Impatiens capensis*
Oxeye daisy	*Leucanthemum vulgare*
Painted trillium	*Trillium undulatum*
Partridgeberry	*Mitchella repens*
Pinxterbloom azalea	*Rhododendron prinophyllum*
Pond water-starwort	*Callitriche stagnalis*
Purple trillium	*Trillium erectum*
Purple-flowered raspberry	*Rubus odoratum*
Purple-stemmed angelica	*Angelica atropurpurea*
Pussytoes	*Antennaria* spp.
Queen Anne's lace	*Daucus carota*
Ragged robin	*Silene flos-cuculi*
Ramp	*Allium tricoccum*
Red baneberry	*Actaea rubra*
Red clover	*Trifolium pratense*
Red elderberry	*Sambucus racemosa*
Robin's plantain	*Erigeron puchellus*
Small white leek	*Allium tricoccum*
Smooth Solomon's seal	*Polygonatum biflorum*
Solomon's plume	*Maianthemum racemosum*
Spotted joe pye weed	*Eutrochium maculatum*
Spring beauty	*Claytonia virginica*
Squirrel corn	*Dicentra canadensis*
Saint-John's-wort	*Hypericum perforatum*

HERBACEOUS PLANTS

Starflower	*Trientalis borealis*
Stinging nettle	*Urtica dioica*
Tall blue lettuce	*Lactuca biennis*
Tall goldenrod	*Solidago altissima*
Tall meadow rue	*Thalictrum pubescens*
Trout lily	*Erythronium americanum*
Tufted vetch	*Vicia cracca*
Turtlehead	*Chelone glabra*
Two-leaved toothwort	*Cardamine diphylla*
Virginia saxifrage	*Micranthes virginiensis*
Virginia waterleaf	*Hydrophyllum virginianum*
Virgin's-bower	*Clematis virginiana*
Water forget-me-not	*Myosotis scorpioides*
White avens	*Geum canadense*
White clover	*Trifolium repens*
White snakeroot	*Ageratina altissima*
Whorled wood aster	*Oclemena acuminata*
Wild grapes	*Vitis vinifera*
Wild sarsaparilla	*Aralia nudicaulis*
Wild strawberries	*Fragaria vesca*
Wintercress	*Barbarea* spp.
Wintergreen berry	*Gaultheria procumbens*
Wisteria	*Wisteria* spp.
Wood anemone	*Anemonoides quinquefolia*
Woodland forget-me-nots	*Myosotis sylvatica*
Yellow jewelweed	*Impatiens pallida*

GRASSES, SEDGES, AND REEDS

Bladder sedge	*Carex intumescens*
Bottlebush grass	*Elymus hystrix*
Common reed	*Phragmites australis*
Crested sedge	*Carex cristatella*
Dark green bulrush	*Scirpus atrovirens*
Fringed sedge	*Carex crinita*
Sallow sedge	*Carex lurida*
Timothy grass	*Phleum pratense*
Wood meadow-grass	*Poa nemoralis*
Woolgrass	*Scirpus cyperinus*

MOSSES

Haircap moss	*Polytrichum* spp.
Knight's plume moss	*Ptilium crista-castrensis*
Peat moss	*Sphagnum* spp.
Red bogmoss	*Sphagnum capillifolium*
Stairstep moss	*Hylocomium splendens*
Ulota moss	*Ulota crispa*
Windswept broom moss	*Dicranum scoparium*

FERNS AND FERN ALLIES

Bracken	*Pteridium aquilinum*
Christmas fern	*Polystichum acrostichoides*
Cinnamon fern	*Osmundastrum cinnamomeum*
Evergreen wood fern	*Dryopteris intermedia*
Fan clubmoss	*Diphasiastrum digitatum*
Hay-scented fern	*Dennstaedtia punctilobula*
Interrupted fern	*Osmunda claytoniana*

FERNS AND FERN ALLIES

Marginal shield fern	*Dryopteris marginalis*
Northern maidenhead fern	*Adiantum pedatum*
New York fern	*Thelypteris noveboracensis*
Polipodes fern	*Polypodium* spp.
Stag's horn clubmoss	*Lycopodium clavatum*
Shining clubmoss	*Huperzia lucidula*

FUNGI

Angel wing fungus	*Pleurocybella porrigens*
Ash-tree bolete	*Boletinellus merulioides*
Black trumpet	*Craterellus cornucopioides*
Chicken of the woods	*Laetiporus* spp.
Common earthball	*Scleroderma citrinum*
Crimped gill	*Plicaturopsis crispa*
Crowded parchment	*Stereum complicatum*
False turkey tail	*Stereum ostrea*
Fly amanita	*Amanita muscaria*
Golden chanterelle	*Cantharellus cibarius*
Hemlock varnish shelf	*Ganoderma tsugae*
Leafy brain	*Phaeotremelia foliacea*
Orange jelly fungus	*Dacrymyces palmatus*
Scarlet elfcup	*Sarcoscypha coccinea*
Suede bolete	*Xerocomus subtomentosus*
Tiger's eye (brown funnel polypore)	*Coltricia cinnamomea*
Turkey tail	*Trametes versicolor*
White coral fungus	*Ramariopsis kunzei*
Witch's butter	*Tremella mesenterica*
Yellow fairy cups	*Calycina citrina*

SLIME MOLDS

Chocolate tube slime mold	*Stemonitis splendens*
Scrambled egg slime mold	*Fuligo septica*

LICHENS

American starburst	*Imshaugia placorodia*
Boreal oakmoss	*Evernia mesomorpha*
Common goldspeck	*Candelariella vitellini*
Common greenshield	*Flavoparmelia carperata*
Common toadskin	*Lasallia papulosa*
Concentric boulder	*Porpidia crustulata*
British soldiers	*Cladonia cristatella*
Many-branched cladonia	*Cladonia furcata*
Fishnet beard lichen	*Usnea filipendula*
Ghost antler	*Pseudevernia cladonia*
Granite-speck rim lichen	*Lecanora polytropa*
Gray reindeer	*Cladonia rangiferina*
Hammered shield	*Parmelia sulcata*
Hooded tube	*Hypogymnia physodes*
Pink earth lichen	*Dibaeis baeomyces*
Powdered sunshine	*Vulpicida pinastri*
Powderhorn	*Cladonia coniocraea*
Red-fruited pixie cup	*Cladonia pleurota*
Reindeer	*Cladonia mitis*
Smokey-eyed boulder	*Porpidia albocaerulescens*
Smooth rock tripe	*Umbilicaria mammulata*
Snow lichen	*Stereocaulon glaucescens*
Speckleback	*Punctelia rudecta*
Variable rag	*Platismatia glauca*

LICHENS

Yellow ribbon	*Unsocetraria oakesiana*
Sea storm	*Cetrelia* spp.

BIRDS

American robin	*Turdus migratorius*
Bald eagle	*Haliaeetus leucocephalus*
Barred owl	*Strix varia*
Black-and-white warbler	*Mniotilta varia*
Black-capped chickadee	*Poecile atricapillus*
Black-throated blue warbler	*Setophaga caerulescens*
Black-throated green warbler	*Setophaga virens*
Blue jay	*Cyanocitta cristata*
Brant goose	*Branta bernicla*
Chipping sparrow	*Spizella passerina*
Common raven	*Corvus corax*
Common starling	*Sturnus vulgaris*
Dark-eyed junco	*Junco hyemalis*
Downy woodpecker	*Picoides pubescens*
Eastern towhee	*Pipilo erythrophthalmus*
Eastern wood peewee	*Contopus virens*
Golden-crowned kinglet	*Regulus satrapa*
Great blue heron	*Ardea herodias*
Hermit thrush	*Catharus guttatus*
Ovenbird	*Seiurus aurocapill*
Prairie warbler	*Setophaga discolor*
Red-breasted nuthatch	*Sitta canadensis*
Red-eyed vireo	*Vireo olivaceus*
Red-shouldered hawk	*Buteo lineatus*

BIRDS

Rose-breasted grosbeak	*Pheucticus ludovicianus*
Ruffed grouse	*Bonasa umbellus*
Scarlet tanager	*Piranga olivacea*
Swainson's thrush	*Catharus ustulatus*
Turkey vulture	*Cathartes aura*
Veery thrush	*Catharus fuscescens*
Warbling vireo	*Vireo gilvus*
White-breasted nuthatch	*Sitta carolinensis*
Wild turkey	*Meleagris gallopavo*
Wood thrush	*Hylocichla mustelina*
Yellow-bellied sapsucker	*Sphyrapicus varius*
Yellow-rumped warbler	*Setophaga coronata*

MAMMALS

American black bear	*Ursus americanus*
Eastern chipmunk	*Tamias striatus*
Eastern cottontail	*Sylvilagus floridanus*
Eastern coyote	*Canis latrans*
Eastern gray squirrel	*Sciurus carolinensis*
Fisher	*Pekania pennanti*
Porcupine	*Erethizon dorsatum*
Snowshoe hare	*Lepus americanus*
White-tailed deer	*Odocoileus virginianus*
Woodland jumping mouse	*Napaeozapus insignis*

REPTILES AND AMPHIBIANS

American toad	*Anaxyrus americanus*
Coal skink	*Plestiodon anthracinus*
Common garter snake	*Thamnophis sirtalis*
Eastern newt	*Notophthalmus viridescens*
Green frog	*Lithobates clamitans*
Leopard frog	*Lithobates* spp.
Northern red salamander	*Pseudotriton ruber*
Pickerel frog	*Lithubates palustris*
Smooth greensnake	*Opheodrys vernalis*
Spring peepers	*Pseudacris crucifer*
Wood frog	*Lithobates sylvaticus*

INSECTS AND MOLLUSKS

American dagger moth caterpillar	*Acronicta americana*
American dog tick	*Dermacentor variabilis*
Bald-faced hornet fly	*Spilomyia fusca*
Black fly	*Chrysops* spp.
Blue blowfly	*Calliphora vicina*
Crane fly	*Tipulidae* spp.
Definite tussock moth caterpillar	*Orgyia definita*
Eastern comma	*Polygonia comma*
Eastern tiger swallowtail	*Papilio glaucus*
Friendly probole moth	*Probole amicaria*
Giant leopard moth	*Hypercompe scribonia*
Hickory tussock moth caterpillar	*Lophocampa carya*
Inchworm	*Geometridae* spp.
Katydid	*Tettigoniidae* spp.
Millipede	*Xstodesminae* spp.

INSECTS AND MOLLUSKS

Mosquito	*Culex* spp.
Mourning cloak	*Nymphalis antiopa*
Pale beauty	*Campaea perlata*
Prominent moth caterpillar	*Lochmaeus* spp.
Red admiral	*Vanessa atalanta*
Roundback slug	*Arionoidea* spp.
White admiral	*Limenitis arthemis*
White-striped black	*Trichodezia albovittata*
Hemlock looper moth	*Lambdina fiscellaria*

APPENDIX C

RUNNING-RELATED INJURIES

1979–1992	Chronic anterior compartment syndrome
1987	Hip flexor strain
1992, 2008–2010	Iliotibial band syndrome
2011	Plantar fasciitis
2011	Posterior tibialis tendonitis
2013	Achilles tendonitis
2015	Piriformis inflammation
2015–2016	Groin strain
2015	Unidentified ligament strain, top of right foot
2016	Quadriceps tendonitis, left knee
2016–2017	Calf strains
2017–2018	Quadriceps tendonitis, right knee
2016–2017	Unidentified ligament strains in the left foot
2016–2018	Posterior tibial tendonitis
2017	Stress fracture of the navicular
2018	Peroneal brevis tendonitis

SAMPLE OPERATIONAL PLAN

ON OCCASIONS WHEN I FEEL A HIKE HAS A SOMEWHAT HIGHER RISK profile than normal, I'll write up an operational plan to ensure that I'm thoroughly prepared. This is the plan I wrote up before the November 29, 2018, ascent of Friday Mountain.

OBJECTIVE

Complete the Grid for November by climbing Friday Mountain, and return safely and without injury, in position to begin work on December's remaining 10 peaks on December 1.

RISK ASSESSMENT AND MITIGATING STRATEGIES

Snowbase estimated at 1+ foot, resulting in slow/difficult travel.
   * Carry snowshoes and spikes or crampons and ensure gear is properly secured when not in use.

Cold weather, potentially in the 20s with high winds at elevation, posing risk of hypothermia and frostbite if not properly dressed and/ or injury prevents mobility. Of note, fingertips still feel a little numb following yesterday's ascent of five peaks.

- Conservative load-out with warm/windproof clothing, shelter, and backup/extra layers. Avoid overheating by frequent gear changes if necessary.

Off-trail route in remote area on a weekday. In the event of injury, highly unlikely that anyone else will be out there and no cellphone coverage in the area, making it impossible to call for help.

- Ensure plans are left with emergency contact. Carry and activate personal locator beacon.
- Create and memorize detailed route plan. Use standard navigational gear with plastic sleeve to keep phone warm, and check battery charger is fully charged.

Steep/rough terrain, taxing on the ascent, with the risk of slips and falls that could lead to injury.

- Plan for slow, steady pace throughout. Ensure that route follows ramp up to summit.

Head cold, with symptoms limited to mild headache.

- Assume slow pace <1 mph on ascent.

WEATHER OUTLOOK

WEATHER.COM

- Weather in Phoenicia projected at low 30s all day, with near-zero probability of precipitation, and winds in the mid-teens from the NW, with a nighttime low of 25°F.
- Weather on Friday Mountain projected at 22–24°F, dropping to 19°F overnight. Precipitation probability at 20%, and winds 16–19 mph out of the NW.

MOUNTAIN.FORECAST.COM

- Summit at 3,691 feet: 0.4" snow projected Wednesday night. Temperature projected 23–27°F, with winds 20–35 mph out of the NW, and no precipitation.
- At 1,641 feet: 30–32°F, dropping to 28°F overnight, with winds 10–20 mph out of the NW, and no precipitation.

INFORMATION ON THE SUN

* First light 6:31 a.m., sunrise 7:02 a.m. Sunrise azimuth: 118 degrees (ESE). Due south at 11:44, 27-degree altitude at culmination, 241 degrees (WSW) at sunset.
* Sunset 4:26 p.m., last light 4:57 p.m.

NOTIFICATION PLAN

* Text Sue with parking area, destination, and expected time of return/check back in.

EQUIPMENT LIST

CLOTHING

* Black knit cap
* Neck warmer
* Wraparound mountaineering headgear and balaclava carried in waterproof bag
* Wool long underwear, top and bottom
* Wool socks, plus extra pair carried in waterproof bag
* Fleece jacket
* Extra fleece sweater carried in waterproof bag
* Mountaineering Gore-Tex shell
* Extra shell carried in pack
* Mountaineering bibs
* Gore-Tex pants carried in pack
* Hiking pants
* Sunglasses
* Mittens

WAIST BELT

* Standard load: tape, compass/thermometer, reading glasses, Band-Aids, jacknife, cordage, loupe, ibuprofen

PACK

- ✴ Sleeping bag in stuff sack, liner, inflatable pad, ground cloth, tent, tent stakes
- ✴ Trekking poles
- ✴ Crampons
- ✴ Waterproof bag with extra warm gear
- ✴ Personal locator beacon
- ✴ Headlamp and flashlight
- ✴ Waterproof bag with first aid kit, extra batteries, phone charger

SCHEDULE

WEDNESDAY EVENING

- ✴ Lay out gear and clothing
- ✴ Pack gear
- ✴ Test phone charger
- ✴ Charge phone

THURSDAY

0600	Alarm
0630	Breakfast
0700	Text Sue with destination
0715	Depart
0830	Arrive at trailhead (via I-87 and Route 28), activate personal locator beacon
0930	Complete leg 1
1100	Complete leg 3 (arrive Pregnant Tree intersection)
1130	Reach summit
1330	Descend to car
1500	Return home. Text Sue

ROUTE PLAN

1. FIRST LEG

After short distance along the road, look for moderate track heading WNW and gradually ascending ridge.

(MILES)		ELEVATION (FEET)			
Distance	Direction	Start	Finish	Change	Grade
1.1	WNW	1100	2000	900	15%

> ✳ Emergency exit option: Heading straight downhill will lead to a stream that runs SE to Moon Haw Rd.

2. SECOND LEG

Climb straight uphill onto ridge crest.

(MILES)		ELEVATION (FEET)			
Distance	Direction	Start	Finish	Change	Grade
0.2	S	2000	2350	350	33%

> ✳ Emergency exit option: Straight downhill leads to same stream.

3. THIRD LEG

Unmarked trail follows south edge of ridge crest, turning WSW as it nears intersection.

(MILES)		ELEVATION (FEET)			
Distance	Direction	Start	Finish	Change	Grade
0.9	W	2350	3250	900	18%

> ✳ Emergency exit option: Dropping downhill would hit a streambed leading SE to Shuttis Lane, make a left on Moon Haw and walk north to parking lot.

4. FOURTH LEG

From "Pregnant tree" intersection, turn N. Steep climb to "ramp."

(MILES)		ELEVATION (FEET)			
Distance	Direction	Start	Finish	Change	Grade
0.1	N	3250	3350	100	19%

> ✳ Emergency exit option: Must move back south, do not drop down steep cliffs.

5. FIFTH LEG

From ramp to summit, move NNE along terrace then NNW on final scramble to summit vantage/canister.

(MILES)		ELEVATION (FEET)			
Distance	Direction	Start	Finish	Change	Grade
0.2	N	3350	3694	344	33%

✽ Emergency exit option: Must return the same way to the ramp; very thick on top and many steep cliffs.

6. CUMULATIVE

(MILES)	ELEVATION (FEET)	
Distance	Change	Grade
2.5	2594	19%

REFERENCES AND SUPPLEMENTAL INFORMATION

CHAPTER 1: A SIGNAL FROM THE NORTH

* Walt Whitman, "Song of Myself," in *Leaves of Grass*, 1855.
* Information on the Escarpment Trail Run at www.escarpment trail.com and 2005 results at http://escarpmenttrail.com /results/2005.html.
* Muir's comments come from *My First Summer in the Sierras* (Houghton Mifflin Company, 1911) and *The Mountains of California* (The Century Co., 1894).

CHAPTER 2: HOOKED BY A NEW CHALLENGE

* The Emerson quotation comes from Robert D. Richardson, Jr., *Emerson: The Mind on Fire* (University of California Press, 1995).
* A full account of my Badwater Double run is contained in Kenneth Posner, "Running the 292-Mile Badwater Double: Lessons Learned," in *Marathon & Beyond*, November/ December 2014, accessed at https://marathonandbeyond.com /wp-content/uploads/2014/10/18.6_EditorsChoice.pdf.
* Keizer's Catskill run and other accomplishments are documented on his website, www.thedogteam.com.

✸ Interview with Keizer in *The New York Times*: http://www
.nytimes.com/2002/11/10/sports/outdoors-he-s-a-speed
-marathon-climber-they-call-him-cave-dog.html.

CHAPTER 3: RACING AFTER CAVE DOG

✸ Information on Rock The Ridge is available at https://
www.mohonkpreserve.org/rock-the-ridge/rock-the-ridge
.html. Results for 2015 are available at https://ultrarunning
.com/calendar/event/rock-the-ridge/race/12417/results.

✸ *The Illiad,* by Homer, translated by Robert Fagles (Penguin
Classics, 1998). Later, as I recalled this vision, I read the
description of Achilles's shield: From the flames emerged
a magnificent shield, a "world of gorgeous immortal work"
depicting earth, sun, moon, and constellations, as well as two
fine cities. It showed marriage feasts, dancers, two armies
clad in armor, farmlands, vineyards, herds of straight-horned
cattle, and around the rim the mighty ocean was inlaid in
glittering silver.

✸ It occurred to me that Hephaestus might have a forged just as
beautiful a shield embellished with scenes from the Catskills.

CHAPTER 4: BATTLING WITH NATURE OFF-TRAIL

✸ Jim Mattis and Bing West, *Call Sign Chaos: Learning to Lead*
(Random House, 2019).

✸ Marcus Aurelius, *The Meditations,* translated by George
Long and first published in 1862, contained in *Stoic Six Pack*
(Enhanced Media, 2014).

✸ The data on American time budgets comes from Neil E.
Klepeis, William C. Nelson, Wayne R. Ott, John P. Robinson,
Andy M. Tsang, Paul Switzer, Joseph V. Behar, Stephen C.
Hern, and William H. Engelmann, "The National Human
Activity Pattern Survey," *Journal of Exposure Analysis and
Environmental Epidemiology* 11, 2001.

✸ Thoreau's comment comes from his essay "Walking," in *The
New Atlantic,* June 1862.

CHAPTER 5: SLIPPING FROM MY GRASP

✷ For an account of Manitou's Revenge, see Kenneth Posner, "A Hellish Path in the Hudson Valley," *Ultrarunning Magazine*, September 2015.

✷ Results for the 2015 edition of Manitou's Revenge are available at http://www.manitousrevengeultra.com/wp-content /uploads/2015/06/results-with-splits.pdf.

✷ Christopher McDougall, *Born to Run: A Hidden Tribe, Superathletes, and the Greatest Race the World Has Never Seen* (Knopf, 2009).

CHAPTER 6: A NEW OBSESSION

✷ Burroughs's quotations from Edward J. Renehan, Jr., *John Burroughs: An American Naturalist* (Chelsea Green Publishing Company, 1992); John Burroughs, *Winter Sunshine* (Houghton Mifflin Company, 1875); and John Burroughs, *Leaf and Tendril* (Houghton Mifflin Company, 1871).

✷ For Burroughs's view on Walt Whitman, see *Whitman: A Study* (Houghton Mifflin Company, 1896).

✷ Emerson's quotation is from his essay "Self-Reliance," first published in *Essays: First Series*, 1841.

✷ Henry David Thoreau, *Walden, or Life in the Woods*, first published in 1854.

✷ David Horton quoted in Scott Jurek, *North: Finding My Way While Running the Appalachian Trail* (Little Brown & Co., 2018).

CHAPTER 7: GOING LIGHT

✷ J. R. R. Tolkien, *The Lord of the Rings* (Harper Collins Publishers, 2005).

✷ Story of the hiker who died in the Adirondacks available at https://www.adirondackalmanack.com/2016/03/analysis-of -the-macnaughton-hikers-death.html.

CHAPTER 8: TAKING MINIMALISM TO THE NEXT LEVEL

✳ Luis E. Navia, *Diogenes the Cynic: The War Against the World* (Prometheus Books, 2005).

✳ *The Golden Sayings of Epictetus,* translated and arranged by Hastings Crossley (Amazon.com Services LLC, 2012).

CHAPTER 9: SHIFTING GEARS AGAIN

✳ For discussion of the Bhagavad Gita, see my blog post accessible at https://thelongbrownpath.com/2016/01/24/a -fresh-look-at-the-bhagavad-gita.

✳ Jan Wellford and Cory DeLavalle's unsupported record for the Catskill 35: http://www.vftt.org/forums/showthread .php?37734-Northeast%92s-Fastest-Known-Times.

✳ Ben Nephew's account of his record-setting Devil's Path run is available at https://www.mountainpeakfitness.com/blog /2015-devils-path-fkt-ben-nephew.

CHAPTER 10: THE 35-PEAK CHALLENGE

✳ Mike Siudy's record for the Nine is at https://fastestknown time.com/route/catskill-9-ny and his report on completing the Grid is available at https://www.mountainpeakfitness .com/blog/2016-catskill-grid-mike-siudy.

✳ Pam Reed, *The Extra Mile: One Woman's Personal Journey to Ultrarunning Greatness* (Rodale, 2006).

CHAPTER 11: CHRISTMAS IN THE MOUNTAINS

✳ Earl Shaffer, *Walking with Spring: The First Thru-Hike of the Appalachian Trail* (Appalachian Trail Conservancy, 1983).

✳ Henry David Thoreau, *The Maine Woods* (Ticknor & Fields, 1864).

✳ John Muir wrote his sister Sarah Galloway in a letter dated September 3, 1873: "The mountains are calling, and I must go, and I will work on while I can, studying incessantly"; accessed from "Quotations from John Muir," https://vault.sierraclub .org/john_muir_exhibit/writings/favorite_quotations.aspx.

✳ Muir sketching from *My First Summer in the Sierras.*

✳ Henry David Thoreau, "Autumnal Tints," *The Atlantic Monthly*, October 1862.

❋ John Burroughs, "The Heart of the Southern Catskills," from *In the Catskills* (Houghton Mifflin Company, 1910).

❋ John Burroughs, *Locusts and Wild Honey* (Houghton Mifflin Company, 1879).

❋ Thoreau's comment on "quiet desperation" comes from *Walden, or Life in the Woods*, (Thomas Y. Crowell & Co., 1854).

CHAPTER 12: WINTER TINTS

❋ Muir's usage of "plant people" is from *My First Summer in the Sierras*. Companion's observations are from Reverend S. Hall Young's *Alaska Days with John Muir*, 1915, excerpted in Lee Stetson, *The Wild Muir: Twenty-Two of John Muir's Greatest Adventures* (Yosemite Conservancy, 1994).

❋ John Muir, "Wind-storm in the Forests of the Yuba," *Scribner's Monthly*, November 1, 1878.

CHAPTER 13: FIFTY MILES THAT NEVER END

❋ See William Lewis Manly, *Death Valley in '49* (1894), which also contains the account of the White explorers and the Shoshone Indians.

❋ For a discussion of drinking too much fluid during races, see Tim Noakes, MD, DSc, *Waterlogged: The Serious Problem of Overhydration in Endurance Sports* (Human Kinetics, 2012).

❋ Muir's journal entry is taken from his book *My First Summer in the Sierras*.

CHAPTER 14: FLOWING DOWN AND UP

❋ Thoreau's comment comes from his essay "Walking," in *The New Atlantic,* June 1862.

❋ The Walt Whitman quotation comes from his poem "Song of the Open Road," in the 1856 collection, *Leaves of Grass*.

❋ Mihalyi Csikszentmihalyi, *Flow: The Psychology of Optimal Experience* (Harper Perennial Modern Classics, 2008). For a discussion of other approaches to flow, see my article "The Problem with Seeking 'Flow'" in *The New Ambler Review of Books*, accessed at https://newramblerreview.com/book -reviews/psychology/the-problem-with-seeking-flow.

CHAPTER 16: RACING THE SUN

✴ For references to articles written under the name Mose Velsor, see Walt Whitman, *Manly Health and Training: To Teach the Science of a Sound and Beautiful Body* (Regan Arts, 2017).

✴ For references to the Yurok Indians, see Peter Nabokov, *Indian Running: Native American History and Tradition* (Capra Press, 1981) and Thomas Buckley, *Standing Ground: Yurok Indian Spirituality 1850–1990* (University of California Press, 2002).

✴ Albert Camus, *The Myth of Sisyphus,* translated by Justin O'Brien (Vintage, 1942).

✴ Kevin Lacz with Ethan E. Rocke and Lindsey Lacz, *The Last Punisher: A Seal Team Three Sniper's True Account of the Battle of Ramadi* (Simon & Schuster, 2016).

✴ Emerson's comment on patience is from his lecture "Education." See Peter Knox, PhD, editor, *The Ralph Waldo Emerson Collection* (Annotated Classics, 2014).

CHAPTER 17: A SPEAR OF SUMMER GRASS

✴ Harold Gatty, *Finding Your Way Without Map or Compass* (E. P. Dutton & Company, 1958).

✴ David Barrie, *Supernavigators: Exploring the Wonders of How Animals Find Their Way* (The Experiment, 2019).

✴ For background on Whitman, see John Burroughs, *Whitman: A Study* (Houghton Mifflin Company, 1896), and Harold Bloom's comment, "Whitman's full aesthetic achievement is still undervalued and misunderstood. He is the greatest artist his nation has brought forth," in Harold Bloom, "Walt Whitman, America's Greatest Artist," *Wall Street Journal*, July 29, 2005.

✴ The clock reference is from John Zerzan, *Running on Emptiness: The Pathology of Civilization* (Feral House, 2008).

✴ Erwin Schrödinger, *What is Life?* (Cambridge University Press, 1967) and *"Nature and the Greeks" and "Science and Humanism"* (Cambridge University Press, 2014).

CHAPTER 18: BRINGING FRIENDS AND FAMILY TO THE MOUNTAINS

* For a discussion of katydid singing, see https://www.research
gate.net/publication/232710356_Katydid_synchronous
_chorusing_is_an_evolutionarily_stable_outcome_of_female
_choice, accessed September 22, 2017.

CHAPTER 19: LEARNING TO TOE THE LINE

* For an account of Muir's visit with Burroughs, see Edward J. Renehan, Jr., *John Burroughs: An American Naturalist* (Chelsea Green Publishing Company, 1992), p. 205, and H. A. Haring, *The Slabsides Book of John Burroughs* (Houghton Mifflin Company, 1931), p. 29.

* Emerson's quotation is from his essay "Self-Reliance," 1841, and Thoreau's is from *Walden*.

* Muir's comment on Yosemite is from *First Summer in the Sierras*. For his account of the meeting with Emerson, see the excerpt from *The Life and Letters of John Muir*, accessed at https://vault.sierraclub.org/john_muir_exhibit/writings /people/emerson.aspx.

* "Blind watchmaker" and concept of nature as devoid of purpose come from Richard Dawkins, *The Blind Watchmaker: Why the Evidence of Evolution Reveals a Universe Without Design* (W. W. Norton and Co., 2015).

* Dogen quotation is from Kazuaki Tanahashi, *Moon in a Dewdrop: Writings of Zen Master Dogen*, accessed at https:// zendogen.es/textos-zen-pdf/Moon-in-a-dewdrop.pdf.

CHAPTER 20: FACING THE WINTER PROBLEM

* Fenwick Lumber Railroad is described in Michael Kudish, *The Catskill Forest: A History* (Purple Mountain Press, 2000).

* Wim Hof and Justin Rosales, *Becoming the Iceman: Pushing Past Perceived Limits* (Mill City Press, 2011) and Scott Carney, *What Doesn't Kill Us: How Freezing Water, Extreme Altitude, and Environmental Conditioning Will Renew Our Lost Evolutionary Strength* (Rodale Books, 2017).

✻ Alan D. Fletcher, MD, *Sioux Me: Stories from the Reservation* (iUniverse, 2009).

✻ John Burroughs, *Accepting the Universe: Essays in Naturalism* (Houghton Mifflin Company, 1913).

CHAPTER 23: A GRUESOME SLOG

✻ Robert Frost, "Birches" in *Mountain Interval* (Henry Holt, 1916).

✻ Sophocles, *Antigone.*

CHAPTER 24: THAT SPECIAL SONG

✻ Pindar's comment on the daemon is from E. R. Dodds, *The Greeks and the Irrational* (University of California Press, 2004), first published in 1951.

✻ John Burroughs, *Accepting the Universe: Essays in Naturalism* (Houghton Mifflin Company, 1913).

CHAPTER 25: A NEW RECORD FOR THE CATSKILLS

✻ Ralph Ryndak, "A Windy, Cold Night at 4,500 Feet," in *Adirondack Peak Experiences: Mountaineering Adventures, Misadventures, and the Pursuit of "The 46,"* edited by Carol White Stone (Black Dome Press, 2009).

✻ For the story of Jim and Joe's record-setting thru-hike, see Tobie Geertsema, "Ambitious Climbers Conquer 35 Lofty Catskill Summits," *Daily Freeman,* 1978.

CHAPTER 26: A NEW RECORD FOR THE LONG PATH

✻ Will and Dustin's FKT report is available at https://www.hogandfox.com/runningandfitness/longpathfkt.

✻ John Burroughs, *Accepting the Universe: Essays in Naturalism* (Houghton Mifflin Company, 1913).

CHAPTER 27: AN UNCONVENTIONAL UNIFORM FOR SUMMER BUSHWACKING

✻ For a discussion of Native American marker trees, see Sarah Laskow, "Did Native Americans Bend These Trees to Mark Trails?," *Atlas Obscura,* January 5, 2016, accessed at https://www.atlasobscura.com/articles/did-native-americans-bend-these-trees-to-mark-trails.

✳ Daniel E. Lieberman, *The Story of the Human Body: Evolution, Health, and Disease* (Random House LLC, 2013).
✳ Muir quote from *My First Summer in the Sierra*.

CHAPTER 28: BACK TO WORK

✳ John Muir, *My First Summer in the Sierra* (Houghton Mifflin Company, 1911).

CHAPTER 29: A LOST GOOSE

✳ The Emerson quotation comes from Robert D. Richardson, Jr., *Emerson: The Mind on Fire*.
✳ Edvard Munch, *The Private Journals of Edvard Munch*, edited and translated by J. Gill Holland (University of Wisconsin Press, 2005).
✳ Jake Haisley, "Goose in the Spruce: A Fowl Out on West Kill," *The Catskill Canister* 52, no. 1 (January–March 2019), accessed at https://www.catskill3500club.org/_files/ugd/f103b2 _47417d15877e47bcb54cc4e573a3ec11.pdf.

CHAPTER 30: THE NINE, THE SIX, AND THE ONE

✳ Muir comment on cherry farming is from Samuel Hall Young, *Alaska Days with John Muir* (Fleming H. Revell Company, 1915).
✳ Muir's success as a small businessman is from Donald Worster, *A Passion for Nature: The Life of John Muir* (Oxford University Press, 2008).

CHAPTER 31: THE FINAL ASCENT

✳ Ligurius's words are from William Shakespeare's *Julius Caesar*, first performed in 1599.
✳ The Emerson quotation is from "Self-Reliance," Whitman quotations from "Song of the Open Road" and *Manly Training and Health*.
✳ Galloway comment comes from Gail Waesche Kislevitz, *Running Past Fifty: Advice and Inspiration for Senior Runners* (Skyhorse Publishing, 2018).
✳ Pam Reed, *The Extra Mile: One Woman's Personal Journey to Ultrarunning Greatness* (Rodale Books, 2006).

✸ For a discussion of transhumanism, see Meghan O'Gieblyn, *God, Human, Animal, Machine: Technology, Metaphor, and the Search for Meaning* (Doubleday, 2021).

✸ Muir's running quotes are from *The Wild Muir* and *My First Summer in the Sierra.*

ACKNOWLEDGMENTS

TO ALL THE KINDRED SOULS WITH WHOM I'VE SHARED THE mountains, some of whom were mentioned in the text, and many who were not, I count you as my friends. Odie got too old for the Catskills' rugged trails. He preferred to spend his days sleeping on the sofa, rising from time to time to bark at passing neighbors or rummage in the kitchen. Even if we no longer ran together, we were still partners. I had his back. Until one day he could not stand up, and in his eyes I saw the resignation and sadness.

A special thank-you to friends who helped me identify species in the forests and who provided comments on various drafts of the book, including Bob Eby, John Franklin, Charlie Gadol, Thea Gavin, Heather Houskeeper, Whitley Kaufman, Mike Kudish, Fred Miller, James H. Ottaway, Jr., Heather Rolland, Michael Simon, and Clay Spencer. A special thank-you to Stephany Evans of Ayesha Pande Literary and Kierra Sondereker and Renee Rutledge of Ulysses Press, whose critical comments were instrumental in improving the narrative.

I'd like to recognize a number of organizations that play a role in preserving, managing, and stewarding the Catskills, including the Catskill Center, Catskill Mountainkeeper, Catskill Mountain Club, Catskill 3500 Club, John Burroughs Association, John Burroughs Natural History Association, New York–New Jersey Trail Conference, Open Space Institute, and State of New York Department of Environmental Conservation.

ABOUT THE AUTHOR

Kenneth Posner's running credentials include completing over 100 races of marathon distance or longer and setting the fastest known times for the 294-mile Badwater Double in Death Valley and New York's 350-mile Long Path. As a barefoot athlete, he has run over 100 races of distances from 5k to 50 miles, climbed more than 500 mountains—including every 4,000-footer in the Northeast—and thru-hiked the John Muir Trail. As board chair for the New York–New Jersey Trail Conference and Run Wild, Inc., he supports land conservation and stewardship and advocates for connecting young people with nature.

Following service as a US Army infantry officer, his business career now spans 30 years as a Wall Street analyst and corporate executive. He is currently serving as senior vice president of strategic planning and investor relations at Mr. Cooper Group, the nation's largest mortgage servicer.